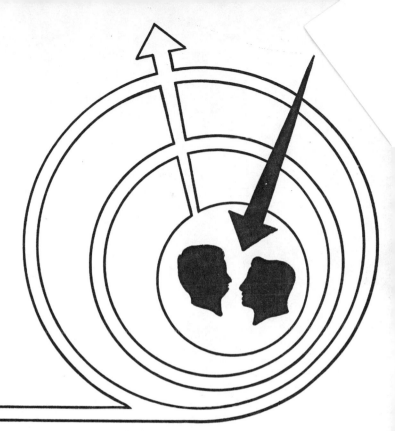

UNDERSTANDING PSYCHOTHERAPY

comparative perspectives

GEORGE J ALLEN

Research Press Company
2612 North Mattis Ave.
Champaign, Illinois 61820

L

The University of Texas
At San Antonio

To
Lynne
Michael and Leslie

With Love

Contents

Foreword

Psychotherapy deals with people. It is an interchange between therapists and clients within a social context that provides explanations and
legitimizes interventions to alter changeworthy behavior. The actions of
therapist and client would be considered unusual, even "deviant," if the
relationship were not a recognized social role. Understanding the nature
of psychotherapy provides a model for understanding many complex,
"special," social relationships.

It is within such a people-oriented context that Dr. George Allen
investigates the history of psychotherapy, the models employed, and
the social processes of labelling behavior as changeworthy and seeking
assistance. With great open-mindedness he covers the currently popular
therapeutic orientations and sketches their procedures and their likely
benefit to clients. A first valuable result of his work is a good introduction for students and general readers as to what presently exists.

A second accomplishment by Professor Allen, one that hopefully
will receive the acclaim it deserves, stems from his approach to his
material. In the midst of the welter of theories, procedures, targets for
change, and different client populations, both the author and the reader
need a guiding set of criteria. Professor Allen takes the position that
data justify theories and applications, and therefore concepts and procedures must be evaluated as the independent variables that they are. It
is in this context that Dr. Allen introduces material on scientific method that is novel yet welcome in a volume devoted to psychotherapy.
But beyond this stance, which is claimed by most psychologists who
have not slipped into solipsism, Professor Allen extends the data range

of psychological treatment to include social influence research. Dr. Allen's judicious blending of epistemology and social psychological data is outstanding and stimulating. His writing combines accuracy with clarity.

Reading this volume highlighted a number of theses with which Professor Allen might agree in varying degrees. A first one is that we must study therapists as closely as clients, and that such study should pit personality differences against procedural ones. It is quite likely that as techniques become more clearly specified as to when they should be used, for what target behaviors, and with which clients, in a manner that is documented and teachable, individual differences among therapists will steadily assume less and less importance. That is, as methods improve, professional knowledge and training increase in importance and personality differences steadily decrease in importance.

A second thesis brought to mind by reading this book is that we will need to devote increasing efforts to the study of what conditions maintain behavior. Another way of saying this is that therapists will have to provide clear reasons for generalization of their interventions over time and place.

As we seek behavioral changes beyond the psychotherapy interaction, we will increasingly be on the interface of psychotherapy and community interventions. If this is the case, both for change and prevention, we will have to develop ever clearer formulations and data bases for our actions as they impinge on the domain of other professional and special interest groups. Professor Allen is particularly well qualified in this area, and his remarks on ethics are an indication of but one of many new subjects that psychotherapists will have to master.

We are already seeing some lines being drawn. On the one hand, there may be an increasing emphasis on the medical model because this justifies intervention on the basis of the presence of the "deviance" per se and locates such deviance within the individual as a result of personality dynamics or physiological error. As such, changeworthy behavior is without reference to the person's social role, age, sex, social class, marital status, or varying and changing social values. Further, this orientation is readily understood by legislators and qualifies the psychotherapist for third-party payment. We are currently seeing the development of lobbying groups, pressure tactics, and *Health* registers.

If, however, changeworthy behavior is a social evaluation of learned behavior, then the psychologist must face up to all the ethical and legal problems of intervening in a private citizen's life. Legal stipulations and challenges to the unconsidered use of psychological testing and treatment are increasing. Noteworthy among indicants of this direction are increasing specification of the rights of those who are incarcerated or in danger of losing their civil rights. The psychotherapists' claims to confidentiality or other special privileges in their records and reports are being challenged. Rather than that of physician, the model of a therapist may become that of teacher, and this model imposes new and different responsibilities. It is a harder model in the short-run, less remunerative yet more demanding, but in the long-run, it may be the best path for psychological interventions.

There are two reasons for this last assertion. The first is increasing consumer awareness as well as legal safeguards for clients. The overtness of action and outcome demanded by consumers and in law will force greater specification of what acts the therapist takes to provide what outcomes with what degree of likelihood. In short, there is pressure towards explicitness and accountability. The second reason is that the teaching, social scientist role is one that in the long-run is more professional, if by professional is meant the development and responsible use of specialized knowledge.

Given increasing attention to preventive measures, professional, legal, consumer, and ethical pressures, and the over-riding scientific need for accountability, there are two interrelated likely outcomes. The first is that goals will be specifiable and measurable so that the therapy contract will deal with results as well as the rules of the therapist and client roles. The second result will be an increasing emphasis on self-modification methods and the clients' selection of both change methods and goals. The ultimate target of all intervention should be that the therapist becomes unnecessary as clients become their own guides and teachers. We are likely to see a growing emphasis on instructing people in methods for coping with future problems rather than merely ameliorating prior mishaps and deficits. We will have to test whether this will be best accomplished indirectly through alteration of inner-personality constructs or directly by arranging interpersonal and environmental conditions.

We should be wary of "cookbooks" and procedures that are organized by types of clients or targets. Every person's call for assistance deserves an individualized assessment and a program fitted to that individual. Rather than therapy routines, we should encourage the development of thinking that is critical, abstract, and flexible. To be most effective, we should strive to specify terms that currently are used as explanations but in the long-run may obscure therapy procedures. For example, what is a "constructive relationship"? What are the observed results of interpersonal interactions that would lead us to apply the designation? What do we mean by "expectancies" and how may such "cognitions" be manipulated? And if we can successfully define and manipulate what are now called "expectancies," will we use the term or will we merely designate the conditions which are the independent variables for obtaining the effect? Is the major problem in behavioral difficulties a general drive such as "anxiety" or is it a lack of competence to deal with specific situations? The former is likely to lead to Hullian and Freudian formulations, the latter to neo-Skinnerian ones. Put differently, does anxiety so disrupt performance that it leads to social incompetence, or is a lack of knowing how to deal with situations the reason for "anxiety"? If the former is the case, indirect, general methods of anxiety reduction may be successfully used; but if the latter is true, the path most likely to benefit the client is direct training in social skills relevant to effectiveness in the situation. In short, are we most useful when we alter personality constructs or when we alter problem-solving strategies?

Other related questions deal with assumptions about psychotherapy. What exactly is "emotion" and is emotional expression necessarily good? We must ask under what conditions and for what reasons is it to the client's benefit to express "feelings." What do we mean by "warmth" and "empathy," and rather than selecting people who have these qualities or providing them with indirect experiences such as therapy, can we increase these qualities by direct instruction? In fact, we might think of making warm and empathic responses contingent on client behavior in order to determine if such a strategy is more effective in obtaining new behavior than acting in a totally unconditional, non-contingent manner. Can we go beyond "faith" and "placebo" by designating what social processes are covered by these terms, and then move from non-specific factors towards a systematic application of effective psychological variables? Do we need to accept psychotherapy as "incredibly complex"? It may well be that we are looking in the wrong places for the variance in behavioral interventions, and it may be that it is our ignorance that leads us to perceive what is simple as complex. In all these instances, work must start on strict, reliable, public definitions, and there must follow the type of scientific investigation that has been our most useful guide in making decisions.

Dr. Allen gives us an accurate picture of the many alternatives that make the field of psychotherapy so interesting and tumultuous. It is to his credit as a teacher and guide that he is even-handed. But breadth of coverage which is a teacher's obligation does not mean that all procedures and models are equally true or equally valuable to clients. To the contrary, the variety of orientations is a circumstance calling for the most careful evaluation and decision making among alternatives. The student must know what exists now, but the student must also learn how to choose from among alternatives. Only by a process of constant evaluation will both the student and the profession be able to steadily improve and meet the obligation of service based on knowledge. The measure of improvement lies in the outcome of our efforts to serve clients, and this service, in turn, is dependent upon ever broadened, improved, and documented psychological theory. Scientific method is not something after the fact or ornamental, much less something that is antithetical to humane treatment of people. Scientific method is a moral and professional necessity. It is what legitimizes and justifies our efforts.

Psychotherapy is currently at a major choice-point with many alternatives available to the student who will be the professional worker of tomorrow. Preparation now will be measured by professional service and client growth in the years to come. Students must know not only what to choose, but how to make choices. In moving towards the future, Professor Allen has provided a bridge: we can only hope that many people will use it as they move from students to providers of service, from readers to scholars, and from being consumers to becoming creators.

Leonard P. Ullmann
University of Hawaii
Honolulu, Hawaii

Preface

When I announced my intention to write a book about psychotherapy, a common reaction was "Why another one? We have books about theories of psychotherapy, books about psychoanalysis, client-centered therapy, Gestalt therapy, behavior therapy, cognitive therapy, and numerous other approaches. We are swamped with various how-to-do-it manuals. We have books dealing with self-help therapy, and even books describing therapeutic forms of anti-therapy. In short, we have confusion, we have conflict, we have controversy. Why do you want to add to it?"

My aim in writing this book is *not* to add to the confusion, conflict, and controversy that has polarized many experts into warring factions. Rather, my aim is to explore many facets of the complex helping endeavors that we label as *psychotherapy* so that the reasons for current theoretical and professional schisms can be better understood. The practice of psychotherapy has enormous political, social, and personal consequences for the participants involved, and for society as a whole. Yet, psychotherapy is an invisible enterprise in many ways; an activity that is shrouded in magic and misunderstanding. It is my belief that understanding psychotherapy requires that the helping process be examined from a wide variety of viewpoints. The contents of this book reflect this basic assumption.

In Chapter 1, historical and sociological perspectives are employed to foster understanding of how the major therapeutic professions of psychiatry, clinical psychology, and psychiatric social work developed. Chapter 2 explores the major schisms and controversies that currently beset the helping professions. It is argued that, even though the controversies are expressed as theoretical differences, their roots lie in the maneuvering of various professional groups toward maintaining and extending their social, political, and economic power.

In Chapter 3, we examine some of the major theoretical underpinnings of therapeutic practices. Psychodynamic, humanistic, and behavioral systems are presented as spectrums. The theme of this chapter is that as much diversity exists within any of these broad spectrums as can be found between them. Chapter 4 explores the relationship between art and science in psychotherapy as complementary and relativistic. The application of scientific criteria and methods to clinical operations has yielded much valuable information about psychotherapy, but in the process, it has also caused some serious conceptual and practical problems.

In Chapters 5 and 6, the fruitful knowledge gained through empirical inquiry into psychotherapeutic processes is presented. Complex interactions between characteristics of clients and therapists are simplified into components that have been consistently related to successful and unsuccessful therapeutic outcomes in Chapter 5. This same strategy of simplification is employed in Chapter 6 in an examination of setting and time influences on therapeutic process and outcome. These chapters are aimed at destroying certain myths about the uniformity of these components (for example, the belief that all therapists are alike simply because they are therapists). Chapter 6 ends with an overview of therapeutic operations that are commonly found in all forms of psychotherapy.

Chapter 7 describes the complex interplay between the scientific and artistic aspects of psychotherapy in terms of complex interpersonal processes by highlighting four emerging frameworks that are commonly employed by clinicians. Conceptualizations of psychotherapy as a problem-solving process, attributional systems, a series of interpersonal games or terms expressing cognitive beliefs, and body language were all developed through clinical intuition and have been subjected to increasing empirical analysis. Chapter 8 provides an overview of some important ethical issues in the practice of psychotherapy. Particular emphasis is placed on examining the issues of sexism and racism.

The one unifying theme that runs through all the chapters is that knowledge about the complex human activity we call psychotherapy is gained through systematic observation. Whenever we observe complicated interactions within a system, our perception is guided toward certain features and away from others. This makes all frameworks, regardless of whether they involve theoretical or empirical criteria, essentially relativistic. Thus, what constitutes a satisfactory explanation for one person may well be viewed as fiction or fantasy by others.

Systematic observation requires that complex clinical phenomena be simplified. Whenever we simplify what occurs in psychotherapy, we obtain a coherent view of some aspects of the phenomenon under study, but we lose sight of the overall picture. Failure to distinguish between coherence and comprehensiveness has led many to assume that their view of clinical reality is the correct one, alternate viewpoints are erroneous, and those who hold them are misguided or misinformed. The relativistic theme of this book represents an attack on this sort of thinking. Any framework that guides our observations of psychotherapy provides new insights about the complex interpersonal processes involved.

A relativistic approach is bound to make some people unhappy. Those who firmly believe that their approach is the best will undoubtedly argue that some of my conceptualizations are overly simplistic, if not wrong. If such accusations are based on theoretical beliefs about the superiority of a particular system, the critic must then resolve the dilemma of how others, who are equally as informed, can reach dramatically different conclusions when operating within an alternative framework. If such accusations are based on the argument that the extensive breadth of coverage contained in this book precludes full, in-depth analysis, I concede the validity of the argument. I have endeavored to balance breadth and depth within the page limitation imposed upon me and with the knowledge that entire books have been written on most of the topics I cover. I view this work as a source of rudimentary knowledge about many aspects of psychotherapy, which hopefully will spur you to investigate topics of interest more fully.

The final product of my efforts owes much to discussion with and critical feedback from my colleagues: Evelyn Guillen, Teresa Huey, Pauline Murray, Leonard Ullmann, Ingrid Winslow, and David Zuroff. Len Ullmann and Dave Zuroff, in particular, provided insightful and penetrating analyses of my writing. I am grateful to all of you for your efforts on my behalf. I also wish to thank Teri Huey for cheerfully and conscientiously typing the manuscript. The cover design is the creation of Gregory Makoul, a very talented young artist. The fine efforts devoted to turning the manuscript into a book by the staff at Research Press are also deeply appreciated.

Two sources of inspiration deserve special mention. Professor Leonard Ullmann was a profound source of intellectual stimulation during my graduate career at the University of Illinois. He served as an extraordinarily capable role model of the scientist-practitioner, combining critical thinking and a respect for scholarship with warmth and genuine concern.

Finally, I wish to express my deepest gratitude to my wife, Lynne, and my children, Mike and Leslie. All of them endured episodes of craziness and periods of neglect during the birth of this work. They were always there whenever I needed them, providing recreation, joy, and delight.

1
Conceptual and Historical Foundations

CONTROVERSIES AND CONFUSION

Perhaps no other word generates more confusion or evokes a greater array of emotional reactions than does *psychotherapy*. Despite an ever increasing level of psychological sophistication among the general public, many people continue to regard psychotherapy as a complex, mysterious ritual that contains many magical elements. The more cynical, however, question whether talking with a therapist can really help anyone resolve a life difficulty. Some individuals regard psychotherapists with considerable awe, viewing them as wise individuals who have solved the riddle of human happiness. Others condemn psychotherapists as charlatans who make big money by doing little or nothing. Much is written about psychotherapy in popular books and magazines, yet, in many ways, therapists practice an invisible profession. Most people have little idea of what therapists actually do, or how to go about finding one. Entering therapy almost always evokes conflicting feelings of shame and hope which often add to the helpee's confusion. Finally, many are unclear about what sorts of difficulties might be profitably brought to therapy or what might be expected from the therapeutic experience.

Professional therapists themselves add to this confusion in a number of ways. They have difficulty agreeing on the range of helping activities that should be considered as psychotherapy. General consensus among the experts is found on only the most broad and innocuous generalizations: that psychotherapy is a uniquely human endeavor, that it has deep historical roots, or that it involves a professional relationship, for example. About the only statement that practically all therapists would agree on is that the term *psychotherapy* is too vague to adequately describe the wide variety of helping activities to which it is applied. It has proven almost impossible to distinguish psychotherapy from counseling, consulting, or re-educative efforts, faith healing, witch doctor rituals, or other forms of helping interventions.

Intellectual and theoretical dilemmas abound within the discipline of psychotherapy. Controversies exist about whether the therapeutic change effort is best directed at hidden motivational forces existing within people, at modifying overt behavior, or at changing the social systems within which the help-seeker operates. Psychotherapists have been polarized into numerous competing camps because of issues such as this one. As a result, communication among professionals suffers.

Over the years, much vicious infighting among various professional groups has occurred. The potential conflict that stems from differences in orientation is heightened because psychotherapy provides substantial financial and social rewards for those who practice it. Many of these conflicts have admittedly self-serving overtones, as various professional in-groups seek to restrict the right to conduct therapy to their own members. The public image of psychotherapists as altruistic service providers consequently has begun to suffer.

In subsequent chapters, we will attempt to highlight many of these issues and explore them in detail. This chapter provides an overview of what is to come by setting forth a conceptual framework for understanding the complexities of psychotherapy and by providing a brief synopsis describing the emergence of therapeutic service-providers as institutionalized professions.

ASSUMPTIONS ABOUT THE RELATIONAL NATURE OF PSYCHOTHERAPY

Psychotherapy is an incredibly complex process, not only because it makes complicated human behavior its focus, but also because we can look at what goes on from many different perspectives. Choosing a particular viewpoint enables us to make sense of some aspects of the helping process but causes us to ignore other facets that are equally as important from a different framework. The following assumptions are designed to emphasize the relativistic nature of psychotherapy.

Psychotherapy Is A Process
Of Mutual Influence

There are two important points to be made about the assumption that psychotherapy is an ongoing mutual influence process. *First, we cannot lose sight of the fact that psychotherapy is process.* People who occupy clearly defined social roles of helper and helpee come together and interact with one another over time. The word *psychotherapy* itself is misleading, because, as a singular noun, it implies that psychotherapy is a static entity. People are often described as "entering," "being in," or "leaving" psychotherapy as if "it" were some kind of special structural state.

For several decades, a debate has raged over the question, "Does psychotherapy work?" The controversy about the effectiveness of psychotherapy was based on the notion that numerous processes could be considered "a thing" that people went through. That the question is unanswerable can be readily seen by asking whether other life processes "work." Is marriage effective? Does education accomplish what "it" is supposed to?

The second area of emphasis is that of mutual influence. The process of psychotherapy involves interchange between people on many different levels. The helping process is aimed at producing some sort of beneficial change in one of the participants. The type and direction of changes considered most desirable depend upon how one conceptualizes human nature. Some therapists seek to change internal dynamic forces, others focus on shifting attitudes and beliefs, while still others emphasize the alteration of behaviors. Regardless of the theoretical rationale involved, the change effort is based on complex interpersonal influence processes.

Because psychotherapy is a human encounter, it affects both the helper and helpee, although often in very different ways. The clinician and client have diverging perspectives about what occurs during psychotherapy as well as what factors bring about change. The emphasis on mutual influence implies that the most important unit of analysis for understanding psychotherapy is the interaction between helper and helpee. We cannot study clients apart from therapists or therapists in isolation from clients. Further, to avoid arriving at a superficial and ultimately sterile understanding of psychotherapy, we must pay attention to what the helper and helpee do to one another, rather than what each person is apart from the change process.

Therapeutic Processes Occur
In A Social Context

People enter psychotherapy because of failures to meet various social demands or an inability to solve real-life problems that confront them. Therapeutic encounters are themselves social actions between the participants. Until recently, psychotherapy was viewed by many as an endeavor that somehow existed apart from the outside world of daily activities. Today, however, we realize that this view is not only nonhelpful but also nonsensical.

Psychotherapy admittedly has some aspects that are not usually found in other social interactions. Because therapists seek to provide emotional support, psychotherapy has many similarities to friendship. The fact that therapists attempt to use their support as a foundation to challenge the client to change, however, makes psychotherapy something more than friendship and something less.

Two implications stem from viewing psychotherapy as a social process. *First, we need to pay attention to how what is learned in this specialized encounter generalizes to the everyday life of the helpee.* All that the therapist has to offer is wasted unless the client can make practical use of it. Simply being in therapy is not enough to guarantee that successful transfer of more adaptive skills outside of the therapeutic environment will occur. Helping to insure that transfer takes place has always been a difficult problem, but it is unfair for therapists to rationalize this difficulty by defining psychotherapy as being outside of the social sphere.

The second implication deals with psychotherapy as a social institution. Being designated as a socially sanctioned service-provider grants the therapist considerable personal power and yields substantial financial benefits. In a competitive, free-enterprise market, it is natural that those who hold such sources of power will seek to exclude others who might threaten them. Differences among professional organizations about what psychotherapy is and who may practice it are couched in theoretical terms as intellectual issues, but decisions about these questions have enormous financial consequences.

Institutional psychiatry and professional clinical psychology have fought battles dealing with these issues for quite some time. Other professional help-providing organizations, such as psychiatric social workers and family counselors, have been more than casual onlookers, while the insurance industry has taken sides to maintain its own interests. This conflict has been fought far beyond the confines of the therapists' offices; it has involved state legislatures, Congress, and the courts.

The social nature of psychotherapy considered as an institution becomes even more evident when financial issues become entwined with political ones. While the major helping professions hack away at each other, they have all come under increasing attack by both consumer advocate groups and special interest organizations. On one hand, there has been increasing demand by consumer activists for accountability by health-service specialists. The beliefs that people ought to be able to make informed choices in selecting a psychotherapist and that they should receive adequate services for their money are being pushed as basic rights.

On the other hand, several special interest groups are accusing psychotherapists of using their power to maintain the current social structure. Radical feminists, in particular, have described psychotherapy as politically repressive. Their argument is based on the belief that most therapists seek to "adjust" women who are oppressed by other social institutions (e.g., marriage, motherhood) to their unfortunate lot in life. They suggest that the psychotherapy process be radicalized to help women and other downtrodden minorities to successfully change the current social structure. It is impossible to gain a clear understanding of psychotherapy without taking the financial and political aspects of the process into account.

Psychotherapy Must Be Viewed
From Several Frameworks

Human behavior is incredibly complex because actions have multiple causes and multiple consequences. Psychotherapy, as an ongoing interactive process, is even more complicated because it encompasses what each participant contributes as a unique individual as well as in combination with the other. Both helper and helpee bring an almost unlimited number of potential influences into the therapeutic setting, which mold the substance and form of the encounter. Given the continual flow of behavior that occurs, it is impossible to comprehend all that is happening.

We can gain some understanding of psychotherapy by asking the therapist or the client to describe what is taking place, or we can observe the process. By doing this, however, we encounter other impediments. What questions should we ask? What do we observe? How do we reconcile the fact that each of these sources will yield limited, arbitrary, and radically different perspectives of the process?

Although we cannot ever gain a complete knowledge of psychotherapy, we do the next best thing by accepting that whatever information we gain will be limited by the framework we use to collect it. Many different frameworks—called paradigms, theories, and models—exist. Any systematic framework provides a method of deciding what features of the interactive process are important and enables people to mold these aspects into general patterns that make interpretive sense.

The Role Of Language. All systematic frameworks are based on the abstract symbols and rules of convention we know as "language." Language itself provides an incomplete and arbitrary perspective for viewing interactions because words cause us to transform ongoing processes into events and order them into logical sequences such as "cause-effect," and "past-present-future." Concepts of causality and time awareness are learned through the medium of language. We need this simplicity to communicate with one another, but we must realize that language makes human action seem simpler than it really is. We may be satisfied by hearing that the goal of psychotherapy is to "make the unconscious conscious," but, in reality, we have learned nothing. All we have done is to transform one hypothetical entity into another hypothetical concept. The statement provides no better understanding of the processes that are involved. We acknowledge the same kind of ignorance when we accept the fact that a person "has an inadequate reinforcement history," "suffers from faulty ego development," or "is a schizophrenic" as explanations of behavior.

Limitations Of A Framework. All knowledge we have accumulated about psychotherapy has come from inquiry conducted within specific, systematic frameworks. There are three implications that arise from this fact which have importance for understanding therapeutic processes. *First, any systematic framework guides our perception in selective and arbitrary ways.* A system draws our attention to particular elements of the therapeutic process, making them appear to be recurring patterns which have specific consequences. The discovery of certain patterns causes us to view other aspects as nuisance or "error" variance which we either ignore or attempt to rule out. Portions of the process that appear haphazard from one perspective will, however, form meaningful patterns from another viewpoint. For example, both humanistic and behavioral clinicians are concerned with the role of the therapist in the treatment process. The general paradigm that most humanists subscribe to emphasizes the type of person that the therapist is, while the behavioral paradigm stresses what the therapist does. Thus, humanistic clinicians make the study of the therapist's personal characteristics a central topic. Behavioral clinicians are more interested in determining whether specific therapeutic procedures are effective when employed by different therapists.

Second, a systematic framework guides the actions of those who employ it. A paradigm helps us ask meaningful questions about the patterns that are observed and provides guidance in developing a technology to investigate the phenomenon that aroused our curiosity. Behavioral clinicians have developed numerous therapeutic strategies for treating specific complaints such as phobias. Their paradigm emphasizes learning-related constructs as the basic processes by which their procedures operate. They are, therefore, less interested in individual differences than their humanistically inclined colleagues.

Selective guidance of perception and action by a framework operates in less obvious ways than described above. Any paradigm rapidly produces a specialized vocabulary that aids communication among those who operate within the same framework. This sort of specialization, however, hinders communication between people who subscribe to different paradigms, causing friction and misunderstanding. The connotations that even nontechnical words possess within a framework also have this effect. The term "mental health professional" is a convenient description that can be applied to psychotherapists. Using the term, however, implies that psychotherapists deal with "health" and "sickness." Many therapists reject the view that they treat "sick" people, preferring to view their clients as having problems in living.

Consider the connotations associated with words describing someone who enters therapy: "victim," "patient," "client," or "helpee." A victim has been the unwilling recipient of unfortunate consequences.

Little is implied about the causes of the incident or the person's need or willingness to change. A patient, however, is someone who has been victimized by sickness. A sick person is not usually held responsible for creating this unfavorable condition nor expected to actively participate in the medical treatment process. A client is a person who seeks aid from a professional who possesses specialized knowledge and skills. A client is generally seen as a person having a more responsible and dynamic role in implementing a helping strategy. Finally, a helpee is anyone who requests help. The source and nature of aid is not specified nor is anything about the person's motivation to change. Historically, the poor have been bad bets to improve in psychotherapy when treated as patients, but they have proven much more responsive when dealt with as victims, clients, or helpees.

The final implication is intuitively obvious: *many frameworks exist.* Psychotherapeutic transactions have been conceptualized in terms of cooperation, conflict, power, verbal content, and nonverbal body signals, to mention only a few. Each of these fairly general content areas has been investigated in numerous, specific ways. Knowledge about the effects of nonverbal messages in therapy, for example, has been generated through systematic inquiry within three particular perspectives that center on paralanguage (voice inflection, tone, and other vocal characteristics), kinesics (body orientation and movement), and proxemics (personal space, body buffer zones, interpersonal distance). In addition, new frameworks, such as the study of clothing and other body artifacts, are constantly emerging.

We encounter just as many perspectives that describe the goals of psychotherapy. The helping process has been aimed at lifting unconscious repression, providing a corrective emotional experience, improving body-image or self-concept, integrating existential polarities, challenging irrational ideas, teaching general problem-solving strategies, enlarging the repertoire of adaptive behaviors, and many other outcomes. Each perspective provides a coherent view of some aspects of the therapeutic process. No single framework represents a totally accurate or complete description of psychotherapy, however. We present the following guideline as a fundamental starting point for understanding the process of psychotherapy. *Every systematic framework enables us to perceive some aspects of psychotherapy as a unified whole, but no single viewpoint allows us to comprehend the whole phenomenon of psychotherapy.*

Understanding Psychotherapy Requires
Open-Minded Sophistication

Choices By Individual Therapists. With so many alternative viewpoints available, how does one choose among them? Once again, our starting point for analyzing this issue rests upon diversity and complexity. Individual therapists can and do subscribe to a number of perspectives that interlock in very complicated ways. Fortunately, many perspectives are complementary in the sense that they can be used in combination with others without causing logical contradictions or practical dilemmas. In fact, inexperienced clinicians usually find the conceptual paradigms provided during their training to be inadequate for dealing with the wide range of problems they encounter in therapy situations. As a result, they are forced to learn new models and elaborate on the ones they already hold to improve their effectiveness as helpers.

Three Theoretical Groups. In reality, the way a therapist conducts therapy stems from numerous beliefs about people in general. These beliefs are organized into models which, in turn, form broader theoretical and paradigmatic frameworks. When we attempt to capture what occurs in psychotherapy, we are forced to simplify this complex network of influences. For example, we can group theoretical stances toward psychotherapy into three families: psychodynamic, behavioral, and humanistic perspectives. In some respects, these broad paradigms are incompatible with one another; yet, on many specific issues, areas of overlapping agreement can be found. A careful analysis of these three major perspectives also reveals as much conflict and controversy within each as exists between them.

Behaviorally oriented clinicians debate heatedly among themselves about whether behavior modification is actually based on laws of human learning. They also share widely differing views about the importance of relationship factors as well as the role of cognitive processes in psychotherapy. As a group, however, they share certain fundamental beliefs about human nature that set them apart from their psychodynamic and humanistic colleagues. They are generally united in opposition to perspectives that emphasize internal dynamics, and they reject treatment strategies aimed at restructuring the personality.

Behavior therapists, however, find themselves allied with humanistically inclined clinicians in conceptualizing therapy as a process of re-education that focuses on real-world, here-and-now issues. Proponents of both perspectives are also united in rejecting the belief that human problems are analogous to disease processes, thus setting themselves apart from many psychodynamic clinicians. Humanistic and psychodynamic therapists tend to focus on developmental aspects of personality to a greater extent than behavioral clinicians, but, within each of these perspectives, there is much divergence of opinion about the extent to which developmental factors influence current functioning.

We find a similar situation regarding the role of scientific inquiry in improving our understanding of psychotherapy. Some humanistic therapists reject science because it turns people into objects and thus dehumanizes them. Others argue that empirical inquiry provides the only meaningful reality check on the clinician's activities. Psychoanalysis has been castigated as being unscientific, even though many analysts have engaged in empirical experimentation. The word *science* has different meanings for psychodynamic, humanistic, and behavioral therapists.

The situation becomes even more complicated when we observe the specific activities of individual clinicians who hold competing perspectives. We sometimes find behavioral clinicians conducting retrospective analyses of parental child-management techniques or interpreting dreams. After all, description of dreams represents verbal behavior. Some psychodynamic therapists will assign "homework," an activity that has a decidedly behavioral flavor. These specific strategies are not decreed by the theoretical frameworks held by the respective therapists, but, rather, they are dictated by the needs of the individual in therapy.

Both clinicians and clients subscribe to numerous perspectives for a variety of reasons. Some were discovered during professional training, others fit the personal style of the participants or make sense in terms of their experiences, and others meet hidden emotional needs. Even though a framework about psychotherapy provides a coherent view of the processes involved, we should not assume it is the only legitimate, comprehensive conception. Such assumptions are fundamental errors that have caused much bitter controversy. Therapists who believe that their theoretical framework contains some ultimate truth about people run the risk of turning personal belief into religious dogma and guidelines into commandments.

The Need For Tolerance. *The only way to satisfactorily cope with this state of affairs is to assume a relativistic perspective that is based on tolerance.* Those who subscribe to competing frameworks have good reasons for believing what they do. They are not stupid, misinformed, inadequately trained, or short-sighted. Different frameworks need to be examined, ideally from an insider's point of view, and judged on the basis of a variety of criteria. Any particular perspective can be evaluated in terms of its explanatory scope, logical consistency, scientific adequacy, practical utility, and unintended side effects. Our knowledge about the incredible complexity of psychotherapy can grow to the extent that we are flexible enough to discover the strengths and limitations inherent in each framework.

A Relational Endeavor. Psychotherapy is a *relational endeavor* in two senses of the word. First, it involves complex *relationships* between people. As such, it is a process that has many facets. Second, our understanding of psychotherapy is not absolute; it is *relativistic* in terms of its being tied to the perspectives we use to conceptualize the interpersonal relationship. With this theme as a starting point, we can view the diversity of frameworks with respect. Humility in the face of the complexity we encounter provides the foundation for tolerant appraisal and, ultimately, growth in our understanding of psychotherapy.

THE HISTORICAL ROOTS OF PSYCHOTHERAPY

Emergence Of Three Frameworks

All forms of abnormality are manifestations of the failure of individuals to fit into their social surroundings as others expect them to do. Throughout history, misfitting has been described in numerous ways, including possession by spiritual forces, moral deficiencies, imbalances of body humors, biochemical factors, psychic energies, genetic aberrations, and inadequate or inappropriate learning. The many existing models can be grouped into three broader categories that classify misfitting as stemming from magical-moral, organic, and psychological causes (Alexander and Selesnick, 1966). All of these perspectives share the common property of locating the source of difficulty within the individual rather than in terms of the fit between a person and his social environment. Examples of all three paradigms can be found in every historical period including contemporary thought.

The Magical-Moral Framework

Early Conceptions. Magical conceptions of the causes of disordered behavior date to the dawn of human history. This recurrent conceptual theme stressed that madness was caused by gods, good or evil spirits, or demons who took possession of a person for their own purposes. The influence of the magical perspective peaked during the sixteenth and seventeenth centuries in the form of witch hunts. Since saving one's soul was deemed to be more important than rehabilitating the deranged individual, a preferred method of treatment involved making the body uncomfortable in an effort to drive the devil out. Death as a result of torture was viewed as a rather inconsequential side effect of the attempt to free the soul, although this attitude was probably not shared by those upon whom such methods were used.

During the mid-nineteenth century, demonic conceptions were gradually replaced by the view that human misery, including madness and poverty, was due to ignorance, laziness, and various other moral deficiencies. This shift led to the development of alternative techniques for rehabilitating people who were now considered to be insane rather than mad. Historians refer to this framework as "moral therapy," which was characterized by the belief that even the most deranged individuals would benefit from the good will, firmness, and fairness exhibited by helping agents in total therapeutic environments (Bockoven, 1963). The demise of moral treatment was hastened by medical advances which demonstrated that many mental disturbances had organic causes.

Modern Variations. Although magical-moral views of misfitting are not particularly influential today, modern variants of this ancient theme still exist in our society, especially in subcultures that emphasize fundamentalistic religious doctrines. Although child abuse has many causes, some parents attempt to deal with undesirable behavior on the part of their children by literally beating the devil out of them. Some faith healers argue that human suffering results from religious failings or moral deficiencies. Relief from the misery of psychological distress is promised to those who abandon their sinful ways and embrace whatever orientation the healer espouses. Occasionally, spectacular improvement occurs as a result of such interventions, although the reasons are not at all clear to interested observers.

The Organic Framework

The organic framework originated with the ancient Greeks, who thought the body occupied an intermediate position between the external world and inner self-awareness. Like the magical-moral framework, this conception represented a fairly deterministic and mechanistic view of human nature. Human behavior was thought to be controlled by imbalances of body fluids or the presence of disease-producing organisms. During the late Middle Ages, this paradigm became interwoven with the then dominant demonic viewpoint.

Effects Of Paresis Research. The development of increasingly sophisticated scientific instruments, such as the dual lens microscope, gradually led to discoveries linking mental disturbances to the action of disease organisms. The classic example of success within this perspective was the gradual documentation that general paresis was caused by the same virus that caused syphilis. For hundreds of years, these conditions were considered to be entirely different diseases. Syphilis frequently occurred in young men, particularly soldiers; it was manifested by a relatively brief period of discomfort and inflammation. The symptoms of general paresis involving muscular weakness, disorientation, and delusions occurred later in their lives. Although barely capable of walking, the afflicted individual would claim being capable of carrying out heroic deeds of great strength.

Connecting what were originally considered to be two distinct diseases and isolating a single cause required the efforts of many people for well over a century. Medical researchers ultimately demonstrated that syphilitic spirochete caused the brief, episodic flare-ups of symptoms associated with syphilis and continued to destroy brain and neural tissues even in the absence of these symptoms. The cumulative effect of the disease organisms was the eventual destruction of the nervous system, with the mental disorder of general paresis resulting.

The conquest of general paresis had three important consequences. *First, it provided proponents of the organic approach with evidence that mental disturbances were ultimately caused by disease organisms.* Although this conclusion has proven to be an overly optimistic one, it spurred medical investigators to seek biophysical bases for all types of emotional disturbances. This orientation continues to provide a foundation for the efforts of modern researchers who seek to discover genetic and biochemical origins of "psychotic" conditions like schizophrenia.

Second, the institution of psychiatry, which developed around the theme of treating mental disturbances, became firmly rooted as a medical profession. Psychiatry was provided with a scientific aura which acted as a cohesive force in the development of the profession well before the other helping institutions achieved such status. As a consequence, psychiatrists typically occupy a leadership role in the current mental health establishment.

The third consequence has the most relevance for understanding current psychotherapeutic practices. Demonstrating the existence of a single biological cause for presumably distinct physical and mental disorders fostered the development of the medical model of psychotherapy. The basic assumption of this model is that emotional dysfunctions are analogous to physical disease processes. Disturbances in thinking, affect, and behavior are conceptualized as symptomatic manifestations of specific causes that exist within an individual. The underlying source of disturbance has been defined in numerous ways, but it typically involves some sort of imbalance between structures within the mental apparatus or in psychic energy of various kinds. Several symptomatic complaints are considered to form a syndrome that originates from a clearly defined set of underlying causes. We will extensively examine the medical model in subsequent chapters, because it represents the dominant framework for describing current therapeutic activities.

The Psychological Framework

The psychological framework has its historical roots in the confessional rites of the early Christians, most notably in the writings of Saint Augustine. This practice stimulated the development of introspection as a genuine and valuable source of knowledge (Ellenberger, 1974). Unlike the magical-moral and organic orientations, the psychological perspective places causation within the inner world of the individual. In other words, ultimate responsibility for social and emotional difficulties belongs to the person who is beset with them and cannot be externalized onto demons, faulty genetic structures, or biochemical imbalances.

This framework has developed more slowly than the other two

orientations because it requires both special techniques of self-observation and communication as well as the moral courage to confront the potentially frightening revelations that result from honest self-scrutiny.

Current psychotherapeutic practices are firmly embedded in the psychological orientation. Psychotherapy, as we know it today, is a twentieth-century invention that is attributable to the pioneering efforts of Sigmund Freud. Although many of his theoretical notions had a decidedly pessimistic flavor, Freud never deviated from the position that knowledge about the inner determinants of behavior can free a person from the limitations these forces impose.

The psychological orientation is gaining strength in modern American society. The prevalence of psychotherapy as a social institution is based on the modern and optimistic belief that guided introspection of one's inner cognitive and emotional world can help improve that person's life situation. This emphasis has always been evident in the many derivatives from classical psychoanalysis, and it is a growing influence even within the so-called *behavioristic* psychotherapies.

In recent years, the psychological framework has taken on a more *social* character that enhances its compatibility with the behavioral perspective. The dynamic relationships of primary interest are not considered to be taking place within a person's head, but rather, between an individual and her surrounding social network. The broadening of the psychological perspective toward a systems emphasis has had immense impact on our views about the origins and maintenance of misfitting. Psychological disturbances are considered to result from failures to adequately meet expectations held by important others, rather than to be forms of mental illness. Yet, this shift has had limited influence on the practice of psychotherapy as a whole. Many therapists tacitly accept the notion that their primary responsibility is to adjust the client to the existing social system, rather than to attempt changing the system itself. The individual person remains the object of the change effort in just about every form of psychotherapeutic intervention.

Healing And Helping
As Professional Roles

Characteristics Of A Professional. An important historical underpinning of psychotherapy involves the development of helping activities as professions. A profession is generally considered to be a superior form of occupation, but exactly what distinguishes one from the other is extremely difficult to specify. Moore (1970) suggests that a modern professional possesses at least some of the enumerated characteristics that follow:

1. *Follows a full-time occupation as a calling.* A calling implies that the individual will undergo sacrifices to learn requisite skills and will be committed to the ideals associated with the occupational activity. Professions are generally considered to be service-providing occupations in which the welfare of the client is more important than the personal gain of the helper.

2. *Possesses expert knowledge that is applied to specialized tasks.* Professionals typically receive a great deal of formal training in content areas that are difficult for lay people to fully understand. When practicing their specialties, professionals employ technical vocabularies that facilitate communication among themselves but exclude outsiders from understanding the intricacies that are involved.

3. *Is committed to demonstrating competence and providing efficient and effective help.* Candidates for admission into a profession are required to meet certain standards established by a governing body of the professional organization itself. Receiving a certificate or license is a sign that some minimal requirements have been met. In addition, professionals are expected to seek training experiences to keep abreast of new developments in their areas of expertise.

4. *Maintains loyalty to exclusive organizations that codify responsibilities and duties.* Professional societies seek to regulate the conduct of their members by moral persuasion. Professionals are expected to conduct themselves according to the ethical code of the organization, and, beyond that, to be loyal to their colleagues. It is rare to find one professional who will downgrade the competence of his peers. Sanctions against those who fail to meet the standards of the professional society are levelled within the organization itself.

5. *Has a great deal of autonomy and freedom.* The professional is called upon to provide high-quality service in a specialized area. It is assumed that the professional clearly understands how this goal

can best be accomplished. The client often is placed in a passive role *vis-a-vis* the helping endeavor, being expected to place faith in the professional's competence and commitment.

Professionals typically enjoy high social prestige and status. They operate without a large degree of external regulation, being instead answerable to their colleagues. Professional organizations exert social control over their own members and a great deal of influence over segments of the larger society.

The characteristics of a profession have a number of consequences that affect the individual client as well as the organization. First, standards of practice and patterns of loyalty among professionals may not always be in the best interests of the client. Second, the effects of malpractice or exploitative activities are not readily apparent. Third, some pretty vicious infighting among the members of a professional organization often occurs. Fourth, friction between professional groups who compete in providing overlapping services is almost inevitable.

Elliott (1972) provides a historical analysis of the development of medicine as a profession in England which documents some of these implications. Historically, the role of the healer has rotated from the shaman to the theologian to the highly educated to the physician. In the sixteenth century, medicine was practiced by learned men of good breeding who simultaneously pursued other areas of knowledge. Physicians were first licensed in England around 1518 by the newly established Royal College of Physicians. Assessment involved testing one's knowledge of the classical languages, scripture, and some medical expertise. No practical experience with sick people was required, and portions of the test were waived if the candidate was known to be a gentleman. Passing the examination qualified the candidate for membership in the Royal College, but the higher status of Fellow was reserved only for those who had obtained a degree from Oxford or Cambridge. This arbitrary restriction was resented by members who had obtained their degrees from other universities, many of which provided better medical training than the two elite institutions.

During the seventeenth and eighteenth centuries, medicine was practiced by three separate groups. **Physicians,** who were responsible for internal treatment, viewed their activities as the only proper domain of medicine. **Surgeons,** who had emerged as a result of a nasty split with the barber's guild in 1745, treated the external portions of the body.

17

The least prestigious group was the **apothecaries** who concocted and prescribed medication. During the eighteenth century, apothecaries were sued in court by physicians who argued tha the former had no right to charge clients for their advice. At first, the court ruled in favor of the physicians, but, by 1815, apothecaries were given the right to expect payment for both medicine and advice.

It was the apothecaries who were the first to set stringent licensing requirements in 1815. The guild required its member to have some hospital experience and to attend lectures sponsored by the society. As late as 1834, a physicians' committee on medical education continued to emphasize classical language training and general cultivation of the mind as the primary requisites of the practitioner. Over several decades, all three groups used their influence to defeat revisions of the medical structure that would give power to their competitors. Order began to grow out of chaos in 1858, when the guilds were recognized as independent licensing agents but placed under the supervision of a General Medical Council. The link between the university and the hospital, which had been forged in 1827, was strengthened by the Medical Act of 1858. Gradually, the council recognized members of all three guilds as qualified professionals and prepared a registry of these individuals.

The development of autonomous organizations of healers is a result of the specialization of functions necessitated by advances in knowledge. The spread of power among these groups has never been accomplished without much strife, however. Currently, the focal points of conflict within psychotherapeutic professions are found between psychiatrists, psychologists, and psychiatric social workers. The emergence of family and group counselors as a specialized profession portends that they also will become caught in many of the current battles. Before examining the specific sources of strife, however, a brief overview of the development of each profession is necessary.

Psychiatry: From The Asylum To The Couch

Organized psychiatry was born in the asylum, spent its early years wandering through the university, and now rests comfortably on the couch, from which it controls the American mental health establishment. Although historians do not agree about the exact origins of psychiatry, Philippe Pinel may be regarded as the founding father of the profession as a social institution. Pinel's greatest claim to fame is that he freed male inmates from their chains in a Paris asylum in 1793. (Women in a neighboring facility were similarly freed two years later.) From a sociological perspective, however, Pinel represented the prototype of a new breed of physician: one who devoted full-time attention to caring for the deranged. His efforts led to the gradual imposition of medically oriented administration within institutions that were established to house mentally disturbed individuals.

The period of asylum psychiatry reached its zenith around the middle of the nineteenth century in the United States. Although the first state hospital for the mentally ill opened in 1173, by 1850, only 18 such institutions existed in this country (Hamilton, 1944). Figure 1, which was compiled from Hamilton's analysis, documents the dramatic growth in the establishment of state mental institutions between 1851 and 1910. In addition to these institutions, 45 county-operated facilities opened during the same period, while only seven others were established either before or after this period.

The beginning of American psychiatry dates to 1783, when Dr. Benjamin Rush joined the staff of the Pennsylvania Hospital. In 1812, Rush published the first American textbook on mental disorders, which remained in wide use until the turn of the century. In 1844, thirteen prominent hospital administrators met in Philadelphia to discuss common problems. This group founded the Association of Medical Superintendents of American Institutions for the Insane, which was the first association of physicians in this country. It gradually evolved into the American Psychiatric Association.

Around the same time, European physicians were making important discoveries about the biological origins of mental disorders. Advances in medical technology gradually made it more difficult to study mental dysfunctions in institutional settings. This influence, combined with the development of more rigorous training requirements for physicians, moved psychiatry toward the university. The search for underlying disease entities helped establish psychiatry as a legitimate branch of medicine, and it enabled physicians to claim the treatment of mental dysfunctions as a medical specialty.

Freud was instrumental in establishing the dominance of the psychological orientation in organized psychiatry. His novel approach to investigating human motivation helped free psychiatry from the limitations of a strict biological model by legitimizing the analysis of

FIGURE 1. ESTABLISHMENT OF STATE MENTAL INSTITUTIONS IN THE UNITED STATES

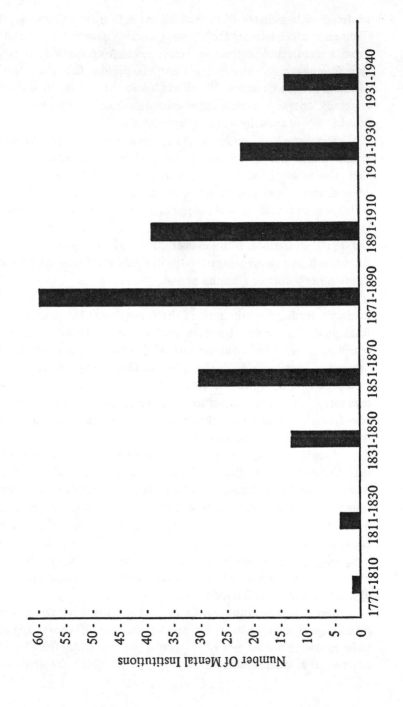

internal dynamics. Freud's mechanistic and deterministic framework, however, made his treatment approaches compatible with the broader specifications of the organic framework. Although Freud's theories received a hostile reception in academic circles, they proved to be a potent source of influence on practitioners.

A psychologist, G. Stanley Hall, also deserves credit for pushing psychiatry toward the couch. In 1909, Hall invited Freud, Jung, and Ferenczi to lecture at Clark University. These addresses had considerable impact on psychiatric practice because they provided a sophisticated, attractive alternative to the increasingly influential behavioristic philosophy, which many viewed as simplistic and sterile.

In 1911, Abraham Brill founded the New York Psychoanalytic Society for the purpose of training professionals in this mode of psychotherapy. A section of psychoanalysis was established within the American Psychiatric Association in 1933, thus helping to legitimize the practice of psychoanalysis within medicine.

Coinciding with the psychoanalytic deluge in this country was the growth of child-guidance clinics. An offshoot of the moral model of treatment, the child-guidance movement was rooted in the establishment of rehabilitation centers for mentally retarded individuals several decades earlier. In 1896, Lightner Witmer established the first such clinic at the University of Pennsylvania. In the early 1900's, several centers for preventing delinquency were established, the most notable being the founding of the Juvenile Psychopathic Institute by psychiatrist William Healy.

Obviously, this brief historical sketch does not do full justice to the many interacting influences that molded the social institution of psychiatry. The interested reader can consult Alexander and Selesnick (1966) for a more comprehensive description of the development of the profession. We have, however, outlined the forces which provided psychiatry with a head start in assuming control of treatment for mental disorders. The basis of power for this group was provided by their exercise of administrative responsibility in institutional settings for the insane and augmented by discoveries linking mental disorders to organic causes. The profession adopted novel treatment strategies that stemmed from psychoanalysis by amalgamating the moral, organic, and psychological perspectives. The prominent social status of psychiatrists during the early twentieth century helped foster the use of psychiatric conceptions in educational settings, primarily child-guidance clinics.

Clinical Psychology: Diagnosis And The Split-Personality

Early Developments. This movement was fathered by Lightner Witmer, spent its earliest years moving from the testing room to the laboratory, and, almost upon graduating from the university, became schizophrenic. The traditional role of the clinical psychologist involved assessment of human behavior and diagnosis of debilitating conditions. This role was fostered by three historical trends: (1) the development of procedures to measure individual differences, (2) the establishment of child guidance facilities, and (3) the spreading impact of psychoanalytic thought (Santostefano and Kahn, 1966).

The measurement of human abilities drew from three distinct lines of influence that arose in Germany, England, and France. The Germanic orientation emphasized the use of experimental methods in laboratory settings. As personified in the work of Wilhelm Wundt and his associates, the intent of these investigations was to describe intellectual and emotional functions in terms of simple associative relationships. In the laboratory, the range of sensory inputs could be restricted and responses accurately measured to achieve the goal of demonstrating causal links between sensory stimuli and behavioral responses. This framework aided the development of early intelligence and personality assessment devices.

The English orientation, which was directed at examining individual differences, facilitated the development of statistical techniques to summarize psychological data. Whereas the laboratory approach emphasized measurement of simple responses emitted by few subjects, English investigators often sampled the responses of thousands of individuals. Contributors like Francis Galton, who made widespread use of questionnaires and developed the statistical normal curve concept, and Karl Pearson, who derived the correlation coefficient, were interested in developing general laws about behavior. The legacy of this approach was providing statistical tools to aid the diagnostic activities of psychologists.

The French orientation stressed detailed case study of the individual to distinguish between various degrees of mental subnormality. Detailed observation of behavior in naturalistic settings was emphasized. Itard, an expert in methods of training deaf individuals, labored for five years to socialize a feral child—the wild boy of Aveyron. He provided many new sensory experiences in an attempt to raise the child's intelligence. Although he viewed his efforts as a failure, his detailed account impressed the French Academy of Science to the extent that they regarded his work as successful. This approach demonstrated the necessity of attending to the individual and provided a foundation for acceptance of psychoanalytic concepts that came later.

The French psychologist Alfred Binet synthesized the methods of these three orientations while developing an instrument to measure the intellectual abilities of Parisian school children around the turn of the century. Following the adaptation of Binet's test for use with retarded children by Henry Goddard in 1910, interest in assessment grew rapidly in the United States.

Polarization Of Research And Practice. Professional psychology had created a specialized area of expertise for itself. The mental hygiene movement, which led to the establishment of mental retardation facilities, child-guidance clinics, and mental institutions, provided psychologists with a large and varied population on which to practice their trade. It was at this point that the polarization of the profession began. Those psychologists who made pragmatic use of assessment devices in institutional settings came to be regarded as service-providing practitioners. Other psychologists, however, gravitated to the university where they employed assessment strategies in their search to uncover basic laws of human behavior. The role of scientist became the major professional identification of these psychologists. Even though these two groups shared a common interest in assessment, the purposes of their professional activities began to diverge.

The influx of psychoanalytic thought had three important consequences for the development of the profession. *First, it provided an alluring alternative to the behavioristic conceptions that enjoyed considerable popularity at the time.* Early behaviorists, most notably John B. Watson, sought to explain conscious human activity by reducing it to physiological reactions. For Watson, "thought" was nothing more than subvocal throat movement, "love" was reducible to glandular activity around the genital area, and "fear" was simply a classically conditioned emotional reaction. Psychoanalysis provided a framework for understanding behavior as a complex phenomenon with multiple determinants.

Second, psychologists developed more sophisticated and specialized assessment devices as a result of being exposed to psychoanalytic conceptions. With the exception of Binet's test, practically all tests of intelligence involved simple psychomotor tasks that measured reaction time, sensory discrimination, and verbal associations. Unfortunately, these tests were not able to predict complex forms of intellectual functioning, such as success in college. Psychoanalysis alerted psychologists to the fact that certain assessment instruments provided insights about the personality and internal dynamics as well as about intelligence. Within this framework, Hermann Rorschach published his now famous "inkblot" test, along with normative data from 300 mental patients and 100 normal individuals (Alexander and Selesnick, 1966). Psychologists began to develop other assessment devices that enabled them to put their newly discovered dynamic conceptions to practical use.

As a third, and largely undesirable consequence, psychoanalysis aggravated the split between scientists and professionals. The former found simple associative tasks better suited to their purposes than the more complex projective and personality assessment instruments. They also found the psychometric properties of many of these devices to be wanting and viewed their uncritical use by practitioners to be unjustified. The latter suggested that the scientists were producing little valuable information for applied psychology.

This polarization was reflected on an organizational level. The American Psychological Association was founded in 1892 under the leadership of G. Stanley Hall, for the purpose of sharing research findings from academic laboratories around the country. As the interests of its members enlarged, the association formed new divisions. The first divisions reflected the scientific orientation of the membership. The Division of Clinical Psychology was not established until 1921; it followed the formation of interest groups that centered on teaching psychology, experimental psychology, evaluation and measurement, developmental psychology, and physiological and comparative psychology.

Differences between scientists and practitioners were intensified by an influx of European refugees from Nazi tyranny during the 1930's. The immigrant professionals brought with them a commitment to practice psychotherapy within either a psychoanalytic or Gestalt framework. This influx had the social effects of offering psychologists a new role as providers of psychotherapeutic services and of furnishing new theoretical perspectives. Many psychologists viewed the provision of psychotherapy as incompatible with the primary task of discovering laws about human behavior. The addition of new theories further fragmented what little unity was left in the American Psychological Association. By 1940, practitioners left it and formed a splinter group, the American Association of Applied Psychologists, to meet their organizational needs.

Mobilization of resources during World War II moved psychologists toward the role of psychotherapist and helped heal the split between scientists and practitioners within the field. Both types of psychologists were required to perform diagnostic activities and, more importantly, to provide therapy, because not enough psychiatrists existed to meet these needs. The scientists discovered that practical service endeavors were more complex than they had formerly believed, while the practitioners gained new respect for the utility of scientific inquiry. In 1945, the two rival professional organizations were again united as the American Psychological Association, and its members endorsed the dual objectives of advancing psychology as a science and as a means of promoting human welfare. As we shall see in Chapter 2, however, the scientist-practitioner controversy still continues to plague professional psychology.

Psychiatric Social Work:
In Search Of An Identity
The movement of psychiatric social work was born in a poorhouse and developed a strong moral character before marching into child guidance clinics and hospitals. As an adolescent, it became very opportunistic and, as a result, failed to carve out a uniquely specialized role upon which to form a professional identity. The origins of social work lay in the charitable activities of individuals and religious organizations within the Judeo-Christian ethical tradition. Before the seventeenth century, a very fatalistic attitude toward human misery prevailed. The poor were generally blamed for their condition, and societal resources for improving the quality of life were never allocated on a widespread basis (Strean, 1974). In 1601, the Elizabethan Poor Law mandated the establishment of almshouses to shelter children and the "impotent poor." Recognition of personal misfortune as a societal problem became more widespread during the next 300 years, leading to the foundation of numerous charitable organizations.

The establishment of the London Society for Organizing Charitable Relief and Repressing Mendicancy in 1869 is generally agreed to mark the beginning of social work as a profession. Although members of these charitable groups had no full-time occupational identity as helpers, they shared the aim of bringing spiritual and material comfort to the destitute. These "friendly visitors" generally believed that economic and psychological misfortune was due to some sort of moral failing. Within this framework, the classification of misfitting had a decidedly moral (and somewhat moralistic) flavor. The "worthy" poor were viewed as somewhat misguided victims, but those who attempted to cope with their poverty by drinking, begging, or suffering enforced idleness were considered to be "unworthy."

Branches of the London Society soon sprang up in the United States. Volunteers from many agencies began providing a wide variety of services to the poor. Lack of coordination including a duplication of services between agencies resulted in the formation of Charity Organization Societies in many cities. These agencies sought to coordinate the efforts of their participating service groups. During the late nineteenth century, however, these societies became increasingly involved in providing services to families, and, by 1919, had evolved into the American Association for Organizing Family Social Work. The family thus became the target for the intervention efforts of social workers.

Movement toward professional specialization was fostered by three milestones within the field. The establishment of the first training program for psychiatric social workers at the Boston Psychopathic Hospital in 1913 produced a new kind of helper: one who practiced social work as a full-time occupation and was paid for rendering these services. The publication of the first textbook of social casework by Mary Richmond in 1917 provided social workers with a method of collecting and evaluating information about people. The notion of *casework* actually supplied social workers with a functional set of tools without an underlying content area (Reinehr, 1975). Casework was not based upon psychological principles, sociological theory, or a family dynamics framework. This content void was filled by the influx of psychoanalytic conceptions, which provided social workers with a theoretical perspective upon which to base their casework activities.

These three developments caused an identity crisis for psychiatric social workers. As a professionally trained group, they were supposed to practice casework on family units within a theoretical system that emphasized individual treatment, which was considered to be the proper province of psychiatry. The psychoanalytic deluge led to fragmentation within the field that was similar to the rift between applied and scientific psychologists. The organization of the American Association of Psychiatric Social Workers in 1926 reflected this confusion. The association was composed of administrative committees, which had the task of determining the legitimate boundaries of psychiatric social work, and study committees, which were concerned with increasing knowledge about casework methods and mental hygiene.

From the beginning, conflict regarding who could properly be designated as a psychiatric social worker prevailed. Two criteria for membership in the association were established. Candidates who had completed a formal training program or individuals who worked in an agency established to deal with mental illness were eligible. The second criterion proved to be quite vague, because the growth of the profession had been so opportunistic. Case workers operated in many settings, including state welfare agencies, charitable organizations, hospitals, and child-guidance clinics, which conceivably could have some remote connection with mental illness. The professional identity crisis thus worsened as psychiatric social workers sought to create a subspecialty within the field without having unique functions that distinguished them from social workers in general. The association attempted to resolve this dilemma during the 1930's and 1940's by sanctioning the practice of psychotherapy by psychiatric social workers. This strategy, however, brought them into conflict with organized psychiatry, which possessed a much stronger power base. At present, the status of psychiatric social workers as psychotherapists rests in a controversial limbo (Strean, 1974).

FINAL WORDS

Psychotherapy is a complex process of interpersonal influence which never takes place in a social vacuum. In the final analysis, therapists and clients are *people* whose activities are molded by both contemporary social influences and the legacy of history. The relational nature of psychotherapy as a social process between individuals has become more readily apparent in recent years. We have been much slower, however, in recognizing that our knowledge about psychotherapy comes from a variety of frameworks, all of which are relativistic and incomplete.

Historical analysis is one fundamental perspective for understanding contemporary psychotherapeutic practices. The professional schisms, as well as the political and economic controversies that currently plague the helping professions, represent a culmination of long, complex historical trends. We are now ready to examine the major areas of conflict and their consequences on the larger social system. The relevance of these issues will be highlighted, however, if we maintain a people-oriented focus. Stating that psychotherapy has an important political and economic impact on the social system is really saying that it affects you and me.

2
Current Professional Controversies

Although the expressed aim of psychotherapy is to relieve the suffering of individuals, providing help in a socially sanctioned context also yields substantial financial rewards as well as power and prestige for therapists. The practice of psychotherapy is a large business in this country today. Given this fact in combination with the opportunistic development of the major helping professions, it is only reasonable to expect that a certain amount of friction will occur as each profession seeks to extend its influence. Even though existing conflicts are usually expressed as theoretical differences, they appear to be strongly rooted in maneuvering by professional societies for political, financial, and social gain. In this chapter, we will explore the background and consequences of major controversies that currently affect professional psychotherapists. Although these controversies are treated as distinctive, the effects of each are tightly interwoven with those of the others. The practical impact of the controversies on consumers of psychotherapeutic services will then be examined.

DEFINING THE ESSENCE OF PSYCHOTHERAPY

A Range Of Definitions
We have already noted that the term *psychotherapy* is a very elastic concept referring to many multidimensional processes. One of the most convenient methods of making sense out of a complicated phenomenon is to define it. A definition that is generally agreed upon can provide a global understanding of what we wish to study.

In attempting to understand psychotherapy by this method, however, we encounter three serious problems. First, we find that no generally agreed upon definition exists. A careful search of the literature will yield at least 40 different definitions. Wolberg (1967) alone provides more than 20 definitions of psychotherapy. Second, any definition contains inherent theoretical biases which limit its scope. This limitation is unavoidable because of the connotative meanings attached to the very words forming the definition. Third, in accepting a particular definition, one comes under the influence of specific practical consequences (e.g., who may legitimately practice therapy) that logically follow from the choice.

To illustrate these points, let us consider three definitions of psychotherapy. Two represent the extreme ends of the wide spectrum of activities psychotherapists are thought to engage in, and one reflects a more moderate, middle position. The italicized words represent terms that reflect theoretical biases which, in turn, generate practical consequences. Note this definition from Thomas (1973):

> A method of treating *disease*, especially *nervous disorders*, by mental means rather than physical [Reprinted by permission. C. L. Thomas (Ed.). *Taber's cyclopedic medical dictionary, 12th Ed.* F. A. Davis Company, 1973, p. 168].

This definition clearly implies that emotional suffering is at the very least analogous to a physical disease. Although the professional nature of the treating relationship is not specified, again, the implication is that it involves interaction between a physician and a patient. Close examination of the definition reveals a curious anomaly. The healer (not the helper) is supposed to treat a disease that is really not a disease through mental methods that are not appropriate for treating real physical diseases. Despite this logical contradiction, the treatment of nervous disorders is defined as the sole province of healers, that is, those with medical training. Thus, psychotherapy, by this definition, is reserved as a medical specialty.

Now we turn to a different definition by Wolberg (1967):

> Psychotherapy is the treatment, by psychological means, of problems of an emotional nature in which a trained person deliberately establishes a *professional relationship* with the *patient* with the object (1) of removing, modifying, or retarding existing *symptoms*, (2) of mediating disturbed *patterns of behavior*, and (3) of promoting positive *personality growth* and development

[Reprinted by permission. L. R. Wolberg. *The technique of psychotherapy, 2nd Ed.* Grune and Stratton, Inc., 1967, p. 3].

Wolberg's conception represents a middle point on the spectrum. This definition implies that the therapeutic relationship differs from other extended social encounters because it involves a formally trained professional, but the practice of psychotherapy is not implicitly restricted to physicians. Although the professional may either help or heal, the definition does contain a medical orientation, as revealed by the words *patient* and *symptom*. These words imply that treatment is directed at a relatively passive participant who ought not to be held responsible for his difficulties. The inclusion of the final goals of altering behavior and promoting personality growth, however, allow the incorporation of behavioral and humanistic interventions as legitimate forms of psychotherapy. Despite the centrality of Wolberg's definition, however, therapists who follow behavioral and humanistic frameworks would likely find certain portions of the definition objectionable.

Let us consider a definition from Frank (1961):

. . . . psychotherapy is a form of *help-giving* in which a trained, *socially sanctioned healer* tries to relieve a sufferer's distress by *facilitating* certain changes in his feelings, attitudes and behaviors, through the performance of certain activities with him [Reprinted by permission. J. D. Frank. *Persuasion and healing: A comparative study of psychotherapy.* The Johns Hopkins University Press, 1961, p. 114].

Operating from a historical perspective, Frank provides by far the broadest definition of psychotherapy. His emphasis on the healer's role as socially sanctioned implies that it is a culturally relative one which can take many forms. Frank cites parallels between modern therapeutic practices and the behavior influence rituals performed in primitive societies and those rites performed by faith healers. This definition legitimizes the inclusion of emerging helping resources, such as trained paraprofessionals, as psychotherapists, pending general social acceptance of them as such.

Although the psychotherapist is described as a healer, the definition emphasizes the role of helper to a greater extent. The therapist is one who facilitates changes in a distressed individual rather than one who treats the person. This emphasis implies that psychotherapy is an interactive catalyst which helps instigate change as opposed to magical or medical forms of treatment in which the distressed person somehow taps the healing power of the therapist. It also contains the very important implication that psychotherapy is a collaborative endeavor which requires the active participation of both helper and helpee. Finally, the word *distress* suggests that the origin of the disturbance involves social misfitting which can be conceptualized from a medical, psychological, or sociological framework.

Components As Definitions

In an attempt to avoid the theoretical biases inherent in any explicit definition of psychotherapy, other experts have sought to describe the essential components of the process. Winder (1957) and Eysenck (1961) have provided such functional definitions, both of which have enjoyed fairly widespread acceptance among psychotherapists. They view psychotherapy as encompassing (1) a prolonged interpersonal relationship between two or more people, in which (2) one participant is a specialist with formal training in facilitating relationships, and (3) the others are dissatisfied with their emotional or interpersonal functioning, and in which (4) treatment involves psychological methods that (5) are based on formal theoretical principles, and (6) is aimed at resolving the difficulties of the distressed individual.

Although the broad, general scope of such a definition makes it acceptable to many, this very breadth poses other limitations on its utility. It presents a somewhat idealistic view of the professional helping process which neither captures the many controversies that exist nor accurately reflects the manner in which most psychotherapy is actually conducted. For example, vast differences exist in the amount of time people remain in therapy, depending upon whether they are seen by a private therapist or in a public outpatient clinic. Strupp, Fox, and Lessler (1969) reported that private clients averaged 26 months in therapy, but the median duration of the therapeutic encounter in public facilities is between six and seven sessions (Garfield, 1971). In addition, no one is quite sure exactly what the term *psychological methods* refers to, other than talking to a client. The importance of psychological theory in the treatment process is similarly unclear, because adherence to a formal theory seems to disappear as clinicians gain practical experience (Fiedler, 1950, 1951; Strupp, 1960).

Weaknesses Of Definitions

The weakness of all definitional attempts has been aptly summarized by Wolberg (1967), who stated:

> The sundry published definitions of psychotherapy agree on one point; namely, that psychotherapy constitutes a form of approach to many problems of an emotional nature. They do not agree on other aspects, such as the techniques employed, the processes included, the goals approximated, or the personnel involved [Reprinted by permission. L. R. Wolberg. *The technique of psychotherapy, 2nd Ed.* Grune and Stratton, Inc. , 1967, pp. 7-8].

It is precisely these "other aspects," however, that make up the essence of psychotherapeutic processes. Disagreements on the definitional level reflect the major professional schisms that currently exist and serve to worsen their practical consequences.

THE TERRITORIAL IMPERATIVE AMONG PROFESSIONAL PSYCHOTHERAPISTS

One very useful side effect of defining psychotherapy in a particular way is that it justifies the restriction of helping endeavors to those who share a particular philosophy and common training. This tendency has existed throughout history; witch doctors and exorcists grudgingly relinquished their power to physicians, who were antagonistic to the rise of psychiatrists, who fought the development of therapeutic expertise among psychologists, who, in turn, denigrate the activities of social workers and marriage counselors.

Claims And Accusations

For better or for worse, psychotherapists seem to have an emotional investment in extolling the virtues of their own beliefs, often at the expense of colleagues who hold competing views. This tendency has led to some curious distinctions. Freud, for example, compared the "pure gold" of psychoanalysis to the "cheap alloy" of psychotherapy (Alexander and Selesnick, 1966). Carrying on the tradition of psychoanalytic superiority, Tarachow (1963) argued that psychoanalysis results in a *resolution* of the resistances that cause emotional disturbances, while psychotherapy, at best, produces a *limited rearrangement* of these sources of difficulty. The clear implication, which has not received very much empirical support, is that psychotherapy yields weaker and more transitory outcomes than psychoanalysis does.

Reservation of certain helping activities as the exclusive domain of groups sharing a common theoretical orientation is not limited to psychoanalysts. Hans Eysenck (1971), a renowned behavior therapist, presented a strong case against teaching psychotherapeutic skills to clinical psychologists. He contended that psychotherapy was a medical legacy and that it had proven to be ineffective. He further argued that learning the skills appropriate to the psychologist's traditional role (i.e., research and diagnosis) represented a full-time training load. He went on, however, to define psychotherapy "to include all types of interpretative, dynamic or even Rogerian systems" and to distinguish these helping activities from "psychological systems involving re-education, conditioning or behavior therapy" (p. 364). The implication here is that the latter types of intervention are superior to the former. Like Tarachow's claims, Eysenck's contentions that psychotherapy is (1) ineffective and (2) qualitatively different from behavior therapy are both heatedly debated issues.

Professional Rivalry
On The Organizational Level

This sort of theoretical pretentiousness usually occurs in the relative obscurity of professional journals. It is mild compared to the friction that exists between organized professional groups, particularly psychiatrists and psychologists. These two professions have fought a running battle over who has the right to practice psychotherapy for more than two decades. After World War II, the federal government underwrote the training of mental health professionals in an attempt to better meet the emerging demand for services. About the same time, increasing numbers of psychologists began to practice psychotherapy, thus bringing them into competition with psychiatrists. Strife between these professions has occurred on four fronts.

Certifying And Licensing. During the 1950's and early 1960's psychologists fought for recognition as psychotherapists by seeking to obtain state laws which provided certifying or licensing of their activities. Briefly, a certification law restricts use of the title *psychologist* to trained professionals who meet specific criteria established by a state-appointed board of examiners. A license restricts not only the title but also specifies the types of service a psychologist may offer the public. In Connecticut, which has a licensing law, only those who meet certain training requirements and pass a written test after having had two years of postdoctoral experience may legally call themselves psychologists. In addition, an individual is licensed as either a clinical or consulting psychologist (or both, if two examinations are passed), and, as such, may legally perform a restricted set of activities. The licensing board, composed of professional psychologists who are appointed by the governor, forms a quasi-legislative body. During the 1950's, psychologists who conducted psychotherapy in states that had no licensing or certification laws were sometimes brought to court by psychiatrists and charged with malpractice.

During the 1960's, a rapidly expanding market for psychological services helped make relations between the two professional groups more amicable. At this time, physicians were eligible to collect third-party (insurance) payments for their services, while psychologists were not (Meltzer, 1975). Many psychologists worked in collaboration with physicians so that they too could be reimbursed through insurance payments. The prospect of federally sponsored national health insurance has led to a resurgence of professional friction, beginning around 1971.

Recognition By Insurance Companies. This second battleground is an extraordinarily complex one. The major insurance companies have traditionally defined psychotherapy as a form of medical treatment, reimbursing claimants for 80 percent of the cost of outpatient treatment, if it is conducted by psychiatrists or under their direction. Arguing that this arrangement restricts the consumer's freedom of choice in selecting a service provider, psychologists have fought to force insurers to make direct payments for the treatments they provide.

The necessity of "supervision" by a physician has been one central point of contention. In 1974, a spokesman for the American Psychiatric Association testified in Congress against a "freedom-of-choice" resolution, asserting that:

> If physician collaboration is not continued as a condition to the reimbursement of services to psychologists, we will soon be in a situation where physician consultation will be minimal or non-existent, to the detriment of the patient [Reprinted by permission. J. Asher. Psychiatrists oppose key bill. *APA Monitor.* American Psychological Association, 1974, *5*, No. 7, p. 1].

This statement is reminiscent of physicians' attempts to obtain the right to search apothecaries in London for "bad drugs" in 1723 (Elliott,

1972). In both cases, the well being of the helpee was the ostensible issue masking a more important power struggle between the professions involved. By 1977, 23 states have adopted freedom-of-choice laws; it appears likely that psychologists will emerge victorious from this skirmish.

In general, the insurance companies have sided with the physicians, contending that recognizing nonmedical practitioners will lead to a drastic increase in insurance premiums. They have, however, taken a number of unilateral steps to maintain their own best interests. Blue Cross, for example, planned to cut reimbursements for psychotherapy from 80 percent to 50 percent after discovering that expenditures for such services exceeded their estimates (Meltzer, 1975).

Regulation Through State Legislation. A third area of conflict has involved attempting to regulate the practice of psychotherapy through emerging state legislation. In 1975, the American Psychiatric Association defined a new concept called *medical psychotherapy* in an effort to restrict practice to its own members. The implication is that real, meaningful, and effective therapy can be carried out only by a qualified physician. Even in light of Thomas' (1973) medically oriented definition of psychotherapy, this new concept is a contradiction in terms. Medical intervention necessarily involves physical, not psychological means. This conceptual drawback has not stopped the introduction of the term into state legislation, however. The outcome of this skirmish is as yet uncertain.

Struggle For JCAH Membership. Attempts by psychologists to establish a beachhead on the Joint Commission on Accreditation of Hospitals is the fourth area of current conflict. The JCAH is an enormously powerful nonprofit corporation, whose membership is drawn from the American medical establishment. Members of the governing board represent the American Medical Association, American Hospital Association, and American College of Physicians and Surgeons, among others. The organization was established in 1918 when the American College of Surgeons began inspecting hospitals to determine if they met minimal safety standards. The finding that only 89 of almost 700 hospitals passed inspection was so embarrassing that the list of offending institutions was burned in the basement of the Waldorf-Astoria Hotel (Trotter, 1976).

Following its formal incorporation in 1951, the JCAH developed specialized accreditation councils for different types of health-care facilities. Currently, the organization has the status of a largely invisible, but powerful quasi-governmental agency. It has the power to set and enforce safety standards for all health-care facilities in the country. By removing its approval of an institution, the JCAH can cause the loss of Medicare and Medicaid funds and private insurance benefits for patients (Trotter, 1976).

Psychologists have recently petitioned JCAH for membership in the organization, contending that medical domination of the group has caused them to be discriminated against regarding staff privileges (e.g., admitting and discharging patients; prescribing various psychological interventions) in institutions. Currently, only physicians and dentists have such privileges. The political lobby of the American Psychological Association complained about the exclusionary policies of JCAH to the Federal Trade Commission in 1976, arguing that psychologists have made significant contributions to knowledge about health care. Their argument further contended that medical control of the organization led to the devaluation of psychologists as health-care specialists.

The common denominator in all four areas of controversy is the attempt by psychologists to gain parity with physicians. The former are actively combatting the generally prevailing belief that medically trained personnel automatically provide a higher quality of service than other professionals. The larger battle is by no means over, and it will likely be a bitter and costly one.

THE ART VERSUS SCIENCE CONTROVERSY
Hard-Headed Scientists Versus
Soft-Hearted Practitioners

The controversy about whether psychotherapy is more an art or a science has caused considerable friction. The art-science polarity cuts across professional lines, although the practical consequences of the split have affected psychologists most seriously. Freud viewed his clinical activities as scientific; this belief is shared by many contemporary psychoanalysts. Critics of this movement, however, have castigated psychoanalysis as unscientific dogma. Behavior therapists proudly wear the mantle of scientist. Yet, they are frequently criticized for being cold, unfeeling, and manipulative. They, in turn, counter these criticisms by arguing that lack of "real" scientific knowledge about psychotherapy by their colleagues makes them *soft-headed*, and, therefore, inadvertently *hard-hearted*.

Such friction results from traditional conceptions of art and science, which suggest that they are qualitatively different from each other. Art is considered to be intuitive, private, informal, creative, playful, and an end in itself. Science, on the other hand, is conceptualized as logical, public, formal, painstaking, laborious, and a means to an end. This traditional distinction emphasized science as a value-free activity that was aimed at discovering objective truths about reality. In contrast, art was viewed as heavily influenced by values and subjective.

Changing Concepts Of Science

Observation And Inference. Fortunately, emerging philosophical conceptions are erasing this illusory distinction between art and science; they are demonstrating that both have their place in furthering our understanding of psychotherapy. Major changes have occurred in how the content and method of science have been conceptualized. The content of science was traditionally viewed as accumulated bodies of factual knowledge that were ordered into models, theories, and laws. Scientific understanding was thought to grow in a slow, incremental manner whereby newly discovered facts triumphed over prevailing but incomplete theoretical formulations. Scientific method referred to formal, repeatable, and presumably objective procedures that were applied to describe, predict, and control environmental events.

Modern philosophers of science (Kuhn, 1962; Reichenbach, 1938; Sjoberg, 1975) have strongly challenged this traditional view. For them scientific inquiry involves the human activities of observation and inference. A number of important implications stem from this shift of emphasis away from the procedures of science per se toward the scientist as an information-processing agent.

First, both observation and inference require simplifying the complexity found in real life. It is impossible to observe everything that occurs around us, and it is even more difficult to tie all that we observe into coherent patterns. Our view of reality is both a restricted and an indeterminant one.

Effects Of Paradigms. Kuhn (1962) calls these restricted frameworks *paradigms*. As noted in Chapter 1, because a particular paradigm provides a coherent scheme for tying observations together, it provides the illusion of representing the total phenomenon of interest. Equating information yielded by a paradigm with objective truth has been the cause of much controversy throughout history.

Second, paradigms are as prescriptive as they are descriptive. Scientists operate in a context of values. They cannot escape being influenced by their beliefs. Regarding empirical procedures, paradigms tend to restrict the types of investigatory techniques a scientist may properly use, and, more importantly, limit the range of topics that can legitimately be examined.

The prescriptive influence of a paradigm extends far beyond the laboratory. People who operate within a widely accepted paradigm often are rewarded by scientific acclaim and positions of social responsibility. They control professional journals, decide which grant proposals are worthy of funding, and write books. These activities steer the accumulation and dissemination of knowledge in directions that harmonize with the prevailing paradigm. Kuhn (1962) argues that scientific knowledge grows by means of a dialectic process of conflict and synthesis between alternate paradigms.

Sjoberg (1975) has taken this analysis one step further by suggesting that scientific inquiry is often deliberately employed to justify social reform. Many experts once believed that black people could not profit from psychotherapy. This notion was supported by solid "scientific" facts that "proved" such individuals had innate defects in their personality structures (Kardiner and Ovesey, 1951). This view is no longer widely held, even though the supporting "facts" have not changed. Alteration of this belief came about as new paradigms arose which led experts to interpret the original "facts" in new and less dehumanizing ways (Gardner, 1971). Reasons for the failure of a black client to improve now implicate defects in the therapy situation or specific failings on the part of the therapist (Wilson and Calhoun, 1974). Such interpretations are themselves derived from paradigms that explicitly support those who are disadvantaged or discriminated against in our society.

Blurring Of Distinctions
Between Art And Science

The contribution of these conceptual innovators was to blur the traditional distinction between art and science. Both art and science are based on observation and inference, and both are subjective and influenced by values. Reichenbach (1938) provided a design for understanding the role of each endeavor in psychotherapy. When dealing with clients, a therapist must achieve a satisfying set of explanations about the causes of their behavior. The typical clinician operates initially in what Reichenbach calls the *context of discovery*. This conceptual state is characterized by inductive thinking, creativity, and procedural vagueness. The therapist forms hunches about the dynamics that underlie the client's behavior and begins to employ flexible and often idiosyncratic treatment procedures stemming logically from these vague intuitions. The typical scientist begins empirical inquiry in exactly the same way. The scientist's hypotheses are nothing more than informed guesses about how particular events will operate.

The scientist, however, is expected to verify informal intuitions within the *context of justification*, according to Reichenbach. The generality of creative insights can be documented through whatever empirical methods are considered acceptable at the time. These procedures share the properties of being deductive in nature, public, replicable, and standardized. Justification is essentially a form of consensual agreement, but along dimensions that transcend groups of like-minded people. Reliability, validity, and generalizability are currently the three major dimensions for evaluating the adequacy of observations as properly "scientific."

Effective psychotherapy requires that the clinician possess the skill of an artist and the talents of a scientist. Ideally, these activities interlock and complement each other. Clinical intuitions provide the raw material for conceptual advances, while scientific inquiry subjects them to public scrutiny. Research activity is ultimately rooted in a creative context of discovery, but it provides an absolutely necessary balance to intuitive flights of fancy. Thus, in the final analysis, the controversy does not center directly on whether psychotherapy is an art or a science. Rather, conflict on a conceptual level stems from differences of opinion about the relative contributions of art and science.

The Art-Science Issue
In Training Practices

When the art-science issue is translated from a conceptual to a professional level, it becomes fragmented into a series of practical controversies between practitioners and scientists. The consequences of this split are most apparent in the somewhat schizoid training practices of clinical psychology. Following World War II, the federal government began to sponsor training for mental health professionals. At that time the American Psychological Association officially accepted a dual mandate for the profession. Psychology was to promote human welfare through practical interventions and to contribute to the body of scientific knowledge. The emergence of many new clinical training programs necessitated a conference to work out guidelines for adequate training.

The Scientist-Practitioner Model. In 1949, the "scientist-practitioner" model of training was officially adopted at the Boulder Conference on Training in Clinical Psychology. The conferees proposed that graduate students should be trained as both scientists and clinicians, but they emphasized that the unique, and primary, contribution of the profession was research. Preparing psychologists for careers as psychotherapists was not deemed to be a primary training goal. Since that time, the practical utility of this training model has been seriously questioned, with both scientists and clinicians expressing dissatisfaction.

Conflict Over Compatibility Of Roles. A central element of conflict has been whether the two roles are incompatible. Albee (1970) has suggested that scientists are trained to be detached, critical observers who make cautious, conservative decisions, but clinicians are expected to be involved, accepting participant-observers who often must employ innovative and radical intervention strategies. Scientific methodology can be taught didactically as applications of formal principles about experimentation. Psychotherapy, however, has traditionally been taught by the apprentice method. Clinical wisdom is passed from expert to novice in the context of extensive and intensive personal encounters. The contradictory demands inherent in training people to be both scientists and practitioners often place graduate students in a confusing double bind.

In contrast to the practical training orientation psychiatrists receive in medical school, the training emphasis for psychologists in university settings has been on developing diagnostic and research skills. Kelly (1961), in a survey of clinical psychologists, discovered a great deal of dissatisfaction regarding both their training and choice of a career. His respondents indicated that this training emphasis was of little value for their primary professional activity—providing psychotherapy. As a result of such widespread dissatisfaction, new training models were generated at conferences in Chicago in 1965 and at Vail, Colorado, in 1973. Movement toward meeting the training demands of practitioners has also been facilitated by the establishment of professional degree programs which function autonomously from traditional academic settings.

These innovations have aroused considerable controversy, particularly regarding how the quality of practitioner training in such settings can be controlled. Critics of professionalization argue that the movement lacks concern with basic theoretical and empirical issues. This flaw will lead to the erosion of excellence (Strupp, 1975) in training psychotherapists because therapeutic interventions must be taught within theoretical and empirical contexts. Without a rigorous empirical emphasis, psychotherapy will forever remain a mysterious art with scientific pretentions. Proponents of professionalization argue that a shrinking job market for traditionally trained psychologists requires the development of new occupational expertise. They further contend that practicing therapists find theoretical and empirical advances to have little relevance for their clinical activities. They also cite the necessity of providing immediate delivery of services to those in need. *The crux of this conflict centers on whether psychotherapy is more art or more science.* Lehner (1952), a participant at the Boulder Conference, summarized this dilemma well:

> I am afraid that in spite of our efforts we have left therapy as an undefined technique which is applied to unspecified problems with nonpredictable outcome. For this technique we recommend rigorous training [Reprinted by permission. G. F. Lehner. Defining psychotherapy. *American Psychologist*. American Psychological Association, 1952, 7, 547].

A recent survey by Garfield and Kurtz (1976) found considerably less dissatisfaction among clinical psychologists than Kelly had uncovered. Fully 77 percent of their respondents expressed at least slight satisfaction with their graduate training, and almost 90 percent were at least quite satisfied with their career choice. Psychologists with academic affiliations, however, rated themselves as significantly more satisfied with their training than their practitioner counterparts.

Although the primary institutional affiliation of the respondents was split equally between the university (22 percent) and private practice (23 percent), a majority considered themselves to be clinical practitioners, as Figure 2 indicates. In addition, one out of every eight of those surveyed spontaneously suggested the provision of more therapy experience under the supervision of an experienced clinician as a necessary training improvement.

Increased satisfaction among professional psychologists has not healed the schism between scientists and practitioners, however. The current debate over quality control has important implications for the selection and training of care-providers. It will likely become a central issue in the interprofessional feud between psychology and psychiatry.

HEALTH VERSUS ADJUSTMENT AS THE AIM OF THERAPEUTIC INTERVENTION

Perhaps the most acrimonious debate among psychotherapists concerns whether emotional difficulties can best be understood within a medical or a social-psychological framework. Like the other controversies, this issue has strong political and guild implications in addition to its conceptual aspects. These practical consequences tend to polarize the experts into taking extreme positions regarding the adequacy of the two models.

The Medical Model

Historical Use. The dominant contemporary framework for conceptualizing maladaptive behavior is called the *medical model*. Within this perspective, dysfunctional conditions are considered to be external manifestations (i.e., symptomatic) of an underlying disease process. The concept of *disease* was vital to the development of medical knowledge from the time of the Renaissance. It provided a structure for linking seemingly random maladaptive behaviors into a coherent syndrome, aiding the discovery of many infectious agents during the nineteenth century. Conceptually, a single foreign agent can be considered to cause a wide variety of symptoms when the notion of disease is employed. This simplification strategy enables one to predict the course of the process, the probable outcome, and the effects of specific interventions. In medicine, three general causes of disease have been formulated: invasion by a foreign agent (syphilis, influenza), internal malfunction of

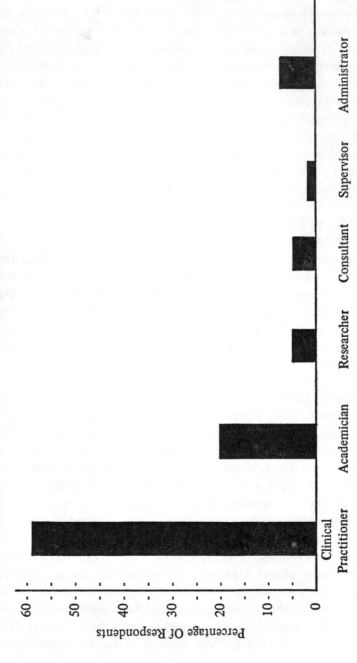

FIGURE 2. SELF-DESCRIPTION OF PRIMARY PROFESSIONAL ACTIVITIES BY CLINICAL PSYCHOLOGISTS

Adapted with permission. S. L. Garfield and R. Kurtz. Clinical psychologists in the 1970's. *American Psychologist*, 1976, *31*, 1-9.

nerves or organs (cerebral palsy, diabetes), and external trauma affecting the systems (bleeding, shock, hypothermia).

Problems With Metaphorical Use. No one questions the utility of these disease models for medical practice. Their historical relevance for linking mental disorders such as general paresis to organic causes is indisputable. Their application as metaphorical descriptions of problems in living has been heatedly contested, however. Sarbin (1967) noted that throughout history the term *illness* has referred to internal discomfort. Around the sixteenth century, the word acquired a second meaning. It was used to describe unacceptable behaviors that disturbed others while causing no subjective discomfort. Deviant individuals were considered to be acting *as if* they were sick, thus turning the term into a metaphor. The meaning of the word *mind* underwent a similar transition from thought processes into an entity several centuries later. Our current concept of *mental illness* derives from the two words. The *mind* is considered to be affected by *disease*, in metaphorical terms. There is a common linguistic tendency to drop the qualifying *as if* and speak of the mind as being literally sick. Sarbin suggests that the term *mental illness* has no real meaning because it is based on a metaphor-to-myth transition.

Proponents of the medical model generally do not believe that emotional or behavioral dysfunctions are caused by real disease organisms. Rather, they currently emphasize that internal malfunctions can create problematic conditions. In some cases, organic or biochemical imbalances are cited; more frequently, the problem is considered to result from psychogenic causes (e.g., imbalances in psychic energies or inadequate development of mental structures). Support for the belief that personal and social problems are analogous to diseases was provided by the publication of a classification manual for mental disorders by the American Psychiatric Association in 1952. This scheme relied heavily on psychoanalytic formulations, postulating the concept of anxiety as the central psychogenic cause of mental illnesses (Sarason and Ganzer, 1968). The manual classified both difficulties that involve personal discomfort (e.g., phobias, depression) and socially inappropriate behaviors (e.g., sexual perversions) as mental illnesses.

Thomas Szasz (1961), a psychiatrist, mounted the first major attack against the medical model, contending that the term *mental illness* could legitimately be applied only to disorders which resulted from clearly demonstrable brain lesions and organic deficiencies. Other critics (e.g., Ullmann and Krasner, 1965) attacked the scientific adequacy of the medical model, arguing that it served as a self-fulfilling theory about human behavior that could not be empirically validated. They listed a large number of hypothetical underlying causes that proponents of the model have generated, pointing out that they have proven impossible to isolate or to investigate. This situation leads to explanatory inconsistency whereby the same symptom may be inferred to stem from multiple causes or different symptoms may involve the same cause.

Sarason and Ganzer (1968) suggest that such criticisms may well be aimed at a straw man; they argue that vilification of the medical model represents an attempt by psychologists to achieve equality with physicians. There is much validity to this argument. The medical model is the major topic of the most widely used psychiatric textbooks, and it is presented as the only view of human dysfunction. More importantly, it provides a comprehensive theoretical justification for medical domination of the *mental health* establishment. The term *mental health* is an incredibly convenient one; it can be used to describe those who provide service, an individual's existential state, a facility, or a helping endeavor. It is also part of the common vocabulary of just about everyone in our society, although its emphasis of medical domination is less clear.

Negative Personal And Social Consequences. It is neither fair nor accurate, however, to suggest that attacks against the medical model are due solely to interprofessional strife. Critics of the model have busily explored its negative personal and social consequences. Adherence to the medical model is thought to foster passivity on the part of the *patient* in psychotherapy. Personal involvement is minimized because both doctor and patient believe that it is the responsibility of the former to *treat* the latter. Proponents of the model are also presumed to spend an inordinate amount of time in diagnostic and classificatory endeavors which have little relevance for treatment.

More serious criticisms have been directed at the social labelling practices that stem from the medical model. It is argued that labelling a person as *mentally ill* leads to the loss of self-esteem, social privileges, civil rights, and economic opportunities (Scheff, 1966; Stuart, 1970).

Not all psychologists share the views of the social reaction theorists. Albert Ellis (1967), who is certainly no avid supporter of the medical model, contends that labels denoting mental illness can be used to positive advantage. Acceptance of the label by a client will enable that person to better take responsibility for the condition and work harder to overcome it. In addition, Ellis argues that such labels will prevent therapists from taking an overly optimistic view of their help-providing capabilities. Slow progress and setbacks can realistically be expected to occur when long-standing illnesses are being treated. Social reaction theorists (Sarbin, 1967; Scheff, 1966), however, argue that these goals can be accomplished without using disease-related labels. Ellis' final contention lies at the heart of the controversy between proponents of the medical model and the labelling theorists. He maintains that such labels can sometimes be used to force socially prominent people to accept treatment. Social reaction theorists argue that such coercion is more likely to involve the poor and socially powerless, and, in any event, represents a serious threat to any person's civil liberties.

PSYCHOTHERAPY AS A SERVICE TO CONSUMERS

The four controversies we have examined have one important element in common. They all involve disputes between professionals who are seeking to maintain and extend their social and economic opportunities. The general public is learning that the best interests of various professional organizations and those of the clients served by their members do not always coincide. Today, professionals too often are viewed as simultaneously attempting to serve their clientele while maximizing their own profit. This emerging portrayal of the professional conflicts with the self-portraits organized professionals provide. Physicians, in particular, have presented themselves as tireless, dedicated, and self-sacrificing individuals who have only the best interests of their patients at heart. Indeed, many physicians actually possess these characteristics. Yet, most find the practice of medicine extremely lucrative, with earnings of $60,000 annually being unexceptional. Kiesler (1977) reported that the average psychiatrist earns in excess of $40,000 annually, and psychologists earn an average of slightly over $20,000. The militancy of consumers is beginning to have impact on the delivery of professional services.

Provider Versus Consumer
Autonomy Of Professionals. Balancing the rights of consumers

against the autonomy of professionals is a delicate and difficult task. When people seek help from a professional, they give up a good deal of power. The professional is presumed to possess expert knowledge about how to best conceptualize and solve complicated problems. The client is essentially purchasing the time and, hopefully, the best efforts of the specialist. It is unethical for a professional to guarantee that the resolution will be successful. Lawyers cannot predict with certainty that they will win court cases, nor can psychotherapists be certain that they can cure depressions or save marriages.

The success rate of professionals depends heavily upon their technical knowledge, strategic skills, and degree of involvement which interact with specific characteristics of the client. Psychotherapy is one of the most complicated professional roles, requiring a tremendous amount of knowledge and effort. In contrast to other professional groups like lawyers who operate within a semi-structured system of legal rules, psychotherapists share no clear consensus of how to best carry out their socially mandated functions. While the ultimate goal of psychotherapy is to improve the life situation of unique individuals, we cannot agree what the necessary and sufficient conditions are for achieving this aim.

Most psychiatrists and an increasing number of psychologists are engaged in private practice. These individuals have been found to possess subjective, intuitive, and "artistic" stances toward psychotherapy; they seem less inclined to engage in public and critical self-scrutiny than their academic colleagues would like (Garfield and Kurtz, 1976). Medical analogies of disturbing conditions as mental illnesses reinforce this artistic stance by providing concepts that are difficult to investigate with currently available empirical methods.

The nature and extent of the therapeutic endeavor are dictated by the clinician's theoretical beliefs about human nature, experience, and personal inclinations. Even though a majority of clients view their therapeutic experiences positively, psychotherapy also can have harmful effects on the individual. All too frequently, therapists foster change by "diddling around," and they themselves are not sure about what went on. These factors often create a situation in which neither the therapist nor the consumer can account for the success or failure of an intervention. This situation is causing considerable friction between professional organizations, consumer groups, and insurance companies.

Stances By Professional Societies. The term *psychotherapy* describes a large number of interactive processes that involve clinicians who differ from one another in terms of education, theoretical beliefs, experience, and competence. Professional societies, which function quite similarly to medieval guilds, deal with the bewildering diversity of their memberships in a most curious manner. They pretend that such differences do not exist and foster the impression on the general public that all their members offer services that are practically identical and equally effective. Professional organizations of mental health specialists will routinely offer a list of practitioners to an interested party, but they will scrupulously avoid describing treatment specialties, theoretical orientations, or fee schedules. The ostensible reason for this practice is to promote freedom of choice by withholding potentially biasing information.

This widespread practice is based on the assumption that all who qualify as members of a society are equally competent to provide quality service. In addition, it is frequently argued that there is no necessity for competition among health providers. There is certainly enough illness to keep everyone occupied, and people ought to be grateful for whatever services their dedicated and overworked specialists can provide.

Efforts At Consumer Information. Consumer groups, however, claim that this orientation is monopolistic (Adams and Orgel, 1975). They contend that a truly informed selection of a professional helper can be made only with the very information that professional societies fail to provide. They also point out that the practice of psychotherapy is big business in contemporary society. In 1974, Americans paid an estimated $1.25 billion to psychiatrists for private therapy, and an additional $116 million went to psychologists (Levine and Willner, 1976). This latter figure was deemed to be a substantial underestimate because it did not include part-time therapeutic activities by psychologists.

The first comprehensive guide to finding a psychotherapist was published by the Public Citizen's Health Research Group, a consumer activist group (Adams and Orgel, 1975). Some of the difficulties encountered by this group illustrate the guildish self-protectiveness of professional societies. A 41-item questionnaire requesting information about professional training, theoretical orientation, fee schedules, and other pertinent data was sent to 719 psychiatrists, 940 psychologists, and 331 psychiatric social workers in the greater Washington, D. C. area. Adams and Orgel reported that an immediate and largely negative reaction to the questionnaire occurred:

Many were angry about the project or wanted to argue, stating that it was "unethical" or "violated their rights;" a few were abusive. Some felt that the Directory might be considered advertising and that they might get in trouble if they responded. A number of mental health professionals called to say that they would not return the questionnaire and warned Health Research Group not to list them as non-responders with statements such as "If you imply that I am uncooperative in the directory or that I am a non-responder, I will regard it as libelous," or "I will take legal action; I did not ask for the questionnaire" [Reprinted by permission. S. Adams and M. Orgel. *Through the mental health maze.* Public Citizen's Health Research Group, 1975, p. 11].

The Washington Psychiatric Society, a branch of the American Psychiatric Association, circulated a letter urging its members not to return the questionnaire because no "important input was given by any serious, experienced psychiatric body" (Adams and Orgel, 1975, p. 70). In actuality, a number of professionals made contributions to the project, but, perhaps fearing reprisals from their colleagues, they did not wish to be identified. This letter appeared to cause a noticeable reduction in the return rate among psychiatrists. Across the three professional groups, the response was quite low, ranging from 16 percent for psychiatrists to 40 percent for social workers, with 26 percent of all psychologists responding.

Analysis of the questionnaires revealed considerable diversity among respondents. Fees for a 50-minute session ranged from $18 to $50 for psychiatrists, $10 to $50 for psychologists, and $5 to $50 for social workers, averaging $39, $34, and $26 for the three respective professional groups. On the average, psychiatrists charged $19; psychologists, $18; and social workers, $16 for a 90-minute group therapy session, although the range was quite wide within each group ($10 - $35 by psychiatrists; $5 - $30 by psychologists; $2 - $30 by social workers). Figure 3 provides additional information about the percentage of therapists in each group who provided weekend coverage, were willing to negotiate fees, and charged for phone consultations.

Some therapists were able to see new clients immediately, while others had waiting lists up to six months. The average waiting period

FIGURE 3. INFORMATION FROM QUESTIONNAIRE TO THERAPISTS IN WASHINGTON D.C. AREA

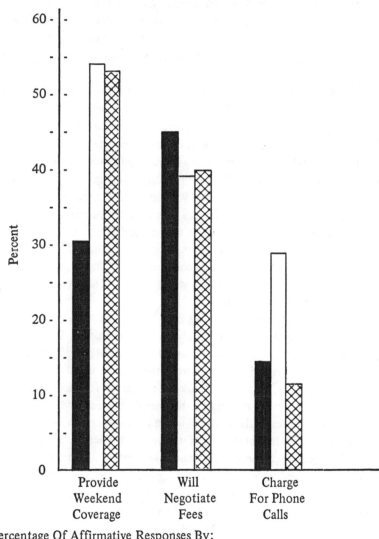

Percentage Of Affirmative Responses By:

Psychiatrists ■
Psychologists □
Social Workers ⬧

Adapted with permission. S. Adams and M. Orgel. *Through the mental health maze.* Washington, D.C.: Public Citizen's Health Research Group, 1975.

was around 12 days for all three groups. The most frequent response to a question asking how long a therapist normally waits before consulting about cases that have not shown improvement was 12 weeks, although estimates ranged from 6 to 30 weeks. One of the potentially most disturbing findings of the survey was the discovery of a surprisingly large percentage (almost one out of five) who did not believe they had any responsibility to report suspected unprofessional conduct by colleagues.

The Collaborative Model. The major dictum of doing business in the open market has always been, "let the buyer beware." Professionals operate under the contrasting dictum, "let the buyer trust" (Lynn, 1965). The major theme of the consumer movement with regard to therapeutic services is "buyer, accept your legitimate responsibilities." The buyer's responsibilities include not only judging the fee schedules and qualifications but also actively working with the therapist to affect change. The therapist's expertise lies in knowledge about general methods for helping people change. The task of molding global rules about human functioning into specific change operations that will be effective for an individual client requires collaboration. The expertise of the therapist must be combined with the expert knowledge clients possess about their own life situations.

A collaborative model of this type assumes that psychotherapy is best conceptualized as a social problem-solving process. Both participants are responsible for contributing to the solution of the client's difficulties. The therapist is freed from the burden of having to apply "treatment" to a passive partner. One vehicle for achieving such mutuality is a formally negotiated therapeutic contract, which specifies the rights and duties of the participants in psychotherapy. The therapist pledges to apply her best efforts to help the client resolve specific difficulties (e.g., become less depressed, understand the origins of one's anger or fear, and so on). The client agrees to reimburse the clinician within a reasonable amount of time and perhaps carry out homework assignments relevant for overcoming the problem.

A contract helps both therapist and client focus on the latter's priorities, which represent the reason he comes for therapy in the first place. In addition, a good contract will specify that a review of progress will occur at periodic intervals. This allows both participants to obtain a general overview of the longer-range therapeutic process and to adjust or revamp specific change strategies to make them more effective.

Although the problem-solving model has certain limitations (see Chapter 7), it is becoming more widely adopted because it provides a means of meeting demands by insurers that wasteful therapeutic practices be curtailed. Contemporary payment practices by insurance companies, however, place therapists in a double-bind situation. Reimbursement is provided for treating certain forms of mental illness. While this scheme is compatible with the activities of physicians, it neglects the fact that neither psychotherapists nor their clients view the latter as being sick.

Responsible spokesmen for both professional psychiatry and psychology are concerned that increased insurance coverage will raise serious problems, including (1) drainage of resources from public health-care facilities into the private sector (Meltzer, 1975), (2) increases in the already inequitable distribution of practitioners, (3) over-utilization of existing services in terms of inordinately long treatment (Marmor, 1975; Meltzer, 1975), and (4) continued adherence to concepts of "psychopathology," which have not proven to be useful (Albee, 1975). Although existing data suggest that clients covered by third-party insurance actually see psychiatrists in private therapy less frequently than uninsured persons (Marmor, 1975), these problems are vitally important ones which will have enormous consequences on the delivery of therapeutic services.

 FINAL WORDS

Although the word *psychotherapy* implies the existence of a singular entity, it actually summarizes a wide range of helping processes. The issues discussed in this chapter clearly suggest that professional therapists find themselves immersed in a good deal of conflict. No clear consensus can be found regarding either the general nature of psychotherapy or the adequacy of specific training and therapeutic procedures. Current controversies are the natural outgrowth of several interlocking historical and contemporary influences.

The first factor is the incredible complexity of human action. Thought and behavior have multiple antecedents and multiple consequences and are determined by complex interactions among biochemical, psychological, and sociological influences. This very complexity requires that human action be analyzed from many different perspectives.

A second influence is the existence of many competing theoretical perspectives. Many of the controversies about psychotherapy are based on clashes between incompatible theoretical viewpoints. It is simply impossible to be a totally unbiased observer. Theoretical and personal belief systems provide coherent conceptual frameworks that enable therapists to better understand their own activities. Unfortunately, strict adherence to particular points of view leads some professionals to argue that their system is superior to others on *a priori* grounds.

A third factor appears to underlie theoretical conflicts, namely, rivalries among professional therapists especially on an organizational level. Controversies about whether psychotherapy is art or science or about the utility of the medical model cannot be fully understood by examining only the intellectual and empirical issues involved. Positions therapists take with regard to these controversies have enormous consequences for them in terms of social prestige, societal power, and financial rewards. Professional helpers typically maintain strong loyalties to the organizations that provide them with professional identities. These organizations seek to maintain control over the quality of service their members provide for the benefit of the general public. They also, however, provide a basis from which professional therapists can exercise influence over the larger society.

Attempts by organizations of professional helpers to further the special interests of their members are bringing them into conflict with consumer groups, who espouse special interests of their own. The likely upshot of this emerging area of conflict is that therapists will be forced toward more rigorous accountability. The burden of demonstrating that their activities are actually helpful will rest squarely on the shoulders of professional therapists themselves.

3
Major Theoretical Stances

The broad historical and social trends highlighted in previous chapters led to the evolution of three major theoretical perspectives about psychotherapy. In this chapter, we examine the basic assumptions and derivative operations of therapists who prefer a *psychodynamic, humanistic,* or *behavioral* model for conceptualizing and dealing with human problems. These descriptive terms are broad and generic. Each perspective actually represents a wide spectrum of both theoretical formulations and concrete therapeutic operations. A careful analysis of the orientations will reveal the existence of as much diversity within a single perspective as can be found across competing ones. In addition, the boundaries between these three general viewpoints are both fuzzy and constantly changing. Describing a therapist as possessing a certain theoretical stance causes us to abstract from and thereby simplify the real complexity of the clinician's activities.

There are many similarities in the ways therapists of different theoretical persuasions actually behave. Those who share a common orientation, however, tend to reduce this diversity by describing their operations with a specialized vocabulary. Psychoanalysts speak of *transference* and *fixation*, humanists refer to *positive self-regard* or to *integration of existential polarities*, and behavior therapists rely on terms like *reinforcement* and *contingency management*. These technical terms facilitate communication among adherents of a particular perspective, but they also foster the impression that all humanists (or behavior therapists) are alike.

The ways in which clinicians of a similar persuasion describe their own activities are less stereotypical than descriptions provided by practitioners who espouse competing theoretical views. Statements like, "psychoanalysis is unscientific," "humanistic therapists do not promote behavior change," or "behavior therapy is mechanistic" are overly simplistic and needlessly polemical. Such stereotypes are the basis of many *uniformity myths* (Kiesler, 1966) about psychotherapy, causing much conflict among professional therapists.

This is not meant to imply that real differences which derive from therapists' theoretical orientations do not exist, only that any generalization will not apply equally to all therapists who give themselves a particular theoretical label. The broad theoretical orientations do provide differing conceptions about the essence of human nature, processes of normal development, and how dysfunctional conditions arise. Specific stances toward these general issues have definite prescriptive consequences for what the goals of therapy ought to involve and what the roles of the participants should be.

Any comparison of competing orientations must involve making generalizations about these important issues. A variety of specific viewpoints within each general perspective is presented to offset the implication that uniformity exists among those who describe themselves as having psychodynamic, humanistic, or behavioral approaches.

THE PSYCHODYNAMIC SPECTRUM

The origin of psychotherapy as a specialized helping endeavor was based upon a psychodynamic conception of human nature. Hence, this perspective is the oldest, and not coincidentally, the most complex of the three orientations. This position encompasses a wide range of viewpoints which share the belief that *human activity results from the operation of internal dynamic forces*. These influences are altered by developmental processes, which themselves are believed to proceed through discrete stages. It is further recognized that an individual will have a varying degree of awareness about the influence of these forces, although the role of conscious volition is generally de-emphasized. Psychodynamic theorists also stress that the development of dysfunctional conditions is due to inappropriate blockage of internal impulses, which impedes a person's ability to adequately meet emerging developmental demands. The importance of contemporary environmental factors as direct causes of disturbances is given considerably less emphasis.

The most widely recognized (and stereotyped) representative of the psychodynamic spectrum is classical psychoanalysis. This model, which was the forerunner of many derivative therapeutic approaches, is thought to have three interrelated facets. It is a theory of human behavior, a treatment strategy for alleviating distress, and a vehicle for conducting empirical research (Blanck, 1976). Psychoanalysis can be understood also as a social force that has shaped the views of the general populace about mental illness and has exerted enormous impact on current therapeutic practices.

Psychoanalysis can be thought of as a particular system within the more general psychodynamic spectrum. Many people confuse psychoanalysis and psychodynamic therapies because, from a historical perspective, psychodynamic viewpoints grew out of classical psychoanalytic theory. Psychoanalysts and psychodynamic clinicians share the belief that human behavior is the product of hidden motivational forces that exist inside people. Differences between them are largely a matter of degree. In particular, psychoanalysts tend to de-emphasize the importance of reciprocal interpersonal influence between the therapist and client to a greater extent than do psychodynamic clinicians. In addition, psychodynamic theorists tend to formulate the nature of motivational energy more loosely than classical psychoanalysts do. In terms of training, psychoanalysts differ from their psychodynamic colleagues primarily on the basis of having undergone psychoanalysis themselves. This distinction is probably the only qualitative criterion that sets psychoanalysts apart from more broadly defined psychodynamic therapists.

Psychoanalysis As A Theory

The writings of Sigmund Freud comprise the most complex theory of human behavior ever formulated. Much of this complexity was due to Freud's scrupulous intellectual honesty. If his observations did not confirm his theoretical predictions, he revised and extended his formulations. Historians differ on the number of evolutionary phases that psychoanalytic thought went through; Ellenberger (1970) notes seven shifts, while Rapaport (1959) describes four basic changes. The latter writer suggests that all of the basic elements in the theory were produced between 1887 and 1897. Dynamic formulations (including the notion of psycho-sexual developmental stages) were generated between

1898 and 1922. The structural components of the id, ego, and super-ego, as well as the description of defense mechanisms, were formulated between 1923 and 1936. The relation of the individual to society occupied Freud's attention until his death in 1939. Each phase represented a transformation of prior conceptions that added a descriptive richness to the entire perspective.

Four Basic Concepts. Freud's theory itself involves four basic concepts for analyzing human action—dynamic, genetic, structural, and economic. Psychoanalysts employ all four vantage points to explain the development of both normal and pathological conditions.

The starting point of the theory is the conception that the personality is a closed system of energy. The energy within the system is called **libido.** Every person has a fixed amount of libido, although different people possess different amounts.

The **dynamic portion** of the theory deals with movement of libido within the personality to provide gratification of instincts that arise as an individual moves through various developmental stages: oral, anal, phallic, latency, and genital.

The **genetic portion** describes these stages as well as the primary instinctual need associated with each. Pleasure, which Freud viewed as the reduction of biological tension, is provided by gratifying the urges associated with each stage. For an infant, pleasure results from satisfying the instinctual need to suck or bite. As the child grows older, the focus of pleasure moves to the anus, then the phallus, and, ultimately, the genitals.

Instinctive strivings for gratification of biological impulses do not occur in a vacuum, however. The toddler encounters hazards in the environment that cause pain, and he simultaneously begins to learn social mores which often prevent immediate biological gratification.

Freud encompassed these influences by describing structures within the personality that mediate the effects of environmental constraints. The **structural portion** of the theory posits the existence of three distinct systems within the personality. The **id** directs the individual toward biological gratification, the **ego** guides the person's interaction with the environment, and the **superego** embodies moral values and social prescriptions about how one ought to behave. Contemporary analysts do not consider these to be real structural entities, but rather view them as motivational systems.

In Freud's theory, libido serves many functions. It is employed to maintain the boundaries of the entire personality system; is used by the id, ego, and superego to meet biological, environmental, and societal demands; and is employed by these structures to repress unacceptable impulses. The three systems are themselves in continual conflict with each other, with the ego attempting to affect compromises between the biological strivings of the id and the harsh dictates of the superego. In a healthy individual, such compromises enable the id to successfully resolve the primary instinctual urges that are associated with successive developmental stages. A proper amount of gratification for the urges that arise at each stage enables the person to progress toward genital primacy.

The development of abnormal conditions is attributed to the dilution of libido in an inordinately expensive manner, thus bringing the **economic concept** of the theory into play. Too little gratification of impulses associated with a particular developmental period leads to **fixation**, impelling the person to seek distorted forms of the thwarted satisfaction throughout life. Overgratification has the same effect because the individual is not driven to further develop. Fixation also creates threats to the person's psychic well being, which take the form of unacceptable impulses.

Inappropriate impulses seek conscious expression; it is the ego's task to repress them into the unconscious. Repression requires a costly expenditure of libido. This state of affairs is worsened by the dynamic nature of the inappropriate impulses, which fester in the unconscious and exert increasing pressure for conscious expression. This pressure is experienced as neurotic anxiety. Neurotic conditions come about as the ego attempts to relieve the building pressure in the personality. The purpose of all defense mechanisms is to permit partial gratification of inappropriate impulses by admitting them to consciousness in symbolic forms. Defense mechanisms thus reduce the build-up of pressure within the personality in a more economical manner than repression does. The type of neurosis one develops is determined by the particular defense mechanism employed to provide disguised expression of the impulse. Anxiety may be *displaced* onto a symbolic representation of the underlying conflict, resulting in a **phobia**; it may be *converted* into a somatic dysfunction, thus leading to a **hysterical conversion reaction**; or it may be mediated by *dissociation*, thus eventuating in **hysterical amnesia**.

The surface manifestations of the conflict, as transformed by the defense mechanisms, are considered to be **symptoms**.

Psychoanalytic formulations of psychotic and characterological disorders also are logical derivatives of these same basic operations. Repression requires that libido be drawn from its task of maintaining the boundaries of the personality. If too much libido is borrowed, the boundary becomes fragmented, and the individual becomes incapable of distinguishing between internal perceptions and external reality. From a dynamic point of view, this is the essential feature of a **psychotic state**.

In a similar fashion, character disorders, such as *sexual perversions,* are viewed as attempts to relieve anxiety that results from fixation. Exhibitionists, for example, are considered to be motivated by castration anxiety, which is generated by fixation at a pre-Oedipal phallic stage of development (Fenichel, 1945). The act of exposing oneself elicits a reaction from the onlooker, thus providing reassurance that the exhibitionist indeed has not been castrated. Over time, however, psychic tension generated by castration anxiety builds up again, and the exhibitionist is compelled to repeat the deviant activity.

Seven Assumptions Of Freud's Theory. Although the theory is extremely complex, it contains seven basic assumptions about human nature.

1. Personality is a closed energy system in the form of instinctive biological urges.
2. These urges are directed toward reduction of biological tensions and come into conflict with environmental constraints and moral prohibitions.
3. Psychic growth results from successfully meeting the changing and conflicting demands of the instincts, the environment, and society.
4. Growth proceeds through fixed developmental stages; the needs associated with each stage must be fulfilled before a person can progress to subsequent stages.
5. Human activities are *overdetermined*—that is, all behavior is the result of *both* conscious and unconscious determinants. Human action is never free in the sense of being random or spontaneous.
6. The unconscious determinants of behavior are rule-governed and operate according to a dynamic-economic model. They are much

more important influences on thoughts and actions than are conscious determinants.

7. Since equilibrium among the complex forces that compete with one another is difficult to maintain, growth is easily thwarted; thus the state of healthy normality is difficult to achieve.

Psychoanalysis As A Method Of Treatment

Given the complexity of psychoanalytic theory, it may seem surprising that psychoanalysis involves a simple treatment strategy that centers on only free association and interpretation. This is less surprising when one remembers that the focus of intervention is on internal forces rather than environmental influences. The process of psychoanalytic treatment is a dynamic and complex one whose major components are outlined in Figure 4.

Relationship Of Free Association And Insight. The goal of psychoanalysis is to ease the repression of unconscious unacceptable ideas by promoting **insight** into their nature and operation. The primary vehicle for achieving this goal is **free association** whereby the patient verbalizes whatever comes to mind. Actually, the term is a misnomer because "free" associations are really totally governed by conscious and, more importantly, unconscious determinants. This primary task of analysis is believed to ultimately produce insight (line 1 on Figure 4). For psychoanalysts, **insight** is more than a sudden realization of how motivational forces operate. Rather, it is viewed as the gradual acceptance of such determinants, which is achieved by repeatedly working through intellectual and emotional defensive resistances.

Acquisition of insight is presumed to be both a necessary and a sufficient condition for restructuring significant aspects of one's personality (line 2) and for promoting the development of more adaptive behaviors in real life (line 3). Behavior changes without the achievement of insight are believed to represent only symptomatic improvement. Analysts believe that this type of behavioral change invariably leads to **symptom substitution** whereby other behavioral manifestations of the underlying conflict will arise in place of the original symptomatic complaint. Because the original symptom was the most psychically economical expression of the underlying conflict, substitution of new symptoms is believed to cause the individual to become even more debilitated.

FIGURE 4. ELEMENTS IN PSYCHOANALYTIC TREATMENT

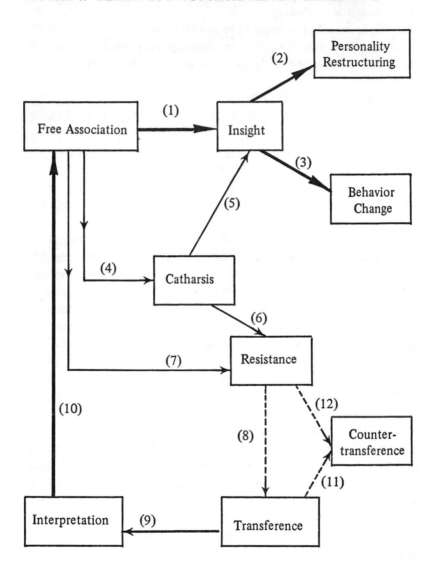

Impediments To Insight. Promoting insight is a slow and difficult process because competing internal impulses cause various forms of blockages to occur. One form of impediment to free association is called **catharsis**, which involves the spewing out of emotionally laden material (line 4). Such emotional outbursts are thought to have a psychic cleansing function, but they do not necessarily result in personality restructuring. Catharsis may help facilitate insight (line 5), but it may also represent a form of resistance (line 6) depending upon how it is viewed by the analyst.

Resistance is defined as any activity that interferes with the primary task of free association (line 7). Resistance may manifest itself in different ways. A patient may suddenly switch topics, engage in long pauses, experience a cathartic outburst, or "forget" what is being verbalized. The most crucial form of resistance is called **transference** (line 8). The patient begins to direct to the analyst positive or negative comments which are based on unrealistic fantasies. In general, the patient acts as though the analyst were an important mother or father figure in the former's early life. Transference is more than just another form of resistance; it represents the most critical point in psychoanalysis because it is considered to be a manifestation of infantile neurotic patterns.

Analysts are trained to recognize transference as a fantasy-based phenomenon, and they attempt to work through it to undo past determinants of the current disability. Resolution of the transference attachment provides a basis for emotional insight, enabling the patient to resume that task of free association more effectively because a strong set of resistances has been nulhfied. The analyst's task is to **interpret** (line 9) transference statements as fantasy projections of the current situation that are distorted by past unconscious influences. Proper interpretation of transference is considered to be objective since it is made without being distorted by the analyst's own needs or personal overinvolvement with the patient. Interpretation is used throughout the entire analytic process (line 10), but it is crucial during episodes of transference.

If the analyst's interpretation of transference is in fact distorted by his or her own hidden needs, **countertransference** results. In this situation, the analyst is personally affected by the patient's positive or negative comments and responds as though they were valid rather than treating them as fantasized projections. Countertransference establishes a vicious cycle of increasing resistance by encouraging further transference projections (lines 11, 12, and 8). Free association is interfered with and the acquisition of insight becomes imperilled. In actual psychoanalytic treatment, these basic elements shown in Figure 4 will form numerous combinations and will recycle themselves throughout the entire process.

The Therapist's Role. Psychoanalysis requires an extensive time investment by both participants, with the tradition of five sessions weekly being standard practice. Despite the high frequency of therapeutic contact, however, mutual interpersonal influence between analyst and patient is minimized. The therapist's role is to serve as a screen upon which the patient projects hidden conflicts. Since the therapist must reflect the distorted nature of these projections back to the patient without adding additional distortions, an attempt is made to keep the patient oblivious to the analyst's personal attributes (Tarachow, 1963). This is generally accomplished by having the patient lie on a couch facing away from the analyst in a dimly lit room. This format also is presumed to minimize external distractions, encourage exploration of inner mental influences, and promote psychic regression, projection, and transference (Blanck, 1976).

Psychoanalysis And Research

Criticisms. Psychoanalytic theory and methods often have been attacked for being "unscientific." This contention is frequently documented by citing investigations that parody psychoanalytic research. This form of satire can be found in Landy's (1967) report that men tend to "castrate" a pack of cigarettes by ripping off the top flap (thus removing a fragile appendage which might become mutilated and arouse castration anxiety), while women obtain cigarettes by forming a cavity and "popping" them out (representing perhaps an unconscious desire to possess a penis?).

Investigation Of Psychoanalytic Theory. The fact is, however, psychoanalytic concepts have provided a system which has been the object of a great deal of serious research involving verification of portions of the theory and investigation of processes and outcomes associated with psychoanalysis.

Unfortunately, some portions of psychoanalytic theory have

been formulated in such a way that they are untestable. No one has quite figured out how to study the pleasure principle or the life and death instincts in a manner that would be considered as scientifically acceptable. Other parts of the psychoanalytic theory require the use of assessment procedures (such as projective tests) whose reliability and validity are doubtful.

The most comprehensive and fairly balanced appraisal of psychoanalytic theory has been provided by Kline (1972), who carefully delineated between speculative and testable portions of the theory and described the methodological difficulties associated with attempting to validate each portion of it. His conclusions, which are summarized below, suggest that very little of the theory has stood up well to empirical scrutiny:

1. Substantial evidence supports the existence of an anal character type, but support for the existence of other types (e.g., oral, phallic, etc.) is weak and tenuous.

2. We currently do not have a technology sophisticated enough to properly investigate relationships between adult character structures and childhood deprivations and gratifications. Current research, therefore, neither supports nor refutes this part of the theory.

3. Assessment inadequacies also have precluded adequate investigation of the theory of neurosis, including the notions of the Oedipal complex and castration anxiety.

4. Although no evidence supports the existence of the id, ego, and superego as distinct physiological systems, factor analytic research tentatively suggests the existence of three broad and distinctive motivational systems that tenuously correspond to the functions of these hypothetical structures.

5. The investigation of dreams has clearly indicated that they possess psychological as well as physiological functions, but research has not yielded much evidence supporting psychoanalytic dream theory.

The key psychoanalytic concepts of repression and projection have received special research attention. Psychotherapists of all theoretical persuasions encounter behaviors on the part of their clients which are interpretable as either repression or projection. The viability of such behaviors as indications of underlying defense mechanisms is both controversial and questionable, however. Both Kline (1972) and Holmes (1968) agree that existing evidence does not support the view that projection operates as a defense mechanism. Kline does conclude that people repress threatening material without being aware of doing so, but Holmes (1974) contends that this does not occur.

The relationship between repression and conscious awareness is complex and tricky. A person's awareness may be assessed by asking the individual to describe the reasons for her behavior or by briefly presenting presumably neutral and threatening words to the client and recording the amount of time it takes for her to recognize the words. Research which employs this latter subliminal perception paradigm has shown that people take longer to verbalize recognition of threatening (usually "dirty") words. This finding by itself, however, does not prove the existence of repression. It may be that people suppress acknowledging what they have indeed observed because they are ashamed or embarrassed. Certainly, in psychotherapy it is not uncommon for people to deliberately withhold sensitive information until they trust the therapist. This, in itself, does not provide evidence supporting a belief in unconscious repression.

The most recent systematic attempt to validate portions of psychoanalytic theory involves the programmatic work of Silverman (1976), who has investigated the relationship between unconscious libidinal wishes and psychopathology. In two lines of research, he has sought to stimulate these unconscious urges by subliminal presentation of eliciting stimuli or through hypnotic suggestion. In one particularly intriguing investigation, Silverman, Frank, and Dachinger (1974) provided evidence for an analytic interpretation of the effectiveness of desensitization in alleviating phobias in terms of activating an unconscious merging fantasy. Twenty women who demonstrated a fear of insects during a behavioral approach assessment were divided into two groups and provided with therapy to overcome this problem. Treatment consisted of having the women imagine scenes involving bugs, which were hierarchically arranged according to the degree of discomfort they elicited. Rather than pairing the visualizations with deep muscle relaxation, they paired them with certain subliminal experiences. After they imagined the discomforting scenes, the women viewed words that were subliminally presented through a tachistoscope.

Experimental subjects were exposed to the sentence, "MOMMY

AND I ARE ONE," while control participants viewed the phrase, "PEOPLE WALKING." The first stimulus array was believed to evoke an unconscious merging fantasy, between the participant and her mother, which would satisfy symbiotic needs and thereby reduce phobic behavior. Participants in this condition were rated as being able to approach caged insects more closely and being less anxious when doing so than control subjects.

Condon (1976) noted a number of methodological deficiencies in this experiment, including failure to assess interobserver reliability, possible interdependence between the outcome measures employed, and use of a single therapist. In addition, significant between-group differences reported by Silverman et al. emerged on the basis of using one-tailed statistical tests, rather than more rigorous two-tailed analyses. Condon replicated the original experiment on a larger sample and added a third condition in which participants were exposed to the words, "DADDY AND I ARE ONE." Based upon the theorizing of Fenichel (1945), the same analyst from which Silverman drew his justification, this sentence was designed to actually increase phobic behavior because it would activate unconscious conflict between unfulfilled Oedipal wishes to have sexual relations with the father and fear of anticipated punishment and retaliation by the mother. Condon found no significant differences between the groups in his study, thus failing to replicate the outcome reported by Silverman et al. Even though Silverman (1976) optimistically suggested that reports of the death of psychoanalytic theory are "greatly exaggerated," the bulk of the evidence indicates that many portions of the theory need to be amputated.

Investigations Of Psychoanalytic Treatment. Another area of empirical inquiry has involved the psychoanalytic treatment process. Historically, the relationship between analyst and patient has been considered by the former to be very fragile. Attempts to record the events that occurred in psychoanalysis or to investigate them by means of simplified analogues were considered to destroy the very essence of the treatment process. This theoretical prejudice inhibited the collection of primary sources of data (other than reports by the analyst) upon which research could be performed. Psychoanalysts also tend to view therapy as an artistic endeavor in which the prediction and control of behavior are deemed to be secondary to the primary goal of describing the richness of dynamic encounters. These orienting beliefs led to a reliance on the case-study approach and to an aversion among analysts to lump cases together for the purpose of quantitative analysis.

Despite these problems, however, Luborsky and Spence (1971) were able to provide a comprehensive review of loosely defined quantitative research on psychoanalytic treatment. Their conclusions suggest that the promise of this treatment modality has yet to be fulfilled:

1. The most suitable candidates for psychoanalysis are relatively intact, young, and highly educated individuals who suffer anxiety-related difficulties.

2. What few studies have been done on the desirable attributes of analytic therapists have primarily involved assessment of supervisor opinions. These investigations suggest that objectivity and self-confidence are desirable characteristics.

3. Very little research has been done on the central topics of interpretation and transference, even though they form the theoretical essentials of psychoanalytic treatment.

Research on the outcome of psychoanalysis is virtually nonexistent. This situation is compatible with the belief of most analysts that the goal of treatment involves restructuring the personality. Unfortunately, such a global criterion is almost impossible to reliably define. A large-scale investigation begun in 1954 as the Menninger Psychotherapy Research Project did, however, yield some findings pertinent to the outcome issue. A vast amount of information was collected from 21 individuals who received psychoanalysis and 21 others who were treated less intensively with other types of psychodynamic interventions. Analysis of information collected prior to treatment, at termination, and after a two-year follow-up period yielded these conclusions (White, 1971):

1. No relationship was found between the ability of the patients to describe what had occurred in therapy and the amount of improvement they manifested.

2. A number of patients experienced symptomatic relief, showed personality growth, and developed more adaptive behavior patterns without having achieved insight.

3. Both therapists and patients would discuss treatment issues more freely and openly if they believed that therapy had been successful.

4. Research participation did not adversely affect patient improve-

ment, but it was very threatening to the therapists, who feared being criticized.

In summary, this serious and extensive research project conducted by investigators with a heavy analytic orientation produced findings that were inconsistent with major psychoanalytic theoretical beliefs. Patient improvement without the acquisition of insight challenges the notion of symptom substitution, while failure to find deterioration as a result of conducting research suggests that psychoanalysis is a less fragile treatment process than many analysts presumed it to be.

Alterations And Limitations Of Classical Psychoanalysis

Alterations Of Theory. Psychoanalytic theory provided a basis for the development of practically every current school of psychotherapy, with the exception of radical behaviorism. Historically, the psychodynamic spectrum developed as innovative clinicians began to reconceptualize major portions of psychoanalytic theory. These alterations led to changes in concrete treatment practices. On a theoretical level, major differences arose about which instinctual strivings were deemed to be most basic, as well as the extent to which these internal forces were affected by environmental and cultural influences. In general, classical psychoanalytic theory itself was castrated by many of Freud's disciples. The psychosexual nature of libido was replaced by drives to compensate for inferiority, become meaningfully productive, escape from alienation, find existential meaning, and integrate experiential polarities.

Further theoretical alterations resulted from the integration of classical psychoanalytic thought with the American value system. Our desire to dominate the environment led to an emphasis on the ego as the primary source of personal control in the writing of "ego analysts," such as Karen Horney and Melanie Klein. Our concern with gratifying social relationships was reflected in Harry Stack Sullivan's view of psychiatry as the study of interpersonal processes, the psychosocial "developmental crisis" framework of Erik Eriksen, and various theories of interpersonal "games" which were formulated by Eric Berne and his associates. Finally, our emphasis on the loving and creative aspects of human functioning can be found in the writings of Abraham Maslow and Rollo May.

Alterations Of Therapeutic Practice. These same influences also dramatically altered concrete therapeutic practices. Many theorists who were trained as classical psychoanalysts rejected psychoanalysis because it de-emphasized the importance of mutual interpersonal influences. Today, many more therapists consider themselves to be psychodynamic rather than psychoanalytic. Few clinicians choose to go through psychoanalysis themselves. Psychodynamic therapists begin with fundamental conceptions about human nature that are similar to those held by analysts, but transform these so that they possess a more interpersonal and environmental focus. Historical factors are still considered to be important influences on current behavior but are not considered to be the sole crucial determinants. Personality is viewed as a system which seeks to maintain equilibrium but is not considered to be a closed system with regard to environmental influences. Psychodynamic therapists also tend to emphasize the role of internal forces, such as drives, motives, and needs, within the personality, but they reject to varying degrees the belief that these forces operate as psychosexual energy flows inside an individual. In fact, the boundary between psychodynamic and humanistic therapists is not at all clear, with the crucial difference between the two groups often being what an individual chooses to call herself.

Contemporary surveys of both psychologists and psychiatrists clearly document the narrow scope of classical psychoanalytic practice. Fully 55 percent of the clinical psychologists sampled by Garfield and Kurtz (1976) described their orientation as "eclectic," while 11 percent considered themselves to be "psychoanalytic," and an additional 5 percent rated their orientation as "neo-Freudian." Among psychiatrists, 29 percent were psychoanalysts, while almost 53 percent described themselves as "generalists" (that is, as nonanalysts) (Marmor, 1975). This latter study also reveals many interesting things about current therapeutic practices.

Marmor (1975) reports results of a survey of 404 respondents out of 606 psychiatrists representing a random sample of 10 percent of all members of the American Psychiatric Association who spent at least 15 hours weekly conducting therapy. The psychiatrists also provided information on roughly 4,000 of their patients, divided into three groups—patients in psychoanalysis, nonanalytic patients of psychoanalytic practitioners, and patients of generalists. A majority of the psychoanalysts' caseload included patients who did not receive psychoanalysis.

Limitations Of Psychoanalysis. Figure 5 [adapted from Marmor (1975)] presents some relevant characteristics of these patient groups and also provides some insight into why psychoanalysis is not practiced on a widespread scale. The clientele for psychoanalysis proper consists of highly educated, fairly wealthy people who are diagnosed as suffering from neurotic complaints. Only 7 percent of the patients in analysis were blue- or white-collar workers, but 66 percent of this caseload possessed managerial and professional occupations. This bias in patient selection is very consistent with Freud's (1905) contention that psychoanalysis should be limited to people with "a reasonable degree of education and a fairly reliable character" (1959, Vol. VII, p. 263).

Other important limitations are operative. Psychoanalysis requires an inordinate amount of therapeutic contact time. Marmor reported that patients in psychoanalysis averaged 139 sessions annually, compared to 51 and 26 sessions for nonanalytic patients of analysts and patients of generalists, respectively. The median number of annual contacts (145) for patients in psychoanalysis was nine times greater than the median number of visits made by the latter two groups combined.

Another limitation resides in the training of analysts. After completing formal degree requirements, analytic candidates are required to undergo psychoanalysis to work through their own unconscious conflicts that might distort their ability to provide objective, unbiased interpretations. This long and expensive process is terminated only when the prospective analyst's own analyst is satisfied that the candidate has obtained objective self-awareness. Besides severely limiting the number of available psychoanalysts, this practice has also had the unfortunate effect of stifling creative innovations within the movement. Attempts to expand classical psychoanalytic thought were often regarded by training analysts as evidence of "resistance," which would be "broken through" once the candidate began to adopt more traditional viewpoints. The most vocal critics of this state of affairs have been analysts themselves, particularly those who went on to make creative advances (e.g., Alexander and Selesnick, 1966).

A final limitation is to be found in the goal of psychoanalysis which is to restructure portions of the personality. Psychoanalytic treatment has little relevance for and impact on the poor, the socially non-elite, or those who suffer from serious thought and behavioral disorders. It is also an inefficient and often ineffective intervention for

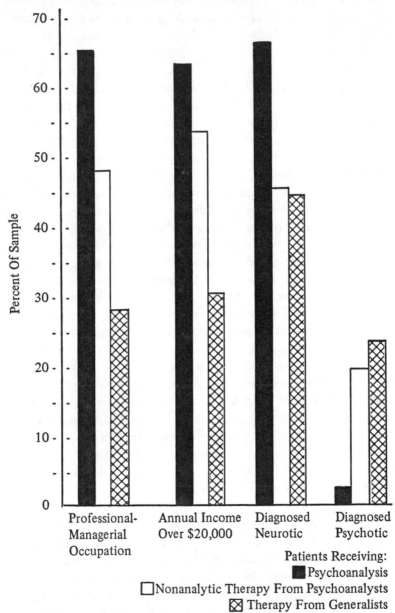

FIGURE 5. CHARACTERISTICS OF PATIENTS
RECEIVING THERAPY

Percent Of Sample

70

60

50

40

30

20

10

0

Professional-
Managerial
Occupation

Annual Income
Over $20,000

Diagnosed
Neurotic

Diagnosed
Psychotic

Patients Receiving:
■ Psychoanalysis
☐ Nonanalytic Therapy From Psychoanalysts
⊠ Therapy From Generalists

Adapted with permission. J. Marmor. *Psychiatrists and their patients.* Washington, D.C.: American Psychiatric Association, 1975.

resolving the life problems even suitable patients bring to therapy. Analysts themselves help perpetuate this situation by refusing to employ conjoint, group, and family modes of treatment. Marmor (1975) termed the fact that only 12 percent of the patients seen by analysts were exposed to such innovative and effective treatment modalities "most regrettable" (p. 69).

Impact Of Psychoanalysis

In summary, even though classical psychoanalysis has exerted tremendous influence on the theory and practice of psychotherapy in a historical sense, the movement has considerably less impact at the present time. Many people confuse psychoanalytic and psychodynamic therapists and criticize the efforts of the latter because of the limitations of the former. Table 1 presents some of the most commonly appearing misconceptions about psychodynamic forms of therapy as a conclusion to this portion of the chapter. We shall see in Chapter 5 that, as therapists become more experienced, they employ a more psychodynamic (but not necessarily psychoanalytic) framework for conceptualizing what occurs in therapy, regardless of their beginning theoretical orientation.

TABLE 1. COMMON MISCONCEPTIONS
ABOUT PSYCHODYNAMIC APPROACHES

1. Most psychodynamic therapists are psychoanalysts.
2. Psychodynamic therapy is a passive form of treatment that ignores "real-world" problems of patients.
3. Psychodynamic therapists are passive, inactive, and silent.
4. Psychodynamic therapy places exclusive emphasis on historical and childhood determinants of present difficulties.
5. Psychodynamic therapy invariably takes years to bring about meaningful improvement.
6. Psychodynamic therapists believe that behavior change is illusory unless preceded by the development of insight.
7. Psychodynamic therapists reject empirical research as meaningless.

THE HUMANISTIC-PHENOMENOLOGICAL SPECTRUM

Calling a therapist a "humanist" may contain the implicit accusation that the individual is a soft-headed, love-freak who employs neither effective therapeutic techniques nor acceptable research methods. Like the stereotyped criticisms of the psychodynamic orientation, such attacks are simplistic, ignoring the wide variety of orientations encompassed within this broad spectrum.

General Assumptions
Of Humanistic Therapists

Humanistically inclined therapists begin with assumptions that are quite similar to those which underlie psychodynamic formulations. These are, however, transformed to provide a more optimistic view of human functioning. Most humanistic therapists would share the following general beliefs, which can be compared with the assumptions underlying psychoanalysis:

1. The personality is an organized system that is open to influence by the environment, and, in turn, can influence the environment.
2. The personality system contains basic, inherent forces that seek to maintain the equilibrium of the system and to promote its growth.
3. The basic aim of the system is the achievement of personal growth, which has been construed in terms of self-actualization (by Carl Rogers), meaning in life (by Viktor Frankl), cognitive complexity (by George Kelly), integration and differentiation (by Fritz Perls), and related ways.
4. Growth is a developmental process which proceeds through phases that are more-or-less distinct from one another.
5. Healthy functioning is based on growth and freedom and is not as difficult to achieve as psychoanalysts would have us believe.

These assumptions are quite similar to those held by many psychodynamic therapists, although humanists consider growth to be a somewhat more fluid process.

Like psychodynamic practitioners, humanistic therapists differ among themselves over important but more specific issues. Some of these differences, as they relate to the role of the therapist and the utility of empirical inquiry, can be seen by comparing the client-centered system of Carl Rogers with the Gestalt approach of Fritz Perls.

Client-Centered Psychotherapy

Basic Assumptions Of Rogers. Like Freud, Carl Rogers is credited with developing a system of psychotherapy, a theory of personality, and a set of methods for investigating clinical phenomena. His writings provided an attractive alternative to psychoanalysis. They have had tremendous influence in the realms of education, clinical psychology, and pastoral counseling. His clearest formulation of personality structure was provided in 1959, which represented an extension of the perspective on psychotherapy he had presented in 1942 and 1951.

Rogers begins with the assumption that people possess an inherent motivating drive to symbolize their experiences into consistent yet increasingly complex patterns. Symbolization of experience enables one to manipulate relevant cognitions to effectively meet new challenges. This developmental sequence leads to the acquisition of a **self-structure**, which Rogers (1951) characterized as an organized yet fluid pattern of perceptions and associated values.

According to his theory, the healthy individual continually moves toward **self-actualization**, which involves incorporating novel experiences in a manner that makes them congruent with one's self-concept. Self-actualized people do not see the world in terms of absolutes or dichotomies. Rather, they are able to act effectively because their cognitive maps of reality are complex and differentiated. Self-actualization is based on positive self-evaluation, which itself involves two processes. **Positive self-evaluation** is generated innately through symbolizing experiences in a manner consistent with one's basic self-concept. It requires that the person be able to interpret her own actions in a favorable, accepting way. Favorably evaluating one's own actions is a learned skill which has its roots in childhood experiences. Before a person can learn to do this, she must receive positive regard from significant others. Movement toward self-actualization through positive self-evaluation is much more difficult for people who did not experience being valued by others in early life. Given that favorable self-evaluation was learned, however, the healthy adult will continue to symbolize experiences congruently with the positive self-concept and thus remain free of tension and anxiety.

Rogers' (1959) conception of how disordered behavior develops is somewhat similar to theory in the psychodynamic framework. Life is filled with situations that can thwart movement toward self-actualization. Meaningful experiences that are incongruent with one's positive self-image sometimes occur. Such experiences are **subceived**, which means they are denied entry into the self-system or they are admitted in a distorted form. Subception is similar to the psychodynamic notions of repression, denial, and projection as defense mechanisms. Subception leads to the **compartmentalizing** of incongruent experiences to reduce feelings of threat. Subception also has the unfortunate consequence of thwarting the innate process of symbolizing experiences consistently with the self-concept. A vicious cycle ensues, whereby incongruent experiences are blocked off from entry into the self-system, thus making the system more rigid and less able to adequately integrate new experiences. As more experiences are compartmentalized, the entire system becomes even more rigid and less effective. Maladjustment involves self-deception, loss of self-esteem, and negation of one's personal value. The behavioral manifestations of these destructive cognitions include deterioration of gratifying interpersonal relationships and an anxiety-ridden ineptitude in meeting the demands of daily life. These outcomes can foster an even greater loss of self-esteem.

Like psychoanalysts, Rogers (1951, 1959) believes that honest self-scrutiny is the only means to alleviate dysfunctional conditions. His therapeutic operations, however, are radically different from those used by analysts. Rogerian therapy is based on the central assertion that the debilitated individual possesses self-curative abilities that can be activated by a warm and permissive therapeutic atmosphere. The client is the center of intervention and is the expert about his current and ideal state of functioning. The task of the therapist is to establish a climate of trust that will enable the client to engage in both intellectual and, more importantly, emotional exploration of the damaged self-concept. Once this process begins, experiences will again be consistently symbolized, and inner tension reduced.

The assumption that people possess an inherent tendency to move toward self-actualization has important practical consequences. The therapist's qualities as a person are considered to be much more important than the specific therapeutic maneuvers that she employs. Client-centered therapists employ a democratic and nondirective focus. They are not concerned with "breaking through" resistances, but rather, they are oriented toward establishing a trusting atmosphere to facilitate communication. This emphasis has led to a great deal of research on the personal attributes of the clinician. Proponents of this system suggest that the effective therapist will be perceived by the client as (1) nondefensive or *genuine* in the therapeutic encounter, (2) able to communicate *accurate empathetic understanding*, and (3) manifesting *nonpossessive warmth* (Truax and Carkhuff, 1967). Rogers originally viewed this latter characteristic as the therapist's ability to demonstrate *unconditional positive regard* to the client.

A multidimensional content analysis of a therapy session conducted by Rogers himself (Strupp, 1957) indicated that his primary mode of intervention involved reflection of feelings. Strupp found Rogers' strategies to be more uniform, less directive, and less inferential, in contrast to a therapist with a re-educative insight orientation. The term *nonpossessive warmth* seems preferable to *unconditional positive regard*. Truax (1966b) found that even the most Rogerian of all Rogerian therapists (that is, Rogers himself) was providing warmth and empathy contingently to a client whenever the latter discussed emotionally involving topics.

Investigation Through Empirical Procedures. For more than three decades, Rogers has been among the strongest advocates of investigating psychotherapeutic processes through empirical methodology. The focus of his own endeavors gradually evolved from demonstrating the effectiveness of client-centered therapy, through a concern with therapist attributes, to examining the nature of interpersonal encounters within the human potential and encounter group movements. His contributions have made an enormous impact on psychotherapeutic practices, clearly demonstrating that the roles of scientist and practitioner are indeed compatible.

Early experimental work by Rogers (1954) and his associates (e.g., Butler and Haigh, 1954) was aimed at demonstrating that client-centered therapy produced greater correspondence between a person's current and idealized self-images. Self-perception was measured by means of a Q-sort procedure in which the participant would sort a series of positive and negative statements (e.g., "My life is very rewarding," "I am an anxious person") into piles representing how well each described the person's perceptions of his present self and ideal self-image. Discrepancies between the self and ideal self were determined by correlating the two sets of rankings. Using this procedure, Butler and Haigh found that client-centered therapy increased this correspondence to a significant degree. Before intervention, the self and ideal Q-sorts of clients were completely independent. Therapy made them moderately consistent with one another.

Even though methodological limitations in this type of research were eventually discovered, such investigations were extremely important because they m de self-assessment by clients a legitimate source of information about psy hotherapy.

In 1957, Rogers published a short article that signalled a shift in emphasis to the importance of the therapist in promoting beneficial change. A number of devices were invented to measure those characteristics which were deemed to be essential in promoting improvement in therapy. We will consider this body of knowledge in Chapter 5.

By his actions, Rogers has demonstrated a deep commitment to understanding psychotherapy through the application of empirical procedures. In 1958, however, he remarked to a colleague that he had learned much more about therapy from his clinical intuition than from any controlled scientific investigation [Bergin and Strupp (1972), p. 313]. This seeming contradiction is explicable if we remember that the major utility of empirical method lies in the validation of clinical insights by public consensus in the context of discovery, rather than in the generation of intuitions within the context of discovery. The willingness of Rogers to expose his clinical hypotheses to empirical scrutiny helped remove the practice of psychotherapy from the realm of magic.

Gestalt Psychotherapy

Studies of perception by psychologists Max Wertheimer and Kurt Koffka, as well as the insight-learning experiments of Wolfgang Köhler, provided the historical underpinnings of the Gestalt approach to psychotherapy. The movement itself coalesced under the direction provided by Frederick ("Fritz") Perls, who began his career as a physician thoroughly trained in psychoanalysis. His clinical experience led him to revise the treatment methods he had learned and to transform psychoanalytic theory into a more socially-oriented system of thought.

Basic Assumptions Of Perls. Perls (1973) begins with the assumption that human beings are unified organisms whose physical and mental activities continually mesh into coherent patterns. All life is governed by **homeostasis**, a dynamic process through which the organism satisfies its complex and ever changing needs. Personality is a system of organized patterns called **gestalts**. These patterns unify experiences into an integrated and continual flow. Perls rejected the numerous experiential dichotomies (e.g., body vs. mind; self vs. external reality; conscious vs. unconscious; past vs. present) that traditional psychoanalytic views have fostered.

In the healthy individual, a fluid, but distinguishable, **contact boundary** exists between the person and the surrounding world. The environment is part of the person and the person is part of the environment. Healthy adjustment results from balancing one's personal needs and desires against the demands of others in the social environment. This ability fosters the smooth integration of novel experiences and enables the person to resolve **existential polarities**.

All people experience such polarities whenever they feel conflicted about choosing a particular course of action. Many of the polarities are seen as illusory, having been fostered by currently dominant beliefs about psychotherapy and the nature of science. For example, Perls, Hefferline, and Goodman (1951) suggest that the split between *infantile* and *mature* itself stems from the preoccupation therapists have with defining cure as a social event, on one hand, and with childhood determinants of behavior, on the other. Perls et al. also point out that, if taken literally, the split between *conscious* and *unconscious* would make therapy impossible, because it is impossible to discover things about oneself that are defined as unknowable. Such polarities have become part of our common culture and have an adverse impact on many people.

Perls (1973) argues that a **neurosis** is an inappropriate defensive maneuver that people use to avoid being overwhelmed by a hostile world. "Neurotics" are unable to prevent others from infringing upon their personal rights. The neurotically crippled individual *needs* to lean on others or *needs* to shut others out of his life. In contrast, the healthy person *wants* (and is effectively able) to have mutual reciprocal influence with others in order to grow.

Perls has made two dramatic reversals of classical analytic thought in his speculating on the origins of maladaptation and one additional transformation regarding psychotherapy. In contrast to the psychoanalytic belief that neurosis is a form of mental illness, *Perls contends that sickness is a form of neurosis.* Adopting the role of a sick person enables weak and insecure persons to manipulate and control those around them. Very often, becoming sick is the least adversive alternative to coping with a difficult life situation. This formulation was highly influential in the development of a framework that defines psychotherapy as a series of interpersonal games.

Perls also changed the basic function of psychoanalytic defense mechanisms from channeling intrapsychic energy to controlling interpersonal events. According to Perls, neurosis involves the inhibition of excitement and spontaneity as well as growth of self-hatred and interpersonal rigidity. Four defense mechanisms are associated with the birth of a neurosis. Each of these involves aggression that is either turned inward against the self or directed outward toward the environment. **Introjection** is the uncritical acceptance of prescriptive modes of thought, feeling, or behavior that belong to others. Introjectors feel compelled to act as they do because their parents, friends, religious leaders, or undefined significant others say that they "ought to." Turned inward, introjection results in feelings of extreme guilt; directed outward, it leads to pathological resignation and helplessness.

Projection involves blaming others for thoughts and actions that belong to the individual. Directed inward, projection leads one to deny or disown the thought or behavior. Directed outward, it causes passive-aggressive behaviors. **Confluence** is the inability to distinguish one's own needs from those of others. Confluent people either inflict their experiences on others, or they allow others to inflict experiences on them, without integrating these into a greater sense of interpersonal awareness. Such individuals are not their own people; they attempt to be whatever they believe others wish them to be, and they demand the same from others. Turned inward, confluence arouses fear of being different; turned toward the environment, it leads to clinging, hysterical behavior. **Retroflection** consists of avoiding direct conflict by erecting a rigid barrier between the self and the environment. Retroflectors "don't care" about anything and do not permit others to get close to them. Turned inward, retroflectors continually undo their successes and experience alienation. When directed toward the environment, retroflection results in obsessive busyness and self-destructive behaviors (Perls, Hefferline, and Goodman, 1951).

Perls (1973) concisely describes the operation of these four defense mechanisms:

The introjector does as others would like him to do, the projector does unto others what he accuses them of doing to him, the man in pathological confluence doesn't know who is doing what to whom, and the retroflector does to himself what he would like to do to others [Reprinted by permission. F. Perls. *The Gestalt approach and eyewitness to therapy.* Science and Behavior Books, 1973, p. 40].

Another major transformation of analytic thought Perls made was to argue that psychotherapy is too good to be limited to the sick. Every person can profit from therapeutic feedback which is aimed at clarifying one's contact boundaries. In Gestalt therapy, heavy emphasis is given to accepting personal responsibility for one's thoughts, feelings, and actions. The therapist serves as a facilitator in this task, which is often conducted in a group setting.

Therapeutic Practices. In Gestalt therapy, a distinction is made between a limited set of rules formalized at the outset and a potentially infinite number of games that represent creative adaptations of the basic rules (Levitsky and Perls, 1970). The purpose of both rules and games is to foster integration of the many polarities that cause people to feel conflicted. Rules are not meant to have the dogmatic quality of commandments, although they do prescribe actions in therapy that are meant to foster acceptance of responsibility. For example, the **principle of the now** is designed to help an individual focus on her present state, rather than on past events which cannot be changed. Similarly, "it" language is to be avoided. **It language** refers to denial of feelings and emotions by attributing their manifestations to a body organ. When a client says "My eyes are filling with tears," the Gestalt therapist will attempt to have the person accept responsibility for the underlying feeling by asking, "Can you say that you feel like crying?" Other rules involve **asking questions** (which involves distinguishing between questions that seek information and those that contain hidden accusations) and **no gossiping** (which prohibits group members from talking *about* others when they should be talking *to* them).

Games encompass exercises aimed at facilitating both intellectual and emotional awareness of how one deals with issues relating to love, fear, expression of feeling, trust, and rejection, among others. For example, group members might form a closed circle with one participant excluded. This person has the task of gaining entry into the circle. When they are outside, some people will demand that they be admitted; others will beg, entice, or seek to induce guilt; still others will try to force their way in physically. The strategies employed are then discussed in terms of the interpersonal impact they had on both the excluded individual and the others. Such games are thought to reveal information about how an individual behaves in the real world.

In contrast to client-centered therapists, Gestalt clinicians are quite active, having a very powerful role in structuring what occurs in therapy.

Attitude Toward Science. Another distinction exists between these two types of humanistic therapists: their attitude toward validation. Gestalt therapists do not engage in empirical validation of their techniques because of their central assumption about science. They believe science has produced prescriptive dogmas which further segment the free flow of experience into polarities. Science has fostered distinctions between body and mind, as well as between subjective and objective knowledge. The goal of Gestalt therapy is to help people learn about their subjective realities instead of adjusting them to fit preconceived scientific notions of what objective reality is. *Perls and his associates reject the view of science as dogma and further reject all forms of dogma as dehumanizing.* About the only issue they seem to be at all dogmatic about is the necessity to reject dogma.

Rational-Emotive Psychotherapy

The system of intervention called *rational-emotive psychotherapy* demonstrates just how fluid and subjective the boundary between humanistic and behavioral perspectives really is. Rational emotive therapy is among the most influential of the existing hybrid models. Like Perls, Albert Ellis operated as a psychoanalyst until his own clinical experience led him to question the value of this approach.

Basic Assumptions Of Ellis. *Ellis* (1962) *views people as essentially processors of information. Environmental events are experienced, evaluated, and acted upon. The most important component of this process, which Ellis describes as an $A{-}B{-}C$ triangle, is the evaluative element.* He contends that exclusive focus on sequences between antecedents (A) and responses (C) provides only superficial knowledge of human action. The most important determinant of adjustment is the self-evaluative meaning (B) that is placed on antecedent external events, which he describes as **what people say to themselves.** A man, for example, might become impotent after hearing his partner belittle the size of his penis. Ellis would argue that the man became impotent, not because of his partner's comment, but rather, as a result of his own evaluative interpretations of the remark. He may have said to himself that he could never satisfy this woman or that he was an inadequate sexual partner because she thought he had a small penis. His dysfunctional condition was the direct result of such negative self-appraisals.

Ellis (1962) described a number of widely held **irrational beliefs** which cause and sustain emotional disturbances. Such beliefs are irrational because no evidence can be provided to justify them and because they contain elements of self-hatred, hostility, worthlessness, and inadequacy. Many people believe that they must be totally competent to be considered worthwhile human beings, that they have no control over their sorrow, that they need to rely upon others who are stronger than themselves to make it through life, or that they cannot overcome the effects of past events. Such beliefs lead to feelings of alienation or depression, psychosomatic complaints, and a "damned if I do-damned if I don't" paralysis of behavior. The no-win situation of a woman client, who believed that everyone must cherish her all of the time, illustrates the dilemma. She felt inadequate at a party where politics was being discussed because she did not say anything. She *thought* that everyone viewed her as *stupid* because she was so quiet. When asked, "Then why didn't you join in?" she replied, "If I had talked, then everyone would have known I was stupid."

Ellis (1973) organized these specific irrational ideas into three interlocking themes that centered on (1) condemning the self for being imperfect, (2) condemning others for being imperfect, and (3) condemning the world for being imperfect. A current of harsh moralism runs through all irrational ideas—the same kind of moralism that causes existential polarities, when it is conceptualized from a Gestalt perspective. *Ellis also contends that irrational components can be found in emotional states as well as in intellectual evaluations.* He distinguishes between fear and anxiety by emphasizing the self-protective function of the former and contrasting this to an element of inadequacy and helplessness that is found in the latter. Fear energizes people to take constructive action, while anxiety causes paralysis.

Goal And Therapeutic Practices. *The goal of rational emotive therapy is to provide clients with methods of self-evaluation that are incompatible with their irrational beliefs.* The therapist engages in active confrontation with the client in an effort to challenge self-destructive beliefs. As the client begins to question these beliefs and develop more self-accepting cognitive appraisals, confrontation is gradually replaced with support. In this way, the rational-emotive therapist essentially functions in a manner similar to a behavior therapist, that is, as a social reinforcement machine (Krasner, 1962). Ellis, however, stresses the humanistic orientation of his approach by contending that individuals are worthwhile in their own right, regardless of their past deeds. *By making the important distinction between what people do and what they are, he is able to challenge irrational beliefs directly without devaluing the individual who holds them.* In fact, such a distinction is made by therapists of almost all theoretical persuasions in an attempt to develop a therapeutic atmosphere of warmth and trust.

Empirical Inquiry Into Effectiveness. Although Ellis himself has produced little empirical evidence about the effectiveness of this treatment method, favorable support has emerged from the work of cognitive behavior therapists (Beck, 1970; Meichenbaum, 1974). The programmatic investigations of both Beck and Meichenbaum have clearly documented the utility of teaching clients to cognitively restructure their self-appraisals. Teaching rational self-talk as a coping strategy has proven useful in inhibiting anxiety, alleviating depression, reducing impulsivity, and enhancing creativity.

Overview Of The Spectrum. Table 2 presents some common misconceptions about humanistic therapies and those who practice intervention within this framework. Our brief overview suggests that obvious differences exist between theorists who wear this particular mantle. Some of the generalizations will apply more to some humanistic perspectives than to others. *As a group, however, humanistic therapists are no more or less committed to empirical inquiry, active, warm, empathetic, genuine, or powerful than therapists who espouse different orientations.*

THE BEHAVIORAL SPECTRUM

Historical Roots

Behaviorism As A Foundation. In contrast to the other approaches we have examined, behavior modification has its historical roots in many different disciplines, including anthropology, sociology, and experimental and social psychology. Behavior modification did not

TABLE 2. COMMON MISCONCEPTIONS
ABOUT HUMANISTIC APPROACHES

---

1. Humanistic therapy is unscientific, and humanistic therapists reject scientific methods and goals.
2. Humanistic therapists are basically passive, nondirective, and reflective.
3. Because humanistic therapists emphasize the dignity of the individual, they are actually warmer and more empathic human beings than other "types" of therapists.
4. Humanistic therapy is not influenced by the values of the therapist.
5. The client is given greater personal power and control in humanistic therapy than in other forms of psychological treatment.
6. Behavior change is not emphasized in humanistic therapy.

---

develop into a social movement until around the middle of the present century. The work of numerous learning theorists, including Guthrie, Hull, Mowrer, Pavlov, Thorndike, and Tolman, provided the intellectual nucleus around which the movement coalesced.

John B. Watson was a particularly influential predecessor of the movement. His views had a profound influence on both the development of a behavioral technology and critics of the movement. Watson (1916, 1924) strongly emphasized that the proper study of psychology ought to be behavior. With his associates (Jones, 1924; Watson and Rayner, 1920) he convincingly demonstrated that seemingly complex "mental abberations," such as phobias, could be produced and eliminated by altering stimulus-response associations. This and other work provided a basis for the development of *methodological behaviorism* which specified methods of empirical inquiry. Methodological behaviorism is characterized by an emphasis on controlled experimentation in which classes of observable events are manipulated and/or reliably measured in order to test the validity of specific hypotheses (Mahoney, 1974). This methodological viewpoint was an extremely important influence on academic psychologists who sought to uncover basic laws governing behavior, and it has dominated conceptions of psychological science for the past 50 years.

Watson also strongly rejected the investigation of mentalistic phenomena as unscientific. His contention that all higher mental processes (like thought and emotion) could be reduced to simple physiological changes has been labelled as *metaphysical* or *radical behaviorism* (Mahoney, 1974). By rejecting the existence of higher mental processes, Watson inadvertently helped further the polarization of academic and practitioner psychologists. Many of the latter reacted against radical behaviorism by embracing psychoanalytic thought.

Another effect of Watson's metaphysical stance was to provide critics of behavioral psychologists with "proof" that documented the empty sterility of the behavioral approach to psychotherapy. Modern behavior therapists are, unfortunately, still all too frequently criticized as being cold, manipulative, or even mindless. We shall shortly see that such criticisms are quite unfair. Nonetheless, the basis of such criticisms was provided by Watson's writings.

Origins As A Social Movement. Ullmann (1969) described behavior modification as an emerging *social movement*. Borrowing from the writings of various social philosophers, he characterized a social movement as involving a collective attempt to reach a common goal by people over an extended period of time and over a large geographical area. Participants in a social movement tend to share common aims and a common identity that is often structured through formal organizations.

The origins of behavior therapy as a social movement can be traced to the work of B. F. Skinner, Joseph Wolpe, Hans Eysenck, and their associates. The contributions of these individuals reflected three general trends that converged to provide behavior therapists with a shared intellectual orientation, common goals, and a professional identity.

Skinner provided a theory of instrumental conditioning that emphasized contingencies be ween responses and consequences within specific settings. His condi ioning procedures soon were being applied to improve the functioning of presumably untreatable people in total treatment settings (Ayllon, 1963; Ferster and Meyer, 1962). Systematic use of behavior management techniques in closed treatment environments resulted in startling alterations in the behavior of retarded and "psychotic" individuals who were considered hopelessly beyond rehabilitation. Skinner, Solomon, Lindsley, and Richards (1953) coined the term *behavior therapy* to describe these contingency management operations. Behavior therapists sometimes rubbed the noses of their psychodynamic counterparts in the interpretative richness of their psychodynamic views. Haughton and Ayllon (1965), for example, systematically reinforced a mute female "schizophrenic" woman with cigarettes for holding a broom. After the woman had been trained to carry the broom everywhere she went, they invited two psychiatrists to provide interpretations of her behavior. One psychiatrist suggested that the broom was a symbolic representation of a child, a phallic symbol, or the sceptre of an omnipotent queen. The nonfunctional utility of this interpretation was then demonstrated by extinguishing the response by no longer making broom carrying contingent for obtaining cigarettes. *The very success of such interventions, however, raised concern about the manipulative and controlling aspects of behavior therapy.*

Wolpe provided the behavioral movement with a theoretical rationale and a derivative method of intervention applicable to people who suffered from "neurotic" dysfunctions. Wolpe (1958) described the successful use of a novel treatment called *systematic desensitization* and provided a theoretical rationale for this procedure based on Pavlovian conditioning principles. *One important consequence of this development was to offer therapists the promise that psychotherapy could indeed be based on scientific laws. A second important consequence of Wolpe's work was the development of a method of therapeutic intervention that complemented the emerging rehabilitative technology of the token economy.* Wolpe's technology has come to have widespread applicability in treatment settings that are more open than those found in residential institutions. Behavior therapy was beginning to enter the private practitioner's office.

Eysenck was the first to question the effectiveness of traditionally defined methods of psychotherapy. In a review of available evidence, he concluded that psychotherapy did not appear to be any more beneficial than no treatment. We shall review this issue in Chapter 4. The controversy over the effectiveness of therapy aroused mutual antagonism between psychodynamic and behavioral therapists. Eysenck also attempted to show that behavior therapy should be set apart from psychotherapy and that it is qualitatively different from psychotherapy. In 1959, he provided 10 polarities that existed between the two approaches. Some of the distinctions he proposed tended to derogate psychotherapy (e.g., as being based on inconsistent and improperly formulated theoretical propositions). Some of his other distinctions presented an overly simplified view of behavior therapy (e.g., the historical development of a problem is largely irrelevant for treatment; cures are achieved by establishing and extinguishing conditioned emotional reactions). Some of his distinctions (e.g., behavior therapy de-emphasizes development of a therapeutic relationship) have provided ammunition to critics of the movement.

Basic Assumptions And Rules

Behavior therapists view themselves as pragmatists, and very successful ones at that. *What theoretical unity can be found among members of this approach rests upon explaining therapeutic changes in terms of learning-based formulations.* We shall see shortly that this is not a very secure basis of unity within the movement. *Beyond this, behavior therapists view their clinical activities as being grounded in "scientific" laboratory-based procedures.* Of major importance has been the emphasis of response-consequence relationships. This emphasis has enabled behavior therapists to produce technological strategies that have proven to be of immense value in total treatment institutions, the classroom, and psychotherapy.

As we mentioned before, the common element in the movement is a specific way of conceptualizing therapeutic processes. Like their Gestalt-minded colleagues, behavior therapists adhere to a few basic rules and have a large number of therapeutic games at their disposal. Krasner and Ullmann(1973) provide the best overview of the rules that comprise the "belief systems" of most behavior therapists:

1. *The functions of treatment and research are inseparable.* Conducting therapy necessarily involves conducting an assessment of a client's strengths and liabilities before, during, and after treatment. Conversely, empirical inquiries into the processes and outcomes associated with specific treatment strategies, such as systematic desensitization, produce benefits for the participating subjects.

2. *The goals of therapy are determined through behavioral assessment procedures.* Behavior therapists are generally disenchanted with traditional diagnostic procedures, many of which stem from dynamic and disease models of human nature. Although not qualitatively different activities, assessment and diagnosis can be distinguished along four interrelated dimensions (Goldfried and Kent, 1972; Stuart, 1970). First, assessment is aimed more directly at gathering information relevant for prediction and control, in contrast to the explanatory function of traditional diagnosis. Second, behavioral assessment involves a preference for short, parsimonious inferential chains that implicate interactions between behavior and the environment in the form of antecedent-response-consequence sequences. Third, in contrast to the emphasis on psychopathology found in traditional diagnosis, behavioral assessment is aimed at discovering a client's strengths as well as his weaknesses. Fourth, behavioral assessment is directed at discovering what a person does, rather than classifying him in terms of traits, types, or presumably underlying mechanisms. Kanfer and Saslow (1965) conceptualize behavioral assessment as probing seven areas of functioning—inquiry into the problem situation, clarification of factors which sustain the difficulty, determination of potentially reinforcing events, discovery of relevant historical and developmental features which affect the disability, analysis of available coping and self-control procedures used by the client, inquiry into immediate social relationships, and assessment of the client's general lifestyle and its fit with larger social values. The wide scope of contemporary behavioral analysis does not justify the criticisms that such assessment is ahistorical or that it provides only a superficial overview of human action.

3. *Basic diagnostic concepts are stated in a manner that enables them to be experimentally tested.* Behavior therapists are not interested in classifying people into categories. The client's difficulties are instead conceptualized as resulting from specific environmental factors. Depression, for example, might be hypothesized as stemming from loss of significant reinforcers, unfavorable work-to-reinforcement ratios, unpredictable punishment from others, or lack of social skill. Such hypotheses are conceptualized to enable the therapist to directly assess changes that result from whatever intervention is attempted.

4. *Explicit strategies are employed to produce beneficial changes.* Diagnostic formulations suggest that specific treatment methods can profitably be used. Behavior therapists rely upon nonspecific therapeutic influences such as therapist warmth and empathy, emphasizing that such factors are necessary but not sufficient for fostering improvement. Beneficial changes in clients are thought to result from what the therapist does, rather than the kind of person the therapist is, through the action of the therapeutic hour, or other mystical forms of influence. In addition, behavior therapists have been busily turning such nonspecific therapeutic influences into specific and effective change strategies. Goldstein (1971; 1975), for example, has transformed the vague notion of "effective therapeutic relationship" into a series of techniques that can be employed to increase the interpersonal influence potential of the therapist.

5. *Research is directed at demonstrating causal relationships between explicit treatment manipulations and changes in the client.* Behavior therapists acknowledge that improvement in therapy can result from a variety of influences that reside in the client, therapist, setting, and specific techniques employed. As a group, therapists with this orientation are more interested in demonstrating that change is a direct function of the intervention itself. Attempts are made to rule out the effects of other sources of influence by having different therapists employ the same basic technique with diverse groups of people in various settings. A causal link between treatment and outcome can be established if the therapeutic procedure is found to be effective across these other varying conditions.

Like our analysis of psychodynamic and humanistic perspectives, our summary of the behavioral framework is more easily described in terms of what it is not, than what it is. The view of behavior modification or behavior therapy as a monolithic system that is qualitatively different from other forms of psychotherapy is both outmoded and inadequate. As much diversity and controversy exists within this perspective as can be found in and between the other major orientations. *Behavior therapy is not simplistic; it is not mechanistic; it is not behavioristic. The movement may be more scientific than artistic, more behavioral than cognitive, and more technological than theoretical, although widespread agreement about even these facets cannot be found.* The exhaustive search for more effective procedures to promote constructive therapeutic change also indicates that the menace of behavior control has been oversold. Contemporary behavior therapists simply do not possess a technology of behavior change that is greatly superior to that of clinicians with different orientations. When faced with clients who are reluctant to change, behavioral clinicians are forced to rely upon the time-honored practices of suggesting, persuading, reasoning, supporting, and challenging.

Commitment To Empirical Inquiry

The general beliefs shared by many behavior therapists suggest that most accept current conceptions of empirical inquiry as having an integral place in their therapeutic activities. Because of this orientation, they have provided an immense amount of research information about both the effectiveness and efficiency of the specific behavior change strategies that they employ. Many different procedures (e.g., systematic desensitization, covert reinforcement, etc.) have been employed with diverse populations in a variety of settings. Most existing procedures have been investigated in numerous ways that differ with regard to the degree of experimental control they afford. Because of these reasons, it is practically impossible to provide a simplified summary of this vast research outpouring.

Certain specific techniques, such as desensitization, have proven to be quite useful in remedying a number of specific complaints. Paul (1969b), in a major review, suggested that desensitization is the only therapeutic procedure to date that has been empirically demonstrated to be helpful beyond a reasonable doubt. Despite such success, many questions about the efficacy of behavioral interventions remain unanswered, particularly questions about the permanence of change and the degree to which change generalizes to the client's real world. Nonetheless, behavior therapists remain committed to developing and empirically validating therapeutic strategies in an effort to improve their effectiveness. We shall examine some of the problematic issues associated with this commitment in later chapters.

Controversies Within The Behavioral Framework

Like the term *psychotherapy*, the words *behavior modification* and *behavior therapy* imply the existence of a uniform set of procedures. In reality, the terms are descriptive summaries of diverse ways of thinking about human behavior. At present, no widely accepted definition of either term exists. About 20 years ago, most behavior therapists were united in believing that their operations were based on clearly defined laws of learning (Eysenck, 1959; Wolpe, 1958). This view very nicely described the activities of those who modified behavior in closed institutional settings.

Development Of Varied Strategies. As treatment methods were increasingly employed in outpatient settings, where direct control of response-consequent contingencies was more difficult to exert, behavior therapists were forced to employ alternative conceptual frameworks. Faced with more complex clinical problems, behavioral therapists have developed an incredibly varied number of relationship-enhancement and cognitive-change strategies. The effect of this expansion was to move behavior therapy away from its foundation in the laws of learning, which never had been particularly secure in the first place (Mahoney, Kazdin, and Lesswing, 1974).

In contrast to the traditional formulations of Eysenck and Wolpe is the technical eclecticism of Lazarus (1973). He views behavior therapy as a multimodal endeavor which is aimed at treating the BASIC ID. This acronym describes seven important areas of therapeutic intervention—Behavior, Affect, Sensation, Imagery, Cognition, Interpersonal relations, and Drugs. Actually, the final focus is not a primary consideration, as most behavior therapists do not directly prescribe drugs; it does round out the acronym nicely, however. Within this model, he contends that the durability of treatment outcome is directly proportional to the number of areas addressed in therapy. Critics of this multimodal position contend that "it" is not *really* behavior therapy.

Conceptual Diffusion. Other kinds of conceptual diffusion have occurred. Some experts argue that psychotherapy is effective because it is *really* behavior therapy; others suggest that behavior therapy is really psychotherapy; still others contend that both psychotherapy and behavior therapy are variants of more fundamental similarities. Thus, it has been argued that psychoanalysis is little more than systematic verbal conditioning (Quay, 1959) or that systematic desensitization is effective because it enables a client to experience merging fantasies (Silverman et al., 1974). The most recent variant of this theme is to suggest that the best features of psychodynamic therapy and behavior therapy can be fused into even more useful conceptual systems such as "behavioral psychoanalysis" or "psychoanalytic behaviorism" (Birk, 1974; Feather and Rhoads, 1972a, b).

Although such integrative attempts have a definite conceptual appeal, they confuse essential philosophical differences with similarities in concrete technique (Franks and Wilson, 1974).

These sorts of conceptual alterations have led to antagonisms among behavior therapists themselves. Wolpe (1976a, b) has reaffirmed his belief that behavior therapy should be defined as "treatment methods derived from experimentally established principles and paradigms of learning and related principles" (1976a, p. 1). He rather uncharitably characterized those who have deviated from this framework as "malcontents." Such individuals are distinguished from people who have made great scientific advances because "malcontents do not understand what they are talking about—at least not entirely" (1976a, p. 2). The clear implication here is that those who disagree with Wolpe's views about behavior therapy are, at the very least, misguided, and, at worst, stupid.

In a rejoinder to Wolpe, Kirsch (in press) has suggested that Wolpe has simply provided a descriptive definition of an artificial phenomenon (i.e., behavior therapy) as it appeared during its early existence and then prescribed this as the essence of the movement as it is today. Taking a prescriptive definition of psychotherapy as a starting point, Kirsch points out that this method of defining a social movement would turn the title of Wolpe's (1958) major book, *Psychotherapy by Reciprocal Inhibition*, into a logical impossibility. Reciprocal inhibition simply would not fit into a prescriptive definition of psychotherapy as conceptualized during the 1950's.

Criticisms From Outside The Movement

Although psychodynamic and humanistic psychotherapists have been subjected to stereotyped criticisms of their activities, those engaged in behavior modification probably have had even more criticism. In fact, behaviorists have had incredibly poor public relations. The mass media typically depict the behavior modifier as manipulating other people in a cold, detached, and malevolent manner. The technology associated with behavior modification has become almost synonymous with attempts to exert mind control reminiscent of *Brave New World* or *Clockwork Orange* through brain stimulation, drugs, and psychosurgery (Andrews and Karlins, 1971). Behavior therapists have been extremely frank in acknowledging that manipulation and control are part of their activities. Roos (1974) has persuasively argued that its very success, coupled with the specificity of techniques and precision of stated goals, makes behavior modification more vulnerable to attack than other strategies that attempt to modify behavior. Analysis of psychotherapy in terms of power and conflict (see Chapter 7) clearly indicates that psychodynamic and even nondirective humanistic therapists exert a tremendous amount of direction and control. However, the extent of the therapist's power within these perspectives is masked by the language used by these individuals in describing their activities.

Related criticisms that behavior modification is dehumanizing, that it is coercive, that it does not involve treatment of the "whole person," and that it is antithetical to fostering human growth also have been raised by influential detractors of the movement. Such attacks have led to legal challenges to behavior modification programs (Martin, 1976; Wexler, 1973) and have increased the threat of external regulation, primarily by the federal government.

Some inherent contradictions in this pervasive stereotype are generally ignored. The use of psychosurgery and convulsive insulin and shock treatment, for example, has long been the sole province of physicians, who generally subscribe to dynamic and disease models of human functioning. We also know that therapists who are generally perceived as cold and aloof by their clients are not likely to be effective helpers. Yet, behavior therapists claim that their interventions are extremely efficacious. In fact, many proponents of the movement argue that the modern "witch hunters" who castigate their activities are upset precisely because behavioral technology represents the only truly effective means of bringing about change.

Much of this vilification has occurred for reasons beyond the control of behavior therapists, although they sometimes have inadvertently contributed to the unpleasantness. Many clinicians continue to equate the views of modern behavior therapists with the metaphysical behaviorism proposed by Watson. Criticisms of this type continue to occur with disturbing regularity, even though almost every behavioral clinician rejects Watson's metaphysical position.

Three contemporary influences reinforce the stereotype of the behavior therapist as a cold and manipulative technologist. First, the *popularized* success of behavioral interventions continues to open them to criticisms of being controlling. The mass media portray behavior modification as a simplistic "thing" that is applied as a panacea for drinking, addictive and gambling problems, marital strife, sexual dysfunctions, and many other life difficulties. Although effective behavioral intervention strategies have been developed to deal with many of these problems, their successful application is by no means a simple matter. Furthermore, the mass media also foster the illusion that behavior modification is *in general* more effective than specific applications often prove to be in real life.

Second, in contrast to other approaches, behavior therapists do not subscribe to theoretical beliefs that prescribe what normalcy should be. They generally find theoretical statements about *universal* stages of human development and criteria of adjustment to be unnecessary. This is not to say that behavior therapists fail to employ criteria of adjustment when doing therapy, only that the criteria they use are quite pragmatic and very relativistic. Life difficulties, for example, are frequently evaluated along three general dimensions: the degree to which they (1) cause discomfort to the client, (2) cause others to become annoyed or disturbed, and (3) diverge from widespread socially defined expectations.

Lack of a unifying theoretical framework that is shared by behavior therapists has some obvious pragmatic advantages. It also has one large disadvantage, however, in that behavioral clinicians cannot use theoretical terms to mask the reality of behavior control that exists in psychotherapy. Skinner (1971; 1974) points out that people seem to have an aversion to viewing their behavior as being controlled by portions of their environment. Behavior therapists simply do not have access to concepts such as "self-actualization" or "genital primacy," which provide satisfying explanations to many people. Without such concepts, the activities of behavior therapists appear to be more overtly manipulative than the strategies used by psychodynamic and humanistic therapists.

Publication policies of the major behavioral journals provide a third source of misconceptions about behavior therapists. Reports of controlled research on therapeutic processes and comparative outcome investigations predominate in behavioral outlets. Space limitations also preclude any extensive discussion of relationship issues in reports that detail the application of behavioral techniques. Readers are thus often left with the mistaken impression that a behavioral clinician will implement a particular treatment (e.g., desensitization, implosion) in a detached manner without making more than a superficial assessment of other important determinants of treatment. Analysis of behavioral assessment procedures (Kanfer and Saslow, 1965) reveals the sterility of this belief.

Table 3 lists some common misconceptions about the behavioral therapies. These contentions are rooted in uniformity myths surrounding the nature of "behavior modification." The vehemence of attacks against the movement has led many behavioral clinicians to cease calling themselves "behavior modifiers" because of the unpleasant associations the term conveys. Krasner (1976) has humorously suggested that the critics of behavior modification have killed "it." Although these detractors have succeeded in destroying the term, behavior modification as a social movement is far from dead. As we have seen, the essence of the movement is a shared set of beliefs about the primacy of functional relationships between therapist and client. This orientation has fostered impressive conceptual advances in many areas of therapeutic endeavor, as we shall discover in subsequent chapters.

FINAL WORDS

A therapist's theoretical orientation is undoubtedly an important influence on her therapeutic practices. Adherence to a particular model of human nature, however, represents only one set of influences, which are open to change over time. In reality, a single clinician is likely to hold some views that are consistent with the dominant theoretical orientation and others that are quite inconsistent. Garfield and Kurtz (1976) documented this point by analyzing the ideological beliefs of clinical psychologists who held competing theoretical views. Factor analysis of their scale yielded three independent dimensions involving beliefs about behavior modification, the intuitive versus objective nature of psychotherapy, and psychodynamic and psychoanalytic conceptions. Of particular interest was the finding that clinicians who generally subscribed to a behavior modification ideology did not agree that, in the etiology of mental illness (1) "recent events are almost

**TABLE 3. COMMON MISCONCEPTIONS
ABOUT BEHAVIOR THERAPIES**

1. Behavior therapy is useful only for changing symptomatic behavior because underlying causes are not dealt with.
2. Behavior therapists tend to be colder, less empathic, and more manipulative than psychodynamic or humanistic therapists.
3. Behavior therapy is no more than applied common sense.
4. Establishing a trusting relationship built on mutual respect is not necessary in behavior therapy.
5. Behavior therapy procedures cannot produce meaningful personality change and therefore cannot be applied to the whole person.
6. Behavior therapy is ultimately based on the laws of human and animal learning.
7. Drugs and brain stimulation are routinely employed by behavior therapists and are considered part of behavioral psychotherapy.

always much more important than early childhood experiences," or (2) "intrapsychic factors tend to be more important than biological or social environmental factors" (p.7). Similarly, those who generally held psychodynamic beliefs did not agree that "maladaptive behavior cannot be treated directly because it results from underlying causes" (p. 7).

In fact, with the exception of classical psychoanalysts, a number of important similarities unite clinicians of different theoretical persuasions. Psychodynamic and humanistic therapists share beliefs about the nature of personality as a system of energy, the role of defenses and resistances, and the importance of developmental and historical influences. Humanistic and behavioral clinicians share a distrust of traditional diagnostic practices and reject classification of people in terms of mental illnesses as being either dehumanizing (from the humanistic perspective) or causing detrimental social consequences (from the behavioral viewpoint). In addition, both humanistic and behavioral clinicians emphasize current functioning and are flexible in conceptualizing just how influential past determinants of behavior are for a given individual. Humanists view past influences as "unfinished business," "psychic tape recordings," "echoes," and "scripts"; behavioral therapists see them in terms of problem-solving and coping strategies.

Clinicians of all persuasions are concerned with developing a trusting relationship with the client and using this as a lever to promote constructive change. Within all therapeutic systems, the clinician also serves as a model for adjustment and functions as a source of reward and punishment. Finally, the "whole person" is the focus of intervention within every perspective.

The belief that all therapists of a particular theoretical persuasion hold the same views about people and conduct therapy in a uniform manner is a myth that is fostered by our language. If we describe people as "psychodynamic therapists," "humanists," or "behavior therapists," we must realize the oversimplification in such labelling. Stereotyped criticisms that stem from rigidly adhering to these simple labels retard our understanding of the mutual influence processes inherent in psychotherapy. Fortunately, emerging knowledge about these processes is causing the myth of therapist uniformity to crumble.

4
The Relativistic and Evolutionary Nature of Psychotherapy Research

Throughout history, socially sanctioned healers have gone about the business of treating afflicted individuals by casting out evil spirits, drawing blood, smearing the body with noxious (and much less frequently with pleasant) substances, prescribing vitamins, injecting chemicals, promoting insight, restructuring cognitions, and engineering behavior change. Each treatment procedure made sense within the context of knowledge that was in vogue in a particular place and time.

The history of mental healing has been characterized by the gradual substitution of ever more satisfying explanations of treatment processes and outcomes. What is satisfying for some people, however, is not acceptable to others. The efforts of skeptics and malcontents lead to the discovery of new knowledge that points to inadequacies in current theories and practices. Eventual repudiation of a prevailing paradigm leads people to view the efforts of their predecessors as stemming from ignorance of the *real* causes of therapeutic change. Yet even critics must admit that their new theories are evolutionary products of the work preceding theirs.

Recognizing this evolutionary chain leads us to a basic conclusion: *No system allows us to perceive the whole phenomenon of interest, but every system has contributed to the understanding of some aspects of the phenomenon as a coherent whole.*

Each theoretical perspective about psychotherapy provides a logically interrelated set of statements describing (1) criteria of ideal functioning, (2) how debilitating conditions develop, and (3) how they might be successfully remedied. Each theory contains an explanatory scope wide enough to account for broad aspects of human functioning. Yet, no single viewpoint provides enough scope to satisfy all psychotherapists. In addition, each framework contains prescriptive assumptions which are considered to be inadequate or unacceptable by those who hold different beliefs.

Given this set of historical facts, we can move to the two-fold purpose of this chapter: (1) to examine how knowledge about psychotherapy has emerged through systematic inquiry and (2) to show that even this systematic inquiry is relativistic.

Systematic investigation of therapeutic phenomena and indeed our conception of science itself are influenced by the investigator. The answers we obtain from empirical procedures depend in large part upon the questions we ask about those issues which aroused our curiosity in the first place. This theme is illustrated by a historical overview of attempts to answer the seemingly simple question, "Does psychotherapy work?" The history of research into the effectiveness of psychotherapy is a tale of excitement and despair, with controversy ever present. The relativistic nature of knowledge about psychotherapy is then further documented by examining how theoretical beliefs influence an individual's conceptions of science and lead to arbitrary decisions about the investigation of therapeutic processes.

CHASING THE POOKA OF PSYCHOTHERAPY

The word *pooka* derives from *puca*—mischievous elves who played tricks on people in ancient Irish mythology. A pooka is a goblin of the mind which exists only because people believe it to exist. Psychotherapy encompasses many complex interpersonal influence processes, but the word itself implies that *it* is a substantive entity. When we speak of psychotherapy as being a monolithic *thing*, we have created a pooka. Although no one has actually defined psychotherapy as an entity, when people began to wonder whether *it* were effective, they in effect did categorize psychotherapy as an entity. The search for the essence of the psychotherapy pooka was a frustrating and futile one, which ultimately led researchers to conclude that they had been asking questions which could not be answered.

Throughout history, the practice of psychotherapy has had many characteristics of a magical mystery tour. Therapists have done their work in relative ignorance of the processes they used to produce change. The status of psychotherapy as a form of magic was aptly described by White in 1956:

> The therapist does a little of this and a little of that, depending upon the circumstances that arise. Often the patient is bettered, but neither he nor his doctor knows just what it was that produced the change [Reprinted by permission. R. W. White. *The abnormal personality, 2nd Ed.* The Ronald Press Company, 1956, p. 313].

At this time, it was generally assumed by both psychotherapists and the general public that therapeutic intervention was invariably beneficial, even if no one was sure how change occurred.

Early Efforts To Assess Effectiveness

Hans Eysenck (1952) was the first to question this state of affairs. He reviewed records reporting the outcome of psychoanalysis on 760 people having neurotic disorders as well as the results of 19 investigations of eclectic therapy involving almost 7300 people. Using clearly specified but necessarily arbitrary criteria, he reported that psychoanalysis was successful in 44 percent of the cases, while eclectic therapy yielded a 64 percent improvement rate. He then compared these figures against records detailing the discharge rate of presumably untreated neurotics from hospitals in New York State and reports documenting improvement in the untreated neurotic disabilities of insurance claimants. He reported the incidence of disappearance of neurotic symptoms without therapeutic intervention (which he called **spontaneous remission**) to be 72 percent and concluded that the available evidence failed "to prove that psychotherapy, Freudian or otherwise, facilitates the recovery of neurotic patients" (1952, p. 322).

Although Eysenck noted the real dangers in drawing conclusions from this sort of actuarial comparison, his paper drew rapid and vehement criticism and led to more than two decades of heated controversy. The thrust of the criticism was that Eysenck's criteria of improvement were too stringent for psychoanalysis. In 1961, Eysenck reviewed subsequent research on therapeutic outcome and concluded that (1) people with neurotic complaints are just as likely to improve without therapy, (2) patients treated by psychoanalysis do not improve as quickly or as certainly as people who receive eclectic therapy, and (3) learning-based behavioral therapies offer more promise for success than other forms of intervention. The debate took on an increasingly polemical character, as evidenced by a rebuttal Eysenck (1964) made to one of his more persistent critics, Hans Strupp (1963). Eysenck declared that Strupp's contentions were "irrelevant, incompetent, and immaterial" (Eysenck, 1964, p. 97).

Although Eysenck's question was reasonable and long overdue, it helped perpetrate the myth that therapy is a uniform entity. It also created a second pooka—spontaneous remission.

Barron and Leary (1955) conducted the first controlled investigation of psychotherapy effectiveness by comparing improvement in people receiving therapy against changes in a group of nontreated individuals. Interestingly, they failed to find differences in the average amount of improvement shown by people in the two conditions. A clear implication of this outcome was that perhaps psychotherapy was indeed a waste of time and effort.

In a reanalysis of Barron and Leary's data, however, Cartwright (1956) noted much greater variability in the changes manifested by those receiving therapy than was found for untreated individuals. The implication of Cartwright's analysis was that psychotherapy seems to affect improvement in some people, but it worsens the condition of others. This conclusion represented a challenge to the belief that therapy was a monolithic and uniform entity. Unfortunately, his findings did not generate much excitement for almost a decade, until they were rediscovered by Bergin (1963).

Eysenck's contentions about the effectiveness of psychotherapy led to an immense upsurge of research activity by interested individuals. In 1958, the American Psychological Association sponsored the first of three conferences on research in psychotherapy. Participants optimistically expressed the belief that the application of scientific methodology would provide clear answers about therapeutic effectiveness. Most of the reports at the conference, however, were devoted to practical problems related to achieving adequate experimental control and to strategies for assessing therapeutic processes, rather than outcome.

A similar emphasis was evident at the second conference held in 1961. Only one of the 11 investigations contained the word *outcome* in its title, and the summary reports of panel discussions focused almost exclusively on the role of the therapist and problems associated with measuring personality change. Around this time, a number of major contributors expressed disillusionment with psychotherapy research in general and its relevance to clinical practice in particular. Colby (1964) characterized the field as "chaotic," while Zubin (1964) chastised researchers for neglecting the outcome problem and engaging in a "flight into process." Astin (1961) called the practice of psychotherapy a "functionally autonomous" activity because clinicians seemed oblivious to the knowledge empirical inquiry was producing. Astin maintained that practitioners continued to go about their business without regard for the potential consequences of therapeutic intervention.

Although all researchers were actually employing strategies to arbitrarily simplify the complexity of clinical reality, the linguistic illusion of psychotherapy as an entity prevented many from realizing the ultimate necessity of this approach. Failure to recognize the arbitrary nature of simplification strategies in the investigation of psychotherapy led to sterile debates that were themselves rooted in illusory distinctions, such as *process* versus *outcome* research. This distinction was one basis for the controversy between Strupp and Eysenck, with the former arguing that what occurs between therapist and client (process) must be understood before we can adequately assess outcome, while the latter contended that, if therapy is really ineffective, then process research is a waste of time.

In retrospect, these signs of confusion and controversy can be considered as healthy growing pains which accompanied the development of empirical knowledge about psychotherapy. Sargent (1961) pointed out that process research involves investigating a sequence of small-scale outcomes, while outcome research consists of examining process at a given point in time. Although this important point was generally overlooked at the time, today we recognize an integral unity between process and outcome.

Other Efforts In The Effectiveness Controversy

A major step toward destroying the pooka of psychotherapy was taken independently by Bordin (1965), Kiesler (1966), and Paul (1967; 1969a). It is interesting to note that Bordin's research identifies him as having a psychodynamic theoretical orientation, and Paul is a renowned behavior therapist.

Bordin called for the use of simplification strategies when investigating psychotherapy, noting the impossibility of ever being able to adequately manipulate and control all facets of the therapeutic encounter.

By discussing three myths about psychotherapy, Kiesler identified psychotherapy-as-pooka as misguided. He argued that much current research was based on the untenable assumptions that (1) all therapists are alike simply because they are labelled as therapists (the myth of therapist uniformity), (2) all patients are alike because they are identified as patients (the myth of patient uniformity), and (3) currently available theories and models (e.g., psychodynamic, learning theory formulations) are adequate representations of therapeutic change processes.

By suggesting that the controversy about therapeutic effectiveness was based on these myths, Kiesler provided researchers with the wisdom that the simplistic question, "Does psychotherapy work?" was the wrong one to ask.

Paul's contribution was to devise a more precise, meaningful, and hence, answerable question:

> What treatment, by whom, is most effective for this individual with that specific problem, under which set of circumstances, and how does change come about [Reprinted by permission. G. L. Paul. Behavior modification research: Design and tactics. From C. M. Franks (Ed.), *Behavior therapy: Appraisal and status*, McGraw-Hill, 1969, p. 44].

Variation In Outcome. This question provides an accurate reflection of the complexity found in psychotherapeutic processes. Variation in outcome is considered to be the product of (1) the specific treatment employed, (2) attributes of the therapist (including theoretical orientation, experience, sex, personality, and so on), (3) characteristics of the client (sex, age, socioeconomic status, race, and so on), (4) aspects of the physical setting, and (5) time limitations, *as well as all possible interactive combinations between these factors*. Each of these general sources of variation can further be broken down into numerous components. We encounter even more complexity when we realize that outcome can be assessed in a wide variety of ways. We can ask the therapist to judge improvement, have clients rate the changes they have experienced, gather information from significant others who know the client well, or have observers judge client behavior. Each of these sources of information also can be divided into many component assessment methods.

As therapists began to realize the complexity of psychotherapy, they also began to acknowledge that the controversy about effectiveness could not be resolved by either a single comprehensive experiment or through actuarial surveys of the literature. Accumulation of knowledge about therapeutic effects can be gained only through the slow, painstaking efforts of many investigators who operate within different conceptual frameworks. In subsequent chapters, we will examine what empirical inquiry has revealed about the major sources of variability in psychotherapy.

The Range Of Conclusions About Therapy Effectiveness

Research Efforts To Assess Effectiveness. We can help bury the twin pookas of psychotherapy and spontaneous remission by reviewing what actuarial surveys and logical speculation have told us about these strange creatures. A graphic demonstration of the relativity inherent in this sort of evaluative research was provided by Bergin (1971) in a reanalysis of the original data Eysenck had reviewed in 1952. Following prior criticisms of Eysenck's review, Bergin pointed out that a very strict criterion for judging the success of psychoanalysis had been employed. Eysenck also had rather arbitrarily categorized people who terminated early or dropped out of psychoanalysis as failures. (This decision was perhaps a reaction against the tendency of many analysts to classify drop-outs as successes.) Bergin adopted a less stringent criterion which was derived from the writings of a prominent psychoanalyst. He then went on to systematically vary these two dimensions (strict versus moderate criterion; include drop-outs as failures versus exclude drop-outs from analysis) and reported the outcomes depicted in Figure 6.

The first column represents Eysenck's original computation of success. In the second column, drop-outs were included as failures, but the less stringent criterion was used. This shift resulted in an increase of almost 40 percent in the success rate, as did the elimination of drop-outs and application of the strict criterion (shown in the third column). Finally, when the modest criterion was used in conjunction with the exclusion of early terminators, the success rate of psychoanalysis was almost double that provided by Eysenck. Bergin's reanalysis of the outcomes produced by eclectic therapy involved applying the less stringent criterion and eliminating drop-outs from consideration. His overall success rate of 65 percent closely corresponded to Eysenck's original 64 percent estimate.

Bergin's intentions were neither to prove that Eysenck was wrong

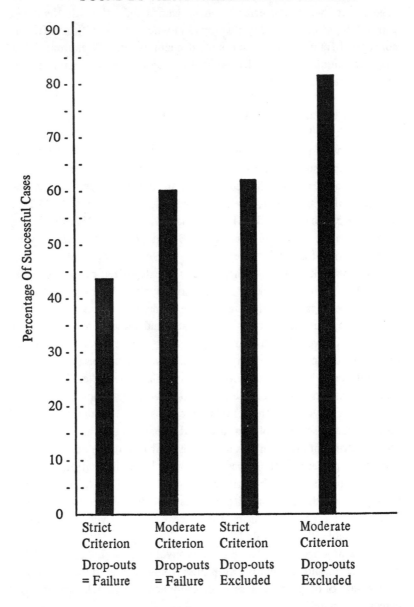

FIGURE 6. RELATIVE EFFECTIVENESS OF PSYCHOANALYSIS
FOUND BY VARYING ASSESSMENT CRITERIA

Adapted with permission. A. E. Bergin. The evaluation of therapeutic outcomes. In A. E. Bergin and S. L. Garfield (Eds.), *Handbook of psychotherapy and behavior change.* New York: Wiley, 1971.

nor to provide some true estimate of the effectiveness of psycho-analysis. His effort, however, clearly demonstrates that the results of any actuarial survey will be heavily influenced by the criteria used to evaluate available research. *Controversy often has arisen because reviewers who have competing theoretical orientations employ different criteria for judging the merits of individual investigations.*

Cross (1964) was able to find only nine investigations which employed some form of control comparison. Although he cited six of these as having demonstrated positive therapeutic outcomes, methodological limitations in the individual studies led Cross to include that the efficacy of therapy "has not been scientifically demonstrated beyond some reasonable doubt" (p. 416).

In his more comprehensive review, Bergin (1971) tabulated the results of more than 50 outcome investigations that had appeared between 1952 and 1969. Dealing primarily with research that involved treatment of neurotic outpatients, he characterized 42 percent of the studies as demonstrating positive outcome, 29 percent as being inconclusive, and 29 percent as indicating negative effects.

Meltzoff and Kornreich (1970), however, reached a much more optimistic conclusion after reviewing 101 investigations. These authors included any study which involved some form of verbal intervention to ameliorate a wide variety of difficulties and which contained some type of control group. Included were investigations of dynamic treatment, group therapy, hypnosis, and behavior therapy conducted with children, adolescents, and adults who had neurotic, alcoholic, delinquency, or psychotic difficulties. Positive results were reported in 81 of the investigations.

These authors documented methodological deficiencies that limited the conclusions drawn in 44 of the studies they reviewed. Of the 57 reports that were deemed adequate, 48 (77 percent) presented evidence supporting the effectiveness of psychotherapy. Of these studies, 54 percent were considered to indicate that therapy produced meaningful benefits in crucial life areas, while 30 percent were classified as having led to less important types of improvement. Meltzoff and Kornreich also suggested that the majority of therapeutic failures involved conditions that are generally considered to be least amenable to psychotherapy, such as delinquency, various addictions, and psychotic states. Their conclusion was clear; in general, the effectiveness of psychotherapy had been amply demonstrated.

The most pessimistic assessment of therapeutic effectiveness was provided by Meehl (1965) in a discussion of one of Eysenck's attacks. Meehl suggested that Eysenck was being much too kind in his assessment, arguing on the basis of probability theory as follows: Only 25 percent of all therapists are actually qualified enough to bring about important and beneficial changes; only 25 percent of those currently in therapy are likely to benefit. The resulting probability of obtaining an optimal match through a random pairing of therapist and client is 25 percent X 25 percent or one out of 16. Thus, therapy is likely to be effective in only 6 percent of all instances! A similar gloomy, but not quite as grisly, conclusion was provided by Truax and Mitchell (1971) in their comprehensive review of therapist characteristics. They argued that fully two-thirds of all practitioners lack the personal attributes of nonpossessive warmth, accurate empathy, and congruent genuineness to function effectively as therapists. Subjecting their contention to Meehl's reasoning would lead to the conclusion that therapy is generally ineffective about 67 percent of the time.

Overview Of Range Seen In Psychotherapy Efficacy. Figure 7 provides an overview of experts' beliefs about the efficacy of psychotherapy. Although a summary of this type is precisely what we have been criticizing, it does yield some interesting implications. The most pessimistic estimates [i.e., Meehl (1965); Truax and Mitchell (1971)] are not based on literature surveys per se; rather, they represent extrapolations from related areas of knowledge. Actual reviews of the psychotherapy literature [i.e., Bergin (1971); Eysenck (1952); Meltzoff and Kornreich (1970)] permit a more favorable conclusion to be drawn, although the range of efficacy is extremely wide. Of particular interest is the difference in efficacy Bergin found in his survey of more recent outcome studies and his reanalysis of Eysenck's compilation of research prior to 1952. This should not be interpreted to mean that psychotherapy was generally more effective prior to 1952, as very different criteria were used to arrive at these figures.

Overview Of Opinions On Spontaneous Remission. An overview of the spontaneous remission controversy provides another example of the relativity inherent in evaluative survey research. The term means that a person's symptoms disappear over time without therapeutic intervention. As early as 1955, Barron and Leary suggested that the term served to hide our ignorance of specific curative influences that

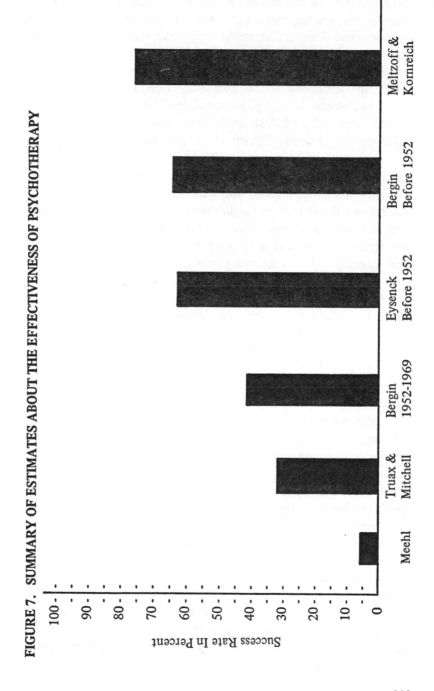

FIGURE 7. SUMMARY OF ESTIMATES ABOUT THE EFFECTIVENESS OF PSYCHOTHERAPY

operate outside of the therapy situation. Spontaneous remission becomes a pooka when it is used to explain how improvement comes about without therapy. The words imply that one's symptoms disappear by themselves.

Eysenck's (1952) estimate of spontaneous remission (72 percent) is generally considered to be excessively high, except by Eysenck (1961) and his colleagues (e.g., Rachman, 1973). Criticisms of the original figure centered on deficiencies in the original data Eysenck used or challenged the comparability of the subject populations and criteria used in estimating improvement. Bergin (1971) reviewed 14 more recent investigations which yielded spontaneous remission rates ranging from 0 percent to 52 percent, with a median of 30 percent. Rachman (1973) was quick to criticize Bergin's estimate by attacking the methodological adequacy of these studies. Rachman reiterated the conclusions Eysenck had reached in 1952 regarding both the ineffectiveness of psychotherapy and the extent to which spontaneous remission occurs.

In a recent reanalysis of the evidence cited by both Bergin and Rachman, Lambert (1976) divided previous investigations into two classes. He noted that, in some cases, minimal therapeutic intervention might have been inadvertently provided; in others, individuals clearly had received no treatment. For the first group of studies, Lambert reported the median rate of spontaneous remission to be 53 percent. A median of 43 percent was computed for the second cluster of investigations.

Like psychotherapy, spontaneous remission is not a uniform entity. From a functional point of view, the term is applied to people who initially seek psychotherapy for specific complaints, cannot be seen immediately, and refuse treatment when it is offered at some future time because they no longer are afflicted by the complaint. Stevenson (1961) has argued that spontaneous remission is not really spontaneous. Improvement results from specific changes in the afflicted individual's environment. People may improve because they receive more respect, reassurance, or affection from others, because they develop more effective coping strategies, or because of shifts in motivational states involving fear, shame, or anger.

Another important source of variability in determining the occurrence of spontaneous remission (as well as the effectiveness of psychotherapy) is who provides the necessary information. Often, therapists, observers, and clients will provide conflicting data about the phenomenon. With regard to spontaneous remission, Sloane, Staples, Cristol, Yorkson, and Whipple (1975) provide a graphic example of how this might occur. These investigators conducted a well-designed comparison of the effects produced by psychodynamic and behavior therapists. Professional assessors rated the symptomology of both clients and untreated control participants at specific times throughout the study. Of particular interest here was that four months into the therapeutic program, these judges rated 77 percent of the untreated controls as having shown improvement. Only 55 percent of these same individuals, however, reported that they had indeed experienced a reduction in their symptomatic complaints.

Realizations About Complexity. Practically every clinical researcher would agree that we know more about therapeutic processes and outcomes at present than we did when White described the nebulous activities of the typical clinician in 1956. Yet, actuarial surveys have permitted only general conclusions to be drawn. It is obvious that psychotherapy of any type is beneficial for some, has little impact on others, and can be harmful for still others. The overall degree of good or ill fostered by psychotherapy is impossible to ascertain, however. It is clear also that some people who suffer from dysfunctional conditions do improve without psychotherapeutic intervention, but, again, no generally accepted estimate of spontaneous remission has been arrived at.

Perhaps the greatest conceptual advance we have made toward understanding psychotherapy has been to realize the tremendous complexity involved in the helping process. We have been forced to admit that knowledge about these processes will emerge slowly and accumulate in a piecemeal fashion.

In short, we have been made more humble as a result of having to investigate psychotherapy within systematic frameworks that are themselves limited. The pooka of psychotherapy has been largely destroyed by the realization that the investigation of clinical encounters involves making some arbitrary choices. Of course, decisions are not totally arbitrary; most choices are based on general guidelines provided by the so-called scientific method. Every decision provides some potential advantages to an investigator, while it also contains some inherent limitations. This situation is an unavoidable fact of life for the psychotherapy researcher.

METHODOLOGICAL GUIDELINES FOR RESEARCH ON PSYCHOTHERAPY

There is general agreement among modern philosophers of science that the mediate goals of scientific inquiry are to describe, predict, and control real-world phenomena (Kaplan, 1964). These philosophers also generally argue that science can no longer be seen as the discovery of basic objective truths about the world. Rather it is an accumulation of guidelines for collecting observations and drawing conclusions from them to establish consensual agreement about the processes under investigation.

The Issue of Control—Desensitization Example

The aims of scientific inquiry can be achieved only by reducing real-life complexity into simpler elements. Because any simplification strategy requires making arbitrary decisions, errors in observation and inference are likely to occur. The issue of control thus is a central concern in scientific inquiry.

In the most general sense, controls are procedures designed to reduce errors by *insulating* observations (e.g., by observing in special settings, or by using standardized, reliable assessment procedures), *cancelling* the effects of extraneous biases (e.g., by randomly assigning people to treatment conditions, or by employing statistics), and *discounting* the influence of potentially important competing factors (e.g., by employing multiple therapists, multiple measures of outcome, or by using factorial experimental designs) (Kaplan, 1964).

Discounting Biases. Although each of these strategies has been utilized in psychotherapy research, discounting biases has been most widely employed, particularly by those who have a behavioral orientation. Discounting biases involves determining the direction and magnitude of a potential error (or artifact) and incorporating this information into the design of an investigation. Discounting strategies depends upon the accumulation of knowledge about processes that influence psychotherapy. Knowledge about artifactual influences grows slowly and evolves through three developmental stages. At first, investigators are *ignorant* of the operation of an artifact, drawing conclusions about factors that presumably cause therapeutic change which may actually be due to the artifact. Discovery of an artifact ushers in a period of *coping*, during which attempts are made to minimize the influence of the potential source of bias. Gradually, the artifact becomes the object of investigation in its own right; researchers *exploit* it in developing new therapeutic procedures (McGuire, 1969). This pattern of ignorance, coping, and exploitation continually recycles as knowledge about psychotherapy grows.

These issues can be illustrated by highlighting the efforts of behavior therapists to demonstrate the efficacy of systematic desensitization. This therapeutic package was developed by Wolpe (1958). It consists of three components that are combined to alleviate phobic dysfunctions.

The therapist first works with the client to develop a series of scenes relating to the fear-producing situation. These scenes, which the client will visualize later, are then arranged in a hierarchy according to the amount of tension they evoke. If a client is fearful of riding in an automobile, for example, scenes might involve walking toward a car, opening the door, seating oneself behind the wheel, turning on the ignition, and so on.

The second component involves teaching the client to become extremely relaxed by tensing and releasing various muscle groups throughout the body. The third element, desensitization proper, consists of having the client work upward through the hierarchy by imagining each scene for a short period of time while being deeply relaxed. The rationale behind this procedure is that the relaxation inhibits feelings of tension usually associated with thinking about the fearful activity and ultimately reduces phobic avoidance.

We have already mentioned that behavior therapists generally view the goal of psychotherapy research to involve the derivation of causal relationships between specific treatment interventions and precisely measurable outcomes (Krasner and Ullmann, 1973; Paul, 1969a). With regard to desensitization, this goal has become ever more closely approximated as hidden artifacts were discovered and exploited.

Pioneering investigations of this procedure involved applying it with individual clients and noting whether they improved. In general, favorable outcomes were noted (Wolpe, 1958; Rachman, 1959). A skeptic, however, could argue that some factor other than desensitization actually produced the change. Perhaps simply deciding to seek help, or talking to a therapist, or winning a new car in a lottery led to improvement. Those who produced simple case-study data would have trouble answering these objections.

The next procedural step behavioral researchers took was to report the results of a string of case studies. Lazarus (1963), for example, reported that desensitization was beneficial in an overwhelming majority of 126 cases of severe disabilities he had dealt with. This evidence is somewhat more compelling because it is unlikely that all of these individuals would have improved because of the unique historical or common maturational influences mentioned above. Our critic, however, might compliment Lazarus on being an outstandingly warm and effective therapist and use this as a justification for suggesting that it was these factors, and not desensitization, that brought about change. To this point, there was no solid evidence that the treatment procedure produced any greater benefits than could be gained by simply going to any professional therapist.

Early Cancellation And Insulation Efforts. Lang and Lavovik (1963) were the first to employ experimental cancellation and insulation procedures when investigating desensitization. A group of snake-anxious people were randomly assigned to receive desensitization or no treatment. They assessed the effects of treatment by having the participants approach and attempt to touch a snake both before and after therapy. By using this specialized assessment procedure and random assignment, they were able to show that brief desensitization therapy was reliably more effective than no treatment. Concluding that the treatment per se was responsible for improvement was justified given the knowledge about therapy then current. As other plausible reasons for change were uncovered, such a conclusion might not be considered justified. Given what we know today, a critic could suggest that the rationale used for the treatment was so believable that it, rather than the desensitization procedure, led the participants to reduce their fear. Or, our critic could argue that improvement was due to the warmth and respect the therapist manifested toward the clients.

First Large-Scale Attempt At Discounting. Paul (1966) provided the first large-scale attempt to actually discount such extraneous influences. In his investigation, he recruited college students who feared speaking in public. Before therapy was begun, each participant had to give a short speech in the presence of observers who recorded the students' overt behavioral manifestations of anxiety. Physiological measures of anxiety also were collected, as were self-reported appraisals of the amount of fear each subject experienced. After screening, participants were randomly assigned to conditions which involved systematic desensitization, insight-oriented therapy, or no treatment.

By assigning some participants to a pseudo-therapy group, Paul also capitalized on emerging knowledge that simply being the focus of therapeutic intervention could be beneficial. These individuals were led to believe that they were receiving treatment, but the actual procedure was not a theoretically justifiable strategy for reducing anxiety. Inclusion of this condition enabled Paul to compare the effects produced by the "true" (i.e., theoretically relevant) procedures against nonspecific curative influences that are inherent in all professional helping endeavors. This was an attempt to cope with such placebo influences via a discounting strategy.

He also attempted to discount potential bias due to specific attributes of the therapist by having each of five experienced clinicians conduct all three forms of treatment. By incorporating these potent sources of influence as independent variables within his research design, Paul was able to measure their direction and magnitude. His results led him to conclude that desensitization reduced self-reported, physiologically measured, and behaviorally assessed manifestations of public speaking anxiety to a significantly greater extent than did psychodynamic insight therapy. This latter treatment was found to be as effective as the pseudo-therapy procedure, with both of these interventions being better than no treatment.

At last, solid evidence had been produced to demonstrate the effectiveness of the desensitization procedure. We shall shortly see, however, that not everyone accepted this evidence as adequate. The strongest conclusion about the *general* efficacy of desensitization was provided by Paul (1969b) in a review of all existing research on this treatment technique:

> The findings were overwhelmingly positive, and for the first time in the history of psychological treatments, a specific therapeutic package reliably produced measurable benefits for clients across a broad range of distressing problems in which anxiety was of fundamental importance [Reprinted by permission. G. L. Paul. Outcome of systematic desensitization. II: Controlled investigations of individual treatment, technique variations, and current status. In C. M. Franks (Ed.), *Behavior therapy: Appraisal and status.* McGraw-Hill, 1969, p. 159].

Citing this conclusion as impressive evidence for a therapeutic procedure might seem unreasonable, given what we have just discovered about the differing results yielded by actuarial surveys of psychotherapy. There is one major difference between this survey and other reviews, however. Comparisons of psychotherapy-in-general represent a mixture of all the interactive ingredients (e.g., treatment strategy, client characteristics, therapist attributes, and so on) mentioned in Paul's (1969a) question about therapeutic effectiveness. Because these factors are combined to varying degrees in the different investigations reviewed, it is impossible to combine them in a meaningful way.

Paul, on the other hand, based his conclusion on a relatively standardized and uniform technique that was applied to clients who differed on many social characteristics by therapists who varied in terms of their training, experience, and personal attributes. These same characteristics which add nuisance variability to assessments of psychotherapy-in-general randomize themselves out in the studies on desensitization. Another way of saying this is that desensitization generally produced positive outcomes regardless (rather than as a result) of its use by different therapists with different types of clients.

Remaining Questions About Desensitization. Even this conclusion, however, provides an overly simplified view of the processes involved in desensitization. The conclusion represents only a *summary of answers* to many more specific questions about the therapeutic package. How durable or lasting are the changes that are brought about? How is effectiveness assessed? Is the procedure more useful for certain sorts of dysfunctions than for others? Is desensitization more useful when combined with other therapeutic strategies? Finding *definitive answers* to such questions is a slow process that is fraught with controversy.

Even though we can be pretty sure that desensitization provides an efficacious method of dealing with anxiety-related disorders *in general*, we have no guarantee that it will produce a favorable outcome for any particular individual. Further, we find disagreement about exactly what the effective ingredients of the treatment package are. Some researchers argue that relaxation is the most important component; others argue that it is the element of visualization; still others suggest that it is the perceived warmth of the therapist or the plausibility of the treatment rationale. Theoretical differences also provide a variety of alternative explanations for the effectiveness of desensitization. Working within a communication-analysis framework, Haley (1963) suggests that this treatment procedure places the client in a therapeutic double-bind situation. The client is instructed to experience anxiety, but acknowledging this emotion slows the treatment process. Faced with this paradox, the only recourse the client has is not to experience the anxiety which necessitated treatment in the first place.

This sort of explanatory relativity is found with every aspect of psychotherapy that has been empirically investigated. This situation itself raises a paradox. How can so many different viewpoints about a single facet of psychotherapy exist among investigators who subscribe to commonly accepted dictates of scientific methodology? To answer this question, we must examine scientific inquiry as a relativistic endeavor.

THE RELATIVITY OF SCIENCE AND EXPLANATION

Alternate Conceptions Of Science

Currently accepted guidelines of scientific research represent simplifications of real-life complexity. We have already noted that any framework of simplification requires making arbitrary choices. Because scientists are human beings, the choices they make are in part molded by the paradigms they subscribe to, the theories they espouse, and the social forces that affect them. One of the most compelling attacks on the view of the *scientist as an objective observer* is provided by Mahoney (1976) who suggests that this view is an illusion which ignores the many reality constraints operating on the researcher. He provides three alternate metaphors which describe science as a passionate romance, a religion, and a game.

Science as romance involves blindly clinging to one's pet beliefs about the world in the face of contradictory evidence. The manifestations of this romance include enchantment with one's own research, resistance to considering alternative views, and biased filtration toward supportive data. **Science as religion** has two components—a certain degree of faith that sometimes borders on fanaticism with which researchers espouse their particular views and various rituals which are followed in the worship of truth. Mahoney compares Nobel laureates to high priests; journal editors have the apostolic function of insuring that the

117

purity of doctrine is preserved; and college instructors preach the gospel in the temple of the classroom.

Science as a game comes complete with players, teams, rules, winners, and losers. Part of the game involves insuring that researchers pass certain tribal rituals (usually in academic graduate training programs) and follow certain rules (to get their name in print). A major portion of the science game is to use the guidelines provided by scientific method to refute views that are contradictory to the beliefs held by a particular scientist. We have already noted several instances of this; for example, Wolpe's (1976a) description of those who do not share his beliefs about behavior therapy as misguided "malcontents." The constant reiteration of the theme that psychotherapy is ineffective by Eysenck (1961) and Rachman (1973) has been based on citing evidence contrary to this theme as being methodologically inadequate. Another example of this strategy is hidden in Chapter 3, and it requires a personal confession. The author personally finds the interpretation of desensitization as involving psychoanalytic merging fantasies (Silverman et al., 1974) to be far-fetched, given his own biases toward a behavioral orientation. So, after presenting the Silverman view, the author naturally put it down by pointing out serious flaws in the empirical investigation and providing more rigorous contradictory evidence.

Varieties Of Explanations

Defining Explanations. We have already noted that the mediate goals of science are to describe, predict, and control naturally occurring phenomena. Although not fully acknowledged until quite recently, the ultimate aim of scientific inquiry is to provide satisfactory explanations about events. Exactly what constitutes an explanation has always been a tricky philosophical issue. Some (e.g., Hempel, 1965) have attempted to define an explanation as a logical derivative of more general descriptive laws, while others (Hancher, 1970) have compared scientific and artistic explanations in terms of their symbolic symmetry.

The simplest and most useful definition of an explanation is based on relativity. *An explanation is anything that puts one's curiosity to rest.* Something has been satisfactorily explained to an individual when that person no longer has any pressing questions about whatever aroused his curiosity. In this sense, it is possible to have explanations without prediction or control, and it is possible to be able to predict and control events without being able to explain them (Kaplan, 1964). It also follows that an explanation will be acceptable to some people but viewed as inadequate (a pseudo-explanation) by others. This situation is obvious when one considers the numerous theories underlying the different "schools" of psychotherapy.

Explaining The Causes Of Behavior. Potential explanations of the causes of human behavior differ along five somewhat interrelated dimensions:

1. The locus of control is within the person (as energy cathexes, drives, or motives) or is external to the individual (as response-consequent contingencies or sociological influences).

2. The presumed control agent is viewed as either a molecular (e.g., germ, virus, ego) or a molar (e.g., socio-economic status, inadequate personal relationships) influence.

3. The effect of the presumed control influence is thought to operate either in a historical (e.g., early childhood experiences determine adult character structure) or in a contemporary (e.g., dys functions result from sudden environmental changes; neurotic symptoms represent a strategy of interpersonal control) time frame.

4. The influence of the control agent is tied to overt behavior by either a long (e.g., obesity is a manifestation of unresolved oral needs) or a short (e.g., obesity is caused by eating too much and not getting enough exercise) inferential chain.

5. Descriptions of presumed causes satisfy either the head (i.e., make intellectual sense) or the heart (i.e., meet one's emotional needs).

Preferences Of Theoretical Groups. The major paradigmatic orientations toward psychotherapy examined in Chapter 3 align themselves fairly consistently along the first four dimensions. Psychodynamic theorists have a preference for internally focused, molecular explanatory constructs that involve historically relevant and long inferential chains. Behavioral clinicians, on the other hand, prefer explanations that embody larger-scale, current environmental factors which are conceptually close to overt behavior. Humanistic therapists tend to occupy the middle ground and tend to be more variable in subscribing to an extreme position on any of the dimensions. These general preferences were documented in the survey of clinical psychologists conducted by

Garfield and Kurtz (1976). The "mental health" ideologies of neo-Freudian or psychoanalytic therapists and behavioral clinicians tended to be farthest apart, with client-centered and other humanistic practitioners expressing more moderate beliefs.

A classic illustration of the psychodynamic preference can be found in Lindner's description of his therapeutic encounters with Laura, "the woman who could not stop eating." Laura suffered from a pathological craving for food which compelled her to go on periodic binges, stuffing herself with any and all available food. At one point, Lindner rushed to her apartment in response to her strangled cry for help made over the phone. He arrived at the apartment to find her lying semi-conscious among rotting food, her body bloated and appearing even more grotesque because she had a pillow strapped to her stomach underneath her nightgown, making her appear pregnant.

This incident led Lindner to construe Laura's compulsive eating as providing distorted satisfaction of an underlying need to have a baby, but he was unable to fathom why this need was so terribly intense. From a "Freudian slip" Laura made, a major therapeutic breakthrough occurred about a week after the orgy of eating. While discussing the device Laura had worn to simulate pregnancy, Lindner jokingly suggested that she might be keeping a replacement in her apartment. He described what happened next as *the end* of his narrative:

> "I doubt it," she replied in the same mood. "I guess I have to mike a new baby every . . ." Her hand went over her mouth. "My God!" she exclaimed. "Did you hear what I just said?" Mike was her father's name; and of course it was his baby she wanted. It was for this impossible fulfillment that Laura hungered—and now was starved no more [Reprinted by permission. R. Lindner. The girl who couldn't stop eating. In H. Greenwald (Ed.), *Great cases in psychoanalysis.* Jason Aranson, 1973, p. 151].

Obviously, Lindner's curiosity had been satisfied. Laura's verbal behavior had provided an explanation that fit his psychoanalytic orientation. Laura had achieved insight into her debilitating condition. His last sentence clearly indicates that he viewed this as both a necessary and sufficient condition for bringing about improvement. Lindner's explanation emphasizes molecular, internal, and historical determinants of behavior. It also contains an extremely long and complicated inferential loop. A verbal statement reflected the sudden acquisition of insight, which led to a restructuring of dynamic forces within the personality, which, in turn, was presumed to cause beneficial changes in the young woman's behavior.

This explanation would not be satisfactory for most behavioral clinicians, many humanistic therapists, and even some psychodynamic theorists. Lindner's explanation would probably raise more questions for these individuals than it would answer. Just what is "insight" anyway? What causes "it" to occur? What is the relationship between insight and behavior change? Those with a more skeptical bent would dispute the existence of a direct causal connection between Laura's acquisition of insight and changes in her behavior (which, incidentally, was never noted by Lindner).

The purpose of this discussion was simply to point out that one person's truth is another's fantasy. This sort of relativity has led to theoretical strife over just about every facet of the psychotherapeutic process. It will be profitable to briefly examine some of the more heated controversies.

COMPARING INTERMEDIATE CRITERIA
AND ULTIMATE GOALS IN PSYCHOTHERAPY

Ultimate Goals of Psychotherapy

On a general level, there is a surprising degree of agreement among professional therapists about the ultimate goals of therapy. Despite theoretical differences, most therapists would endorse six major aims of the therapeutic process—(1) eliminating the presenting problems one brings to therapy, (2) reducing psychological pain and suffering, (3) increasing one's capability to engage in pleasurable activities, (4) improving one's ability to experience on both an intellectual and emotional level, (5) enhancing self-acceptance, self-esteem, and inner directedness, and (6) improving the quality of interpersonal relationships (Mahrer, 1967). In general, psychotherapy is directed toward reducing discomfort, distress, and disability, as well as attempting to insure that the client is better able to cope effectively with future stresses and life difficulties.

Intermediate Criteria

Unfortunately, it is practically impossible to determine whether these ultimate goals have been achieved with any given individual, especially in a manner that is consistent with our current conceptions of scientific inquiry. *Psychotherapists are thus forced to establish intermediate criteria which are designed to permit the public evaluation of their endeavors. All such criteria are presumed by those who employ them to be accurate indicators of more general, far-reaching, and important indicants of adjustment and effectiveness.*

Numerous mediate criteria exist, reflecting the values espoused in different theoretical orientations. Some of these criteria conform to scientific methodological dictates (e.g., they must be reliable, valid, and stated so that they can be empirically tested and replicated), but others are based on conceptions that are important elements within a particular theory. As might be expected, little agreement exists about which of these criteria are really valuable. In some cases, debate rages about whether some are actually meaningful or even detrimental.

Controversies Involving Ultimate And Intermediate Goals

Before highlighting some specific areas of controversy, a general source of conceptual confusion needs to be examined—the relative nature of both ultimate and intermediate goals. For example, Knight (1941) provided five criteria for judging the adequacy of psychoanalytic treatment—(1) reduction of symptomology, (2) increased work productivity, (3) better sexual adjustment, (4) improved interpersonal relationships, and (5) greater adaptive skills in coping with conflict and stress. These goals are remarkably similar to Mahrer's (1967) list of the ultimate aims of all psychotherapeutic endeavors. For the typical analyst, however, Knight's goals are more likely to represent lower-level intermediate goals because changes in these areas would be viewed as evidence that basic portions of the personality have been restructured. Yet, behavioral, humanistic, and psychodynamic clinicians are able to affect improvements in these functional areas without necessarily having restructured the personality. Thus, what some clinicians would consider ultimate therapeutic goals are viewed as only intermediate aims by others.

This sort of confusion shows up in other ways. The specific intermediate criteria of adjustment available to clinicians who possess a certain theoretical inclination often are interpreted in entirely different ways by therapists with different orientations. Consider Mahrer's first ultimate therapeutic goal. Are the dysfunctions one brings into therapy problems in living, or do they represent symptoms of underlying psychopathology? Conceptualizing difficulties in one or the other of these ways has set clinicians of different theoretical persuasions at one another's throats.

The Debate Over Symptom Substitution. During the 1960's there was considerable infighting between psychoanalysts and behavioral clinicians over the issue of symptom substitution. This term, which Ullmann and Krasner (1965) cited as the one testable offshoot of psychoanalytic theory, refers to the presumption that the underlying conflict must be resolved if meaningful behavior change is to occur. Psychoanalytic theory emphasizes the belief that one's manifest symptoms are the most psychically economical way of resolving tensions between intrapsychic forces. Within this framework, it is presumed that, if the symptoms are removed without dealing with the underlying cause, less economical and more debilitating symptoms will replace the original ones.

Both behavioral and humanistic clinicians have criticized this concept. Behavioral therapists (e.g., Rachman, 1963) have sought to determine whether symptom substitution occurs and have indicated that the incidence of this phenomenon is quite rare. From a humanistic vantage point, Haley (1969a) criticizes this concept as representing a rationalization of ineffective therapeutic intervention. Many psychoanalysts, however, adamantly argue that symptom substitution is a clear and ever present danger.

This difference of opinion stems from characteristics of the therapeutic endeavor that clinicians of all theoretical persuasions agree exist but interpret entirely differently. Most clinicians agree that people bring more than one problem into therapy (Kadushin, 1969). Most would agree that clients frequently fail to raise problems of central concern until the therapist has won their trust and confidence. The client is in fact "testing out" the therapist by waiting to see if less important issues can be adequately handled. Most therapists also would agree the client's problems frequently interlock in complex ways. Treating depressive complaints, for example, might involve counseling about marital interactions or career choices.

In many instances, then, it might *appear* that resolution of one specific problem *causes* other difficulties to arise. *If the subsequent difficulty seems to be a more central concern, psychoanalysts have evidence for symptom substitution.* Clinicians who hold different theoretical views, however, would deny that a causal link exists, preferring to interpret the apparent emergence of subsequent problems in terms of more functional influences (e.g., the client has failed to develop adequately generalized coping skills; the client brings multiple difficulties into therapy). Such formulations have generally proven to be more useful for conceptualizing mutual influence processes in therapy than has the notion of symptom substitution.

Additional Theoretical Debates. Other debates have arisen over the meaning of terms that describe specific, theory-bound operations presumed to bring about beneficial change. Disagreements can be found over the value terms like *insight, cognitions, anxiety,* and *personality* have in explaining therapeutic change. The notion of *insight,* for example, refers to entirely different processes for a psychoanalytic and a behavioral clinician. For the analyst (e.g., Lindner), insight represents a growing awareness by the patient about formerly hidden motivational influences. For Lindner, Laura's statements represented insight because they were easily interpretable within his theoretical framework.

Behavioral clinicians are generally concerned with the functional properties of the client's verbal behavior. From this perspective, insight means that the client can describe how dysfunctional conditions came about, and, more importantly, can discuss strategies for effectively dealing with subsequent difficulties. Behavior therapists do not reject the concept of insight. Most would, however, not consider the type of insight Laura showed to be an *automatic* indication that her problem had been resolved. More generally, they would reject the classical psychoanalytic belief (Tarachow, 1963) that insight into motivational determinants is sufficient in itself to cause meaningful behavior change. The psychoanalytic conception of insight might not even be a necessary condition for bringing about improved functioning, as the results of the Menninger study of psychotherapy indicated. The growing concern with teaching problem-solving skills in behavioral psychotherapy (D'Zurilla and Goldfried, 1971) rests upon the belief that clients can profit from functional insight into their difficulties.

THE ASSESSMENT OF INTERMEDIATE CRITERIA

During actual therapeutic encounters, both the therapist and client tend to operate within the context of discovery. A holistic continuity exists in which the client's communications are formed into conceptual themes that make sense to the therapist. Very frequently, skilled therapists employ helping strategies that are based on vague hunches which cannot be independently and publicly verified. Research on psychotherapy is conducted within the context of justification; it requires the imposition of some external structure on the communication process. Events which have an experiential unity for the participants are simplified and segmented into predetermined units of measurement. From the researcher's point of view, the flow of interactive behavior becomes the number of words-per-minute, head nods, smiles, or self-depreciating statements, the distance a client goes toward a feared object, the amount of cigarette smoke emitted during transference episodes, and innumerable other bits of discrete data. The assessment strategies and instruments an investigator elects to employ are partly determined by her preferences for particular paradigms and theoretical views.

Demonstrating the effectiveness of a therapeutic intervention requires that three interrelated problems be surmounted. We have already highlighted one source of difficulty; namely, the fact that competitive theoretical orientations will emphasize some intermediate criteria as more important than others. Even if certain criteria were generally accepted, limitations also exist regarding both the sources of available data and the bias potential of these data.

Range Of Data Sources

Numerous sources of data about therapeutic processes and outcomes are available, but each one is open to certain potentially contaminating biases. One might assess the effectiveness of therapy by asking the client, questioning the therapist, obtaining the opinions of significant others (e.g., parents, spouses, friends), or assessing client behavior in simulated or real-life situations outside of therapy, for example. Each of these broadly defined sources of information must be tapped through more specific assessment channels. The client could be asked to evaluate the therapist, the specific type of intervention, or self-appraised changes in thoughts, feelings, and actions. This could be accomplished by means of standardized psychometric measurement devices (e.g., "objective" personality questionnaires), through "projective" assessment techniques, or by an interview. Many varieties of more precise measurement instruments can be used within each of these channels. As we simplify from general source through specific assessment modalities to even more specific instruments, we often gain precision at the expense of scope.

Bias In Data Sources. All the informants just mentioned have hidden reservoirs of vested interests that will influence their responses. The client might be motivated to please the therapist or to provide favorable responses so that the clinician will not be embarrassed. The therapist desires to appear effective and competent. Significant others might be influenced by the knowledge that the client has undergone therapy. Confusion becomes even more pronounced when changes noted across information sources are not consistent with one another. Can we say that therapy is effective if the therapist reports improvement in the client, but the latter maintains that nothing has changed? Is therapy to be judged effective if the therapist has noted no meaningful changes, but the client reports feeling and acting better?

Reviews of the literature on psychotherapy point up some interesting anomalies regarding how different sources view the helping process. Success from the clinician's viewpoint is typically defined in terms of relief from debilitating dysfunctions or improved social effectiveness, while clients usually view improvement in terms of increased self-confidence and self-acceptance (Sloane et al., 1975; Strupp, Fox, and Lessler, 1969). Therapists also are more apt to indicate that improvement resulted from either the specific therapeutic interventions that were employed or the amount of time the client spent in therapy. Clients, on the other hand, are more likely to attribute improvement to the human characteristics of the therapist (e.g., warmth, attention, understanding, respect), and they do not generally believe that more therapy is necessarily better.

Each source of information contributes relative and limited knowledge to our overall understanding of psychotherapy. Given the inherent potential for bias in every single source, psychotherapy researchers resort to "triangulating" the effects of an intervention by using multiple measures of process and outcome. The measures chosen ideally should be both statistically and procedurally independent of one another. We can be more certain that a particular therapeutic procedure has indeed been effective if the assessments made by the therapist, client, and outside observers are in substantial agreement.

PSYCHOTHERAPY IN REAL-LIFE AND ANALOGUE FORMS

Empirical inquiry into therapeutic processes and outcomes requires simplifying the complex interpersonal interactions that occur during the helping endeavor. The extent to which such simplification is justified has led to a second major controversy among professional therapists. Psychoanalysts, in particular, have been reluctant to allow researchers to study what occurs in therapy, maintaining that investigation of the presumably fragile treatment process will destroy it. Behavior therapists, on the other hand, have emphasized that simplification is an absolute necessity if we are to determine causal relationships between treatment techniques and outcomes in therapy. The major vehicle for accomplishing this goal is the therapy analogue study.

Defining Analogue Investigations

Analogues represent simplified abstractions of real-life events that are systematically examined in more-or-less artificial settings. The purpose of the analogue is:

> . . . to isolate, quantify and experimentally manipulate factors whose direct observation in situ would be obscured or would be prohibitively costly [Reprinted by permission. K. Heller. Laboratory interview research as analogue to treatment. In A. E. Bergin and S. L. Garfield (Eds.), *Handbook of psychotherapy and behavior change*. John Wiley, 1971, pp. 126-127].

In a typical psychotherapy analogue, a carefully limited sample of people who suffer from a clearly defined target problem is selected. Participants are then screened to (1) insure that they are actually debilitated by the problem and (2) provide data for the evaluation of treatment. Participants are then assigned to various experimental conditions in which standardized therapeutic techniques are uniformly applied for a fixed amount of time. Following treatment, the clients are then reassessed to precisely determine the extent to which change has occurred. Sometimes (but not often enough), a follow-up assessment is arranged so that the durability of therapeutic effects can be examined.

The allure of an analogue investigation is its seeming simplicity. Specific intermediate criteria are employed to measure changes in more complex dysfunctions. Factors which might provide plausible alternative explanations of differences between treatments (e.g., differences in therapist attributes or the length of various therapies) can easily be cancelled and discounted. Paul's (1966) comparison of systematic desensitization and insight therapy represents an example of a methodologically sound analogue investigation.

His conclusion about the superiority of desensitization, however, was quick to draw criticism. Strupp (1967), for example, questioned whether what Paul did was *really* psychotherapy, contending that college student "subjects" were not equivalent to real-life "clients." He also criticized Paul's imposition of a time limit on the amount of therapy as a bias unfavorable to insight treatment. While Paul had indeed imposed such a limit, it was based on an estimate made by the experienced therapists in his study, all of whom had psychodynamic or client-centered orientations.

Problems With Analogue Studies

Two types of criticism have been raised by those who object to analogue approaches. One type considers analogues to have no relevance for real-life therapeutic processes on *a priori* theoretical grounds. The psychoanalytic belief that simplification destroys the essence of the transference relationship falls into this category. A second variety of criticism (e.g., Cooper, Furst, and Bridger, 1969) has an empirical basis. According to this criticism, psychotherapy analogues have focused on trite and simplistic problems that are not readily found in actual client populations.

There is, unfortunately, some merit in the second type of criticism. Analogue investigations that do not respect the complexity of clinical reality add more to our confusion than to our understanding. (Analogue investigations are potentially simple to design and easy to execute. This makes them attractive as a way of obtaining publications so that the investigator is not banished from academe.)

Many documentations of the effectiveness of behavioral treatments have been analogues conducted with college students who reported being afraid of snakes, spiders, rats, and other small animals. Animal phobias, however, constitute an extremely small percentage of the problems people bring into clinical settings. Many of these studies were quick and methodologically dirty. It is interesting to note that the strongest criticism of such research has come from behavioral clinicians who are firmly committed to the analogue approach. Bernstein and Paul (1971), for example, provided a damning indictment:

With a few notable exceptions, the majority of these "snake, rat, and spider" studies involve sufficient analogue research errors to limit severely the cogency of their findings to the circumstances in which data were collected, without making significant contributions to clinical practice, or to knowledge of the mechanisms involved in the operation or treatment of anxiety [Reprinted by permission. D. A. Bernstein and G. L. Paul. Some comments on therapy analogue research with small animal "phobias." *Journal of Behavior Therapy and Experimental Psychiatry*, 1971, 2, 225].

This criticism is not limited to research involving small animal phobias. It can be extended legitimately to any content area where researchers fail to adequately discount potential sources of error.

Another general source of criticism could be called *the growth of clinical gimmickry*. Analogue research, especially as used by behavioral clinicians, has made it easy to investigate numerous variants of basic change processes. Many of these presumably new techniques are slight modifications of more widely used therapeutic procedures (e.g., systematic desensitization). Yet, each rapidly acquires a fetching name that implies that it is somehow uniquely different from its predecessors. A cursory examination of the contemporary literature will yield such exotic treatment procedures as accelerated mass desensitization, anxiety-management training, self-guided imagery, cue-controlled relaxation, and autogenic training, to mention only a few.

While any one of these variants might well be demonstrated to be a meaningful clinical advance, current evidence supporting the utility of most is tenuous. This trend is supported by the academic "publish-or-perish" tradition. The net effect of clinical gimmickry on our understanding of basic therapeutic change processes, however, is likely to be unfavorable. The worst consequence that it might have would be to split the behavior therapy movement into "a technique-oriented school of therapists, on one hand, and a behavioral science of little direct relevance to clinicians on the other" (Franks and Wilson, 1974, p. 3).

The criticisms we have examined center neither on the utility of the analogue per se nor on the behavior modification movement. Analogue research is an extremely useful method of inquiry that has been employed by investigators of all theoretical persuasions. It has been used by psychodynamic researchers (e.g., Bordin, 1966; Silverman, 1976) as well as humanistically inclined investigators (e.g., Truax and Mitchell, 1971) to examine therapeutic processes that have relevance to them.

Guidelines For Analogue Strategies

The utility of analogues, however, depends upon the extent to which they do justice to the real-life phenomena that aroused our curiosity in the first place. Bordin (1965) provided three general guidelines that simplification (analogue) strategies ought to reflect. They are paraphrased and expanded below:

1. *Analogue research ought to be an accurate reflection of naturally occurring therapeutic practices.* Analogues ought to contain features that are close approximations of what occurs in actual clinical settings. Generalizing the results of an analogue study which employed undergraduates as "therapists" to settings in which experienced clinicians operate is a violation of this guideline. The same is true of analogues that investigate dysfunctions that are not often the focus of real-life therapy.

2. *Analogue research can safely simplify complex clinical processes only in proportion to what we already know about clinical reality.* Analogues ought to incorporate emerging knowledge about potential sources of error so that these influences can be cancelled and discounted. Simplification strategies involve making numerous trade-offs between the rigorous dictates of scientific method and practical limitations. A researcher, for example, might be forced to choose between using one highly trained and experienced therapist or several novices. Both choices may represent departures from actual clinical practice. The decision should be based on a thorough understanding of the setting to which the investigator wishes to make generalizations.

3. *Empirical bridges need to be established between the analogue and the real-life clinical phenomenon of interest.* This guideline suggests that the distinction between analogue and real therapy is often illusory, or, as Krasner and Ullmann (1973) put it, research is therapy and therapy is research. Sound analogue research can have relevance for clinical reality to the extent that its output is an accurate reflection of the therapeutic phenomenon. Borkovec (1976) has provided an empirical bridge between analogue and real-life therapy by identifying specific target problems as having

relevance for both the analogue researcher and the practicing clinician. His programmatic research has clearly indicated that various evaluative apprehensions (e.g., public speaking anxiety, heterosexual dating anxiety, insomnia) occur with high frequency in analogue populations, cause debilitation in both analogue and real-life clinical populations, and are not susceptible to nonspecific (demand or placebo) influences. Carefully planned analogue research on these target problems can have definite impact on clinical practice.

FINAL WORDS

Growth in empirical knowledge about psychotherapy requires systematic examination of many complex processes. Systematic analysis means that observations are made within a conceptual system which provides a coherent view of certain facets of the therapeutic encounter. Systematic analysis, however, can provide only a limited view of the entire helping endeavor. This inherent limitation has both advantages and drawbacks. One of the most exciting features of empirical inquiry is that new frameworks are constantly emerging. An emerging conceptual scheme enables us to view existing aspects of therapeutic processes in novel ways. Even more importantly, the evolving scheme points our curiosity in new directions, opening up exciting areas of discovery.

The biggest liability systematic inquiry imposes on us is the illusion that one particular coherent view is the only viable view of psychotherapy. The search for the essence of the pooka of psychotherapy-in-general was based on the optimistic premise that science would provide the necessary methodological tools to enable us to examine objective reality and extract the truth. The chase after the pooka ultimately was abandoned as we realized that our conception of science was itself relativistic and limited. Science was not the real villain in this case, however. It has been our collective arrogance in believing that complex processes could be understood through simple strategies.

Perhaps it was not our arrogance after all. Perhaps we were fooled into seeing simplicity where complexity really existed because our language made the complex seem simple. In any event, the application of empirical methodology to psychotherapeutic phenomena has caused us to become optimistically humble. In the years since White's (1956) assessment of psychotherapy, we have learned much about what constitutes the "this and that" which occur during the helping endeavor. Our knowledge has accumulated gradually through the efforts of numerous contributors who addressed different questions from within alternate theoretical perspectives.

Our optimism lies in the fact that indeed we have learned much in the last two decades. As our knowledge about psychotherapy grows, so does our ability to devise more sophisticated strategies of inquiry. These in turn add to our knowledge. Our humility lies in the fact that no single conceptual system has a monopoly on clinical truth. Each paradigm and theory we employ provides conceptual insights that might have ultimate utility in helping people improve their condition. Each framework, however, limits our understanding of other facets of therapy. Inherent in our humility is the potential for wisdom. We are becoming increasingly aware that ever more adequate answers about psychotherapy will evolve from the slow, methodical, and painstaking efforts of many curious people who work within differing paradigms.

5
Therapeutic Components I: The Client and the Therapist

Psychotherapy involves communication between people within a social context. Empirical inquiry has provided us with many frameworks for systematically observing communication processes. The application of these frameworks to psychotherapy enables an astute observer to perceive much more than people simply conversing together. Interaction between the therapist and the client ' ultimately the critical focus for understanding psychotherapy. The interactive interpersonal influences that occur during psychotherapy are incredibly complex. We are just beginning to develop methodological tools sophisticated enough to enable us to systematically examine these complex communication processes.

For our purposes, it is convenient to arbitrarily separate these interactional influences into discrete components that make up the therapeutic encounter. Using Paul's (1969a) question about therapy effectiveness as a guideline, we can specify four major therapeutic components (1) characteristics of the client, (2) attributes of the therapist, (3) influential aspects of the treatment setting, (4) factors relating to time limitations. This basic scheme is a gross simplification of clinical reality. Each component contains numerous elements, all of which have been examined in a variety of ways and all of which combine in an individual therapy session.

In this chapter, we will examine what empirical inquiry has revealed about the client and the therapist. The next chapter will highlight what we know about setting and temporal influences; it also will explore some specific interactive and common elements.

THEORETICAL PREFERENCES TOWARD SIMPLIFICATION

Before turning our attention to these topics, we should reiterate that therapists adhering to a particular orientation tend to selectively emphasize certain therapeutic components. We can illustrate such relativistic preferences by highlighting the attention accorded to each component by psychodynamic, humanistic, and behavioral clinicians. To avoid interpreting these preferences as sterile uniformity myths, we must keep in mind that these broad theoretical orientations encompass many divergent viewpoints about psychotherapy.

Psychodynamic Researchers

Let us begin with orthodox psychoanalysts who represent a clearly defined subset of the psychodynamic spectrum. These practitioners generally believe that the therapeutic process is uniform and fragile, and they view the therapist as a blank screen upon which the patient projects distorted manifestations of underlying conflicts. As a result, little attention has been paid to therapist characteristics in the psychoanalytic literature. Because meaningful change is presumed to require an extensive investment of time, investigations of time-limited arrangements by analysts also are practically nonexistent (Luborsky and Spence, 1971). The occurrence of differential patient responses to the highly standardized treatment format has led to a more concerted focus on client characteristics, which are usually conceptualized in terms of either diagnostic symptom clusters or personality types (e.g., hysterical, narcissistic, and so on). Much of this research has employed analogue simplification. Bordin (1966), for example, systematically examined factors which influenced the ability of real and analogue patients to produce insightful verbalizations during free association tasks. He concluded that meaningful "experiencing" during free association was easiest for people who were generally free from serious pathology and who possessed well-balanced personality structures. These findings agree nicely with Freud's original views about the type of person who was best suited for psychoanalysis.

Psychoanalysts' belief that the treatment process is divorced from mutual interpersonal influence processes has precluded much research attention to setting factors, including nonspecific placebo influences (Luborsky and Spence, 1971). More surprisingly, there has been little investigation of the central psychoanalytic concepts of transference and countertransference. Available analogue research, however, suggests that basic analytic treatment processes are affected by interpersonal influences. The content of free association is reliably altered by the overt presence of a listener, for example (Colby, 1960).

More broadly defined psychodynamic researchers have focused on both client characteristics and therapist attributes. The former set of influences has typically been defined in terms of either personality types or trait characteristics, rather than in terms of concrete behaviors. Research on therapist characteristics has explored differences in the activity of clinicians as a function of experience and theoretical orientation. Little research on the outcome produced by specific therapeutic strategies has been conducted, since process is emphasized. Strupp (1960), for example, had therapists who differed in terms of training and experience as well as theoretical background provide responses to standardized comments by clients. The output of these investigations was the development of multidimensional rating scales to classify the activities of the clinician. Some psychodynamic therapists also have investigated temporal influences on therapeutic outcome (e.g., Shlien, Mosak, and Dreikurs, 1962), but they have paid little attention to nonspecific placebo influences, with some notable exceptions (Frank, 1961).

Humanistic Researchers

One basic concern of humanistic therapists has been the interplay between attributes of the therapist and emotional growth in the client. Client-centered therapists have been among the most active contributors to knowledge about these interactions. Emphasis was first directed toward determining whether therapy (which was conceptualized as a package of general strategies) fostered growth toward an idealized self-image (e.g., Butler and Haigh, 1954). Subsequent investigations were aimed at measuring theoretically relevant therapist attributes (e.g., warmth, genuineness, accurate empathy) and assessing the effects they had on cognitive and emotional self-exploration by clients.

Humanistic researchers emphasize that aspects of the therapist's personality are more important than the strategic helping operations the clinician employs. This focus is in line with their beliefs about the self-curative nature of therapeutic interaction. The orientation de-emphasizes the necessity of formal training and has led to an interest in the use of paraprofessional helping resources (Truax and Mitchell, 1971).

Within this perspective, there has been little research on what sorts of people are most likely to profit from treatment. Investigation of this therapeutic component also has been hindered by the humanistic aversion to categorizing people in terms of predetermined classes (Perls, Hefferline, and Goodman, 1951). In addition, it has been hindered because client functioning is conceptualized in global terms which involve internal, experiential concepts.

While some exploration of time-limited therapy has been undertaken, systematic assessment of the contributions made by nonspecific placebo influences has been neglected. This omission stems from the belief that such influences are part and parcel of the total therapeutic package.

Behavioral Therapists

Behavioral clinicians have devoted most of their efforts to demonstrating the effectiveness of specific treatment strategies by showing them to produce better outcomes than would result from curative influences residing in the therapist, client, or treatment setting. This preference makes behavioral clinicians sensitive to the potential operation of factors, such as therapist warmth. Rather than systematically investigate these influences as important ones in their own right, however, they often view these influences as nuisance variables that need to be discounted lest they obscure presumably more basic relationships between treatment technique and outcome.

In contrast to their psychodynamic and humanistic counterparts, behavior therapists have been in the forefront in investigating expectancy and placebo influences on the therapeutic process. This emphasis probably results from a fortunate blending of the behavior therapist's penchant for precise measurement with the increasing realization of the importance of such cognitive influences. Eclectic and psychodynamic therapists (e.g., Frank, 1961) had discussed the operation of such influences in very general terms (e.g., a patient's faith in a therapist). Early attempts by behavior therapists to demonstrate the efficacy of particular therapeutic techniques sought to cope with these influences by comparing the theoretically relevant procedure against various pseudotherapies (e.g., Paul, 1966). As knowledge about these nonspecific factors has grown, behavioral clinicians have begun to systematically exploit their effects to improve the effectiveness of currently existing therapeutic strategies (Fish, 1973; Goldstein, 1973, 1975; Meichenbaum, 1974).

Behavioral clinicians believe that what therapists do is more important than the kind of people they are. They seek to discount and cancel the influence of the therapist's attributes on the treatment process by having more than one therapist employ a common therapeutic strategy. Therefore they de-emphasize study of these attributes. Measurement of specific therapist characteristics is sometimes conducted (e.g., Allen, 1971), but these data are typically used to covary out differences that affect outcome. Because most behavioral treatments are generally short term, little emphasis has been given to time limitations per se. Some research has been aimed at making existing procedures more efficient.

Like humanistic therapists, behavioral clinicians reject the classification of people according to types, not because of the presumably dehumanizing properties of such categorizations, but because such labelling masks functional properties between treatment strategies and relevant client characteristics. Within the behavioral framework, much effort has been directed toward developing treatment procedures which are effective for seriously debilitated and poor people (Goldstein, 1973; Lorion, 1974). As we shall see, these efforts have been very successful.

Interplay Between Perspectives

Before turning our attention to the basic components, we need to further emphasize a point. No single theoretical domain has provided a better avenue to knowledge about clinical reality than have any of the others. Each has provided a framework for viewing some facets of psychotherapy in a systematic and coherent manner and many useful investigative strategies. Among clinical researchers, there is considerable interplay between the psychodynamic, humanistic, and behavioral perspectives. The reciprocal borrowing process that occurs between researchers of all theoretical inclinations provides a healthy pollinization of methodological strategies and research instruments.

CONTRIBUTIONS OF THE CLIENT

Even the first psychotherapists recognized that their efforts of intervention would be more successful with some people than with others.

Information about the characteristics that influenced such determinations originated in theoretically guided intuitions and has become increasingly systematic and comprehensive over time. White (1956), for example, supplied six criteria that influenced the choice of patients likely to benefit from psychotherapy. The most suitable candidate, according to White, is a person who is young, intelligent, possesses a high degree of motivation, is able to cope with difficulties in life, is free from serious organic or neurological impairment, and is able to alter distressing life circumstances. Despite the fact that the justification for these characteristics was derived from the theoretical writings of psychoanalytic and client-centered clinicians, they have generally withstood the test of empirical scrutiny.

Personal Characteristics

Investigators have conceptualized the assessment of therapeutic outcome differently, depending upon whether their focus is on (1) selection of people to participate in psychotherapy, (2) premature termination of therapy, or (3) comparison against external criteria of improvement. *One general conclusion which all three investigative strategies point to is that psychotherapy appears to be most effective for those who need it least.* Schofield (1964) provides the most succinct summary of the attributes of successful clients by labelling them as YAVIS—*Young, Attractive, Verbal, Intelligent and Successful* individuals.

Youth is seen as an advantage since it is generally believed that oldsters are more set in their ways, finding it harder to promote significant lifestyle changes than younger people. Whether this is actually true is certainly debatable. Oldsters may be less able to change because of age-associated deficiencies or because they have come to believe the myth that old people cannot change radically. This latter view suggests that old people may be victims of a self-fulfilling prophecy. Whatever the reason for this sort of societal devaluation of old people, psychotherapists contribute to it by preferring people between the ages of 20 to 40 as ideal clients.

Attractiveness has had two distinct meanings; the term has referred to an interpersonal quality of social charm and graciousness as well as to physical attractiveness. More research has been devoted to the first aspect of attractiveness. People possessing this quality are perceived as introspective, psychologically sophisticated, insightful, and "good bets" for improving while in psychotherapy. Although little about the role of physical attractiveness in therapy is available, the social-psychological literature suggests that the world is a beautiful place for "beautiful people." A comprehensive review of this topic by Berscheid and Walster (1974) permits the following conclusions to be drawn about the impact of physical attractiveness:

1. Despite much variability in norms that constitute beauty across cultures within our society, attractiveness can be reliably judged by both male and female observers.
2. Individuals' self-ratings of their own attractiveness tend to be only marginally related to judgments made by external observers, however.
3. People generally hold strong positive stereotypes about the physically attractive, believing that they are better adjusted, happier, and more successful.
4. The attractive person is more likely to receive better treatment from childhood on. For example, nursery school children express more liking toward attractive peers, teachers typically view such children as having greater academic potential and as being better adjusted, and dating an attractive person enhances self-esteem.
5. Although there are few investigations relating physical attractiveness to stable personality characteristics, tentative evidence suggests that attractiveness has a slight relationship to positive self-concept.

Many questions about physical attractiveness await investigation. Much of the existing evidence was gathered from rating photographs or having brief interpersonal encounters. It seems likely that prolonged social contact may weaken the influence of physical attractiveness. Yet, it is clear that possessing this characteristic apparently provides one with many social opportunities that might otherwise be unavailable. A study by Dailey, Dailey, Allen, Chinsky, and Veit (1975) documents this point well. A number of demographic and interpersonal variables were used to predict frequency of initial and subsequent visits by volunteers to retarded children in a state training facility. The only significant predictor of first visits was physical attractiveness, as judged from children's photographs by the sample of volunteers. Subsequent visits to the same child, however, were influenced by both physical attractiveness and the perceived social responsivity of the resident. Ratings of residents' attributes were made nearly a month after the volunteers made their visits. At the very least, being physically attractive certainly appears to provide more initial access to occupational and social opportunity.

Good verbal ability is another characteristic of the good-risk client. Every form of psychotherapy, including behavior therapy, involves discussion. Of course, simply talking is not enough. Yet, many studies have suggested that discussion of emotionally laden material promotes greater therapeutic change (Truax and Carkhuff, 1967). The client's intelligence, both in terms of intellectual ability and social skill, also is considered by many to be an important factor in therapeutic success. It is intuitively obvious that working with an individual who possesses these attributes and the ability to build upon successful experiences in other life areas is likely to be a rewarding experience for the therapist.

Another commonly noted positive factor in therapeutic outcome is the degree of motivation the client possesses. This is an elusive variable to deal with. Yet, various investigations (summarized by Garfield, 1971) have suggested that the (1) amount of distress or dissatisfaction about the current situation expressed by a client, (2) suggestibility, and (3) willingness to actively explore problems are stable predictors of both length of stay and favorable outcome in psychotherapy.

Social Class

Ineffectiveness Of Therapy Related To Class. The characteristics of the YAVIS client generally are associated with middle-class values. For many years, it was generally held that people from the lower socioeconomic classes could not profit from psychotherapy. Considerable evidence has been offered in support of this contention which indicates that lower-class individuals are less likely to be accepted into treatment, terminate earlier, and profit less from therapy than their middle-class counterparts.

Interpretation Of The Evidence. This pervasive body of evidence has been interpreted in two distinct ways. Some think the evidence indicates inherent deficiencies in such people. Although this point is difficult to document with glaring examples, the frequently heard acronyms DUD (Dumb, Ugly, and Disadvantaged) and HOUND (Homely,

Old, Unintelligent, Nonverbal, and Disadvantaged) attest to the uncharitable description of lower-class individuals as having deficient personal attributes. Ryan (1971) calls this type of categorization "blaming the victim."

A second and more widely accepted interpretation of the evidence suggests that traditional psychotherapy attempts to foster middle-class values (such as beliefs about the importance of hard work, delay of gratification, the inhibition of aggression, the primacy of emotional and cognitive self-exploration, and others) that simply do not fit the life experiences of many culturally disadvantaged individuals. Rather than blaming the victims of cultural and intellectual poverty, this view suggests that various therapeutic procedures need to be tailored to meet the specific needs particular to the disadvantaged.

Implications Of The Evidence. Very different implications result from accepting one or the other of the interpretations. We shall consider the example of premature termination from psychotherapy. Major reviews (Baekeland and Lundwall, 1975; Lorion, 1973) indicate that low-income clients display higher attrition rates than middle-class individuals. By itself, this fact suggests that therapy may be a wasted endeavor when applied to disadvantaged people. Lorion (1974), however, documented that the therapist exerts greater influence on the decision to terminate treatment than the client does. Thus, lower-class people may be victimized by a self-fulfilling prophecy. Since these clients' conceptions of therapy may be different from the therapist's, the latter holds lower expectations about the probable success of treatment and subtly drives the clients away. This contention is documented in a thorough review of the termination issue (Baekeland and Lundwall, 1975). Fifteen factors were found to affect dropping out of treatment. The socio-economic status of the client was found to be a crucial determinant in 42 percent of the investigations they reviewed, while therapist attitudes and behaviors were implicated in 100 percent of the relevant studies.

There is a second aspect to this issue. "Premature termination" is a relational term indicating a discrepancy between the belief of the therapist that therapy should not be concluded and the decision by the client that it should. Garfield's (1971) review of the termination issue indicated that people of all social classes expect therapy to last for between five and ten sessions and that these expectations closely parallel actual attrition rates. This convergence has been interpreted to mean that people drop out of therapy at meaningful end points for them (Lorion, 1974).

Modifying Interventions. There have been a growing number of attempts to modify therapeutic interventions to better meet the needs of disadvantaged populations. The most systematic program to date, labelled "structured learning therapy," has been implemented by Goldstein (1973). The rationale behind this interventive strategy is based upon employing knowledge about the language processes and lifestyle of lower-class individuals to formulate relevant, highly prescriptive, and time-limited training exercises. The basic elements of the intervention involve observing models, practicing modelled responses through guided rehearsal, and receiving concrete feedback as well as social reinforcement. Many forms of audiovisual aids are employed (e.g., cartoons, comics, short films) that have relevance for the specific population having therapy. Goldstein's systematic efforts represent an important start toward adequately meeting the needs of individuals who have historically been neglected by traditional psychotherapists.

Client Expectancies

Defining The Term. The term **expectancy** refers to a belief that an individual holds. It is convenient to conceptualize an expectancy as a cognitive variable that mediates environmental inputs and response outputs. As mediating variables, expectancies can never be directly manipulated, but they can be measured through self-report instruments. Interest in expectancies emerged from the study of placebo effects in medicine throughout history. The critical role they play in physical healing and mental change processes was graphically described by Frank (1961), who suggested that such diverse procedures as witchdoctoring, religious faith healing, and psychotherapy changed behavior through generating self-curative expectations. He characterized these as faith and hope. Since that time, there has been a geometric increase in the literature on this topic.

Research On Expectancies. Wilkins (1973) has distinguished two general lines of research on the variable *expectancy for therapeutic gain in psychotherapy*. Early investigations focused on expectancy traits, or the enduring attitudes a person brings into the therapy situation. In general, this was accomplished by either correlating some measure of

142

clients' expectations with various indices of outcome or seeking statistical associations between expectancies and stable properties (e.g., age, sex, and so on) of clients.

This line of research has yielded several important conclusions. People who enter therapy with a moderate expectancy for improvement generally manifest greater therapeutic change than individuals who hold extremely low or extremely high expectations (Goldstein, 1962). This finding certainly makes intuitive sense. On one hand, a person who enters therapy with the strong belief that the helping process is going to be unproductive is likely to find it so. On the other, an individual who views therapy as a magical panacea that will insure a problem-free existence is bound to be disappointed.

Differences in expectations about therapists also have been systematically related to several characteristics of the client. Apfelbaum (1958) delineated three general roles clients expected of their therapists: (1) protective and nurturant, (2) nonjudgmental, or (3) critically analytical. Women expressed a preference for more supportive and nurturant clinicians, but men anticipated more critical and analytic behaviors from their therapists. Tinsley and Harris (1976) reported also that expectations about the benefits of counseling among college students vary as a function of age and sex. In general, however, they concluded that clients have a definite preference for being seen by an experienced clinician.

Attempts to relate expectancies for therapeutic gain to stable personality characteristics of clients (e.g., dependency, suggestibility, and so on) have produced inconclusive and contradictory results (Shapiro, 1971). Given the nature of therapy as an interpersonal influence process, failure to isolate trait characteristics is not surprising. Our brief examination of the issue of premature termination supports this contention. Differences in the expectations held by the therapist and client are a crucial determinant of dropping out of treatment. Yet, the actual rate of termination closely parallels the clients' beliefs about how long therapy should last.

Dissatisfaction with the trait approach led to a rise of interest in investigating expectancy states. This line of research typically involves attempting to alter the client's beliefs about some aspects of therapy by providing instructions or other experimental manipulations. Goldstein and Shipman (1961), for example, reported that having clients complete a questionnaire before entry into an initial therapy session led to a reduction in the intensity of the presenting complaint. We shall examine expectancy state research in Chapter 6.

Range Of Presenting Problems

The Choice Of Helper. A final topic worth highlighting is what brings people into psychotherapy in the first place. This is quite a complicated issue with several interrelated aspects. We can begin with the assumption that the practice of psychotherapy is a relatively invisible enterprise. When people experience difficulties, they are likely to seek aid from professionals other than psychiatric or psychological helpers. In a major survey of Americans' attitudes toward mental health, Gurin, Veroff, and Feld (1960) reported that 42 percent of those seeking professional help turned to the clergy and 29 percent consulted the family physician. Less than 18 percent became involved with psychiatrists, and only 6 of 345 respondents specifically mentioned going to a private therapist. Kadushin (1969), in a survey of New York City residents, found that only 15 percent could name a psychiatrist, while even fewer (6 percent) could identify a psychologist. The proportion of prospective clients who seek treatment at outpatient facilities on their own also is quite small. Strupp, Fox, and Lessler (1969) reported that only 11 percent of the clientele seeking treatment at the University of North Carolina Medical School clinic had not sought prior help from an alternate source.

Admission Of The Need For Help. Several reasons for this state of affairs exist. The decision to enter therapy invariably evokes conflicting feelings in the candidate. Taking this step is a tacit admission that the client is dissatisfied with some aspect of her personal functioning and requires outside help. The humiliation and shame inherent in this admission conflicts with feelings of optimism and hope stemming from the belief that therapy will be helpful. The process of psychotherapy is by its very nature paradoxical. The client is inducted into a dependency relationship which is aimed at helping her to accept responsibility and eventually function independently. Many people are ignorant about exactly what therapy entails. Their confusion is a reflection of the many alternative paradigms that are publicized through the mass media.

These factors combine to produce a curious anomaly with regard to seeking treatment. Many clients tacitly accept the tenets of the medical model by seeking to discover an organic basis for their difficulties. This particular model often provides a sense of relief to clients because it legitimates their desire to externalize the causes of their problems. Adherence to this belief is often antithetical to the goals espoused by most practicing clinicians, who desire to foster a sense of responsibility and self-mastery in their clients. Many of these same therapists, however, employ diagnostic and classification procedures that derive from the model.

Classification Of Problems. Most people enter therapy because they suffer from problems which adversely affect their day-to-day functioning. Figure 8 presents the frequency of common presenting complaints people bring to therapy. The figure contains weighted averages that were derived from 131 applicants to a hospital training clinic (Strupp, Fox, and Lessler, 1969) and from 1440 candidates who applied for treatment at various psychoanalytic, religio-psychiatric, and hospital clinics in New York City (Kadushin, 1969). In both investigations, a sociological typology was employed to classify problems. Kadushin's framework involved the following major areas (with subcategories listed in parentheses): (1) *biosocial problems* (physical complaints involving somatic dysfunctions as well as drug or alcohol abuse; and sexual dysfunctions), (2) *inner emotional problems* (cognitive disorientation; cathectic difficulties involving depression, generalized anxiety and phobias; and self-evaluative dilemmas), (3) *social problems* (difficulties with primary love relationships involving spouses, families, and so on; with occupational roles; and with generally getting along with people), and (4) *no problem—others have problem*.

Analysis of the questionnaire and interview data provided by respondents in Kadushin's survey revealed the existence of four problem clusters. The first cluster encompassed classically defined psychiatric symptoms, including physical, cathectic, and cognitive complaints. The second group involved performance problems relating to meeting the demands of daily living. The third group centered on problems closely associated with psychoanalytic therapy and included sexual, interpersonal, and self-evaluative concerns. The final grouping described a tendency to project blame for one's difficulties onto situational factors or onto members of primary social groups. People with particular problem clusters were found to seek treatment at agencies with differing orientations.

FIGURE 8.   PROBLEMS COMMONLY BROUGHT INTO THERAPY

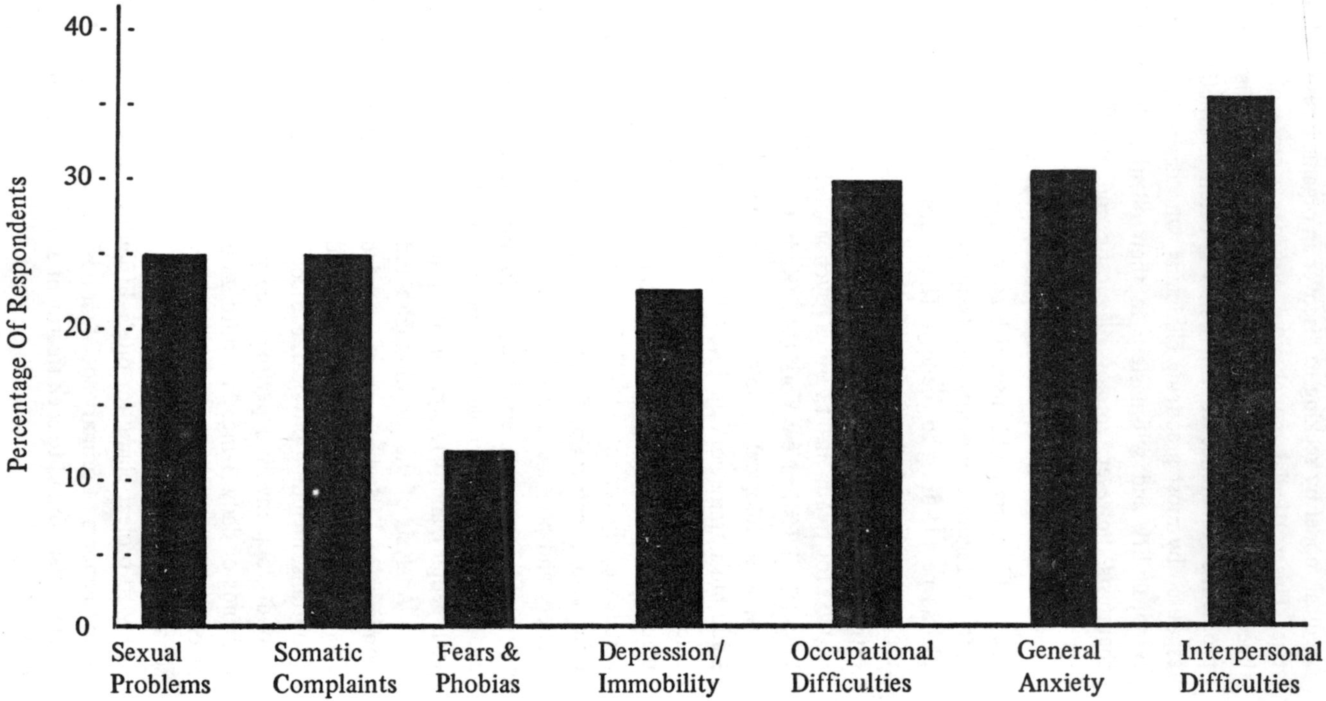

Some interesting implications emerge from analyzing Figure 8 in conjunction with additional findings from the two surveys. Obviously, people do not enter therapy because they view themselves as sick, but rather, because they encounter interpersonal or occupational difficulties and because they suffer from emotional inadequacies. A second implication is that people less frequently seek therapy for more serious forms of maladjustment. Only 5 percent of the presenting difficulties reported by both Kadushin and Strupp et al. involved cognitive disorientations that are typically considered *psychotic*. Only 2 percent of Kadushin's total sample indicated having problems with drugs and alcohol, although the percentage of people who mentioned difficulties with these substances varied from 1 percent of the clientele in analytic clinics to 7 percent of those seeking treatment in hospital clinics. The low overall rate of substance abuse can be partially accounted for by the fact that the sample of analytic patients was more than three times as large as the religio-psychiatric and hospital clinic samples combined.

In Marmor's (1975) survey of psychiatrists in private practice, the respondents classified their patients according to the *Diagnostic and Statistical Manual of Mental Disorders* compiled by the American Psychiatric Association (1968). This scheme, which is based on a disease model of human functioning, provides some interesting contrasts with the sociological typologies used by Kadushin and Strupp et al. Diagnoses were provided for 4342 patients who were clustered into three categories—those receiving psychoanalysis, those receiving nonanalytic treatment from a psychoanalyst, and those being treated by a nonanalyst. For the entire sample, 25 percent were classified as suffering from a depressive neurosis, 23 percent from some other neurotic condition, and 19 percent from a personality disorder. More interestingly, 21 percent were diagnosed as psychotic. Although the distribution of psychosis-relevant diagnoses ranged from 3 percent of the analytic patients to 24 percent of the patients of nonanalysts, the overall figure is four times larger than estimates of psychotic conditions reported when sociological typologies are employed.

Differences In Diagnoses. Kadushin made a direct comparison of both classification schemes and reported that people with the same presenting problem are likely to be diagnosed very differently, depending on the type of clinic in which they seek treatment. For example, a majority of people suffering from feelings of depression and immobility were diagnosed as neurotic at two clinics, schizoid at a third, and schizophrenic at a fourth. The diversity of problems an individual brings to therapy is also not accurately reflected by traditional psychiatric diagnosis because multiple difficulties are typically conceptualized as forming syndromes involving a single underlying cause (e.g., anxiety). Kadushin reported that clients mentioned up to seven complaints during initial screening, with the average being three per applicant. Less than 6 percent of the patients in Marmor's sample, however, received multiple diagnoses.

Mental Illness Versus Problems In Living. In summary, we find a great deal of ambivalence among both therapists and clients regarding whether difficulties represent mental illnesses or problems in living. The sociological typologies clearly suggest that people enter therapy to resolve problems in living, but commonly employed diagnostic practices often obscure this view. On another level, attributing problems to mental illness often provides an emotionally satisfying explanation to a client, although many clinicians find this view to be intellectually untenable.

CONTRIBUTIONS OF THE THERAPIST

Many experts consider the therapist to be the most crucial determinant of success and failure in psychotherapy. In their search for characteristics that contribute to therapeutic effectiveness, however, researchers have encountered some difficult problems. We have already noted that discrepancies often exist between the conceptions of therapists and clients regarding the factors that bring about improvement. Clinicians are more apt to describe the techniques they have employed as the crucial component, while clients are more likely to cite the human characteristics of the therapist.

A similar polarity exists between humanistic and behavioral clinicians, with the former focusing on the personal attributes possessed by a clinician and the latter emphasizing what the therapist does. Humanistic researchers (e.g., Truax and Mitchell, 1971) seem more concerned with validating the therapist, while behavioral clinicians seem more concerned with validating the therapeutic procedure. This contrast is illustrated shortly.

Training Of Professional Therapists

Critical scrutiny of the training practices for psychiatrists, psychologists, and psychiatric social workers would lead to the conclusion that none of the educational programs produces practitioners who are skilled therapists (Reinehr, 1975). This does not imply that professional clinicians are not skilled or helpful, but rather, that current training is not directly related to the practice of psychotherapy. Let us briefly review the typical training sequences of these three professional groups.

Psychiatrists. Psychiatrists begin their professional training in medical schools. During the first two years, most of the prospective physician's time is devoted to attending lectures and working in the laboratory. Heavy emphasis is given to biological foundations of medical practice (e.g., biochemistry, anatomy, pathology, etc.), and the candidate is expected to memorize vast amounts of material. Training as a generalist continues during the second two years of medical school. Classwork is reduced and replaced with **clerkships**, which involve obtaining practical experience in hospitals and clinics. Each clerkship lasts from three to six weeks, with the candidate rotating through a predetermined sequence involving medical specialties, such as gynecology, radiology, surgery, psychiatry, and others.

Completion of medical school requirements entitles candidates to take an examination to receive a license as a physician. At this point, most prospective psychiatrists cannot be regarded as specialists; they have been exposed to perhaps four to eight hours of classwork pertinent to psychiatric practice and six to twelve weeks of practical experience in this area. Medical licenses reflect the generalist emphasis of training. A license permits the holder to practice *any* area of medicine without further legal restriction. Legally, a surgeon may practice psychiatry and a psychiatrist may practice surgery, although, in fact, this does not frequently occur.

After completing medical school, the physician begins to specialize during a one-year internship in an approved hospital or clinic. For psychiatrists, this experience often involves prescribing medication or providing brief counseling to individuals in crisis situations. Demands on the physician's time by the institution frequently preclude exposure to supervised, longer-term therapeutic contact. Further specialized training is provided during a two- or three-year residency following internship. Unfortunately, in many cases, the service demands of the institutional setting again preclude practicing psychotherapy under intensive supervision.

One credential which does indicate some therapeutic expertise among psychiatrists is certification by the American Board of Psychiatry and Neurology. Candidates are eligible after completing a three-year residency in psychiatry and practicing their specialty for two additional years. The first part of the certification examination is written. Criteria for passing are quite high. In 1974, 37 percent of the examinees failed this portion. The second part involves oral examinations and assessment of standardized work samples provided by the candidates. In 1974, only 66 percent of the candidates passed this portion of the examination (Annual Report of the American Board of Psychiatry and Neurology, 1975). Adams and Orgel (1975) reported that only about one-third of all practicing psychologists have obtained board certification.

Psychologists. During their graduate education, clinical psychologists generally receive training that is more directly relevant to therapeutic practice than do psychiatrists. Most training programs in clinical psychology, however, are oriented toward developing skills in research and testing. The typical training program combines course work in theories of personality, advanced abnormal psychology, and perspectives on psychotherapy and counseling, with instruction in experimental design, learning, perception, and statistics. Practicum courses in individual and group psychotherapy are usually provided, but these occupy less of the training load. Considerable time and effort during the four-to-five-year training sequence are devoted to research required for obtaining the master's and Ph.D. degrees.

An integral part of the training program involves a one-year internship in a clinic or hospital setting that is approved by the American Psychological Association. Psychology interns often gain more therapy experience than psychiatric interns because they are not responsible for prescribing drugs or conducting other forms of physical treatment (e.g., electro-convulsive therapy). In some cases, however, interns perform research and evaluative functions for the institution at the expense of gaining supervised therapy experience.

Psychologists who complete training are eligible for certification or licensing by a state-appointed board of examiners. Licenses awarded to psychologists are more stringent than those awarded to physicians in the sense that they limit the activities one may engage in to certain legally defined (e.g., clinical work; consulting) specialties. There is much more variability in certification and licensing requirements for psychologists across states than is found in the licensing of physicians, however. In Connecticut, an applicant for a license must submit evidence of having satisfactorily completed approved training and internship programs as well as having had two years of (very loosely defined) supervised clinical experience. The test itself is entirely written, a short-answer assessment of one's general knowledge about the field, a section on ethical principles, and several essay questions about one's area of expertise.

Like psychiatrists, psychologists may apply for advanced certification through the American Board of Professional Psychology. To become an ABPP diplomate, a candidate must have had at least five years of post-doctoral experience and must pass a rigorous examination. The major emphasis in this examination is assessment of the candidate's ability to formulate diagnoses and conduct therapy with a high level of competence. Only 17 percent of the psychologists responding to the survey by Adams and Orgel (1975) were approved as diplomates.

Psychiatric Social Workers. The training of psychiatric social workers involves a two- to three-year postgraduate educational experience in a school of social work. These training institutions are typically divorced from specific academic departments within a university. The training emphasis is on combining classwork with a series of rotating clerkships in surrounding social service agencies. In the typical program, few, if any, courses are devoted to psychotherapy. Social workers are expected to practice the rather vaguely defined activity of "social casework." Functionally, this means that the social worker is supposed to interview both patients in clinics or hospitals and their families.

Many schools, particularly on the East Coast, orient their training around psychodynamic and psychoanalytic models, without emphasizing contributions from sociological or psychological theories. Research is de-emphasized because training is aimed at turning out practitioners. These models do not appear to have much relevance for the social worker's mission of dealing with the various social systems that affect the patient. What little psychotherapy experience is provided usually involves giving short-term support for people in crisis situations.

Practitioners with at least two years of experience after having obtained the Masters Degree in Social Work are eligible for certification by an in-house agency—the Academy for Certification of Social Workers. Obtaining this credential involves having demonstrated completion of training requirements and passing a test administered by the Academy.

Inadequacies In Training. Again, it should be emphasized that current training practices do not routinely produce poorly skilled or unqualified therapists. Certain tensions within each profession do, however, make training less optimally relevant than it might be. Both psychiatrists and psychiatric social workers are trained as service providers, but they often are not given the technological tools that would enhance their effectiveness in this role. Freud (1926) was among the first to argue that medical training does not provide physicians with the requisite psychological knowledge to practice therapy effectively. He denounced medical education as giving physicians a "false and detrimental attitude" toward the neuroses (1959; Vol. XX, p. 231). Although Freud's attack might have been partly a reaction against the antagonism the medical establishment had to his theory, one must question the relevance of generalist medical school training for psychiatric practice.

The emphasis on providing service in both the psychiatric and social work training models leads to an unfortunate de-emphasis on the importance of subjecting therapeutic practices to empirical scrutiny. For many practitioners with this sort of training, psychotherapy is indeed a functionally autonomous activity. Reliance on training models that translate problems in living into disease processes helps perpetuate this state of affairs.

Clinical psychology trainees are generally exposed to a variety of frameworks for understanding therapy as a mutual influence process. Many also are provided with statistical and methodological tools for evaluating their therapeutic activities. The danger here is that the trainees become overloaded and frustrated; the dual training emphasis as clinician and researcher often prevents the development of expertise in either area. In addition, trainees often find themselves caught on the horns of the scientist-practitioner dilemma.

Personal Characteristics
Although there is no such creature as a "Super Therapist," generally effective clinicians have all the characteristics of a SAUNA: *Sensitive, Active, Unflappable, Nonpunitive, Amoral.* In combination, these characteristics provide the client with a warm healing or enhancement experience.

Sensitive. Personal sensitivity is undoubtedly the primary determinant of growth in psychotherapy. This sensitivity often is labelled as "warmth," "empathy," "genuineness," or "understanding." *Sensitivity ultimately stems from successfully resolving the paradoxical task of becoming emotionally involved enough to support the client while keeping enough distance to effectively challenge the person.* The sensitive clinician listens with the "third ear," weaving verbal material and emotional overtones into meaningful themes about the client's world. Empathic involvement allows the therapist to become part of the client's cognitive framework, using this understanding to provide the person with the courage to undertake change. The sensitive therapist *does not become entangled* in the client's framework, however. Rather, the understanding of the cognitive world is used to formulate strategies that the client can use to rise above currently existing difficulties. Effective therapy is based on being able to support and challenge the client, which is impossible to accomplish without being aware of the client's view of reality.

Active. Sensitivity is molded to meet the dual demands of supporting and challenging through therapist activity. Being active does not necessarily mean that the therapist must talk incessantly or continually seek to control everything that occurs during a therapy session. Activity is reflected on several levels. On a cognitive level, the therapist is continually formulating hunches, operationalizing these into hypotheses, and testing them out. This sort of involvement is reflected even in the actions of therapists whose theoretical beliefs lead them to act very passively during therapy. The reflective statements employed by client-centered therapists and the interpretations of some psychodynamic clinicians represent a very active form of listening. On a more overt level, active therapists constantly approach and deal openly with the client's concerns, regardless of whether they appear to be painful to the client or threatening to the therapist.

Unflappable. Because clients often bring what they consider to be shameful secrets into therapy, it is important that therapists do not lose their composure. Therapists who seem unfazed by hearing seemingly bizarre anecdotes (e.g., "Doc, I need help. Twice a day I am overwhelmed with a compulsion to sexually molest chickens!") rapidly foster a nonjudgmental and accepting atmosphere that facilitates communication. As a professional, the therapist is expected to be unflappable, at ease, and in control. A matter-of-fact acceptance of the client's shameful secrets often indicates to the client that his situation is neither terribly unique nor terribly shameful.

Nonpunitive. Feelings of shame, alienation, and isolation with which people enter therapy are often the result of punitive and moralistic evaluations by other people or by the clients themselves. Depressed individuals often hear (or make) statements like "Stop feeling sorry for yourself"; "You shouldn't be depressed"; "You are lucky to have all your limbs (eyesight, good job, etc.)." Such evaluations often make the client feel guilty about being depressed. A nonpunitive orientation toward the client frequently helps ease some of this evaluative pressure. Nonpunitive therapists do not shy away from making value judgments about the client or from expressing these (this is part of being active). The evaluations are data-based, however, rather than being derived from some hidden agenda held by the therapist. A data-based evaluation involves pointing out the hidden consequences of what the client says and posing these as alternatives open to the client. Nonpunitiveness also implies that the therapist will not reward or punish the client in a capricious manner.

Amoral. Being *amoral* is quite different from being *immoral*. Amorality involves the therapist's ability to distinguish courses of action that will be beneficial from the client's own moral point of view. This is admittedly a complex issue. All therapists operate within a complicated web of social and moral conventions which combine with their own prescriptive moral views to influence the therapeutic intervention. At one extreme, providing direction based on the therapist's belief system, without considering the situation of the client, is clearly counterproductive. Providing advice about obtaining a divorce or an abortion that is dictated solely on the basis of the therapist's values is a subtle form of exploitation. Yet, therapists cannot escape from their own moral dictums, particularly those that relate to sex, aggression, and lifestyle. These beliefs often provide a hidden agenda upon which the advice of the therapist rests. On the other hand, therapists have the responsibility to provide the client with information that will enable the latter to make a more fully informed choice between alternatives.

In seeking to resolve this dilemma, most therapists adopt a laissez-faire stance in their clinical interactions by attempting to neutralize or hide their own moral leanings. Humanistically inclined practitioners have, however, studied the issue of value clarification more directly. Raths, Harmin, and Simon (1966), for example, describe seven criteria for viewing the valuing process. These form three general areas that encompass (1) choosing a value after thoughtful consideration of alternative possibilities, (2) publicly proclaiming the value as a prized and cherished one, and (3) acting upon the value frequently enough so that it makes a discernible difference in one's life pattern. The amoral therapist will share her beliefs with a client as one potential influence on the latter's own decision. The amoral therapist will neither be forced into actually making ethical decisions for the client nor deny the fact that moral decisions are an integral part of the therapeutic process.

Relational Nature Of SAUNA Characteristics. Describing therapists in terms of SAUNA attributes is a concise and rather slick presentation. In reality, these characteristics do not reside inside the therapist, although they have hidden cognitive and attitudinal components. Clients perceive their therapists to have particular attributes as a result of how the therapist behaves. The therapist's concrete actions are used by the client to form impressions about the kind of person the therapist is. This is an extremely important point to keep in mind. For a therapist to be perceived as having a certain characteristic, the responses she makes must be contingently related to particular responses in the client.

The prototype of research demonstrating this point was provided by Bandura, Lipsher, and Miller (1960). In their experiment, clients' statements were rated as to whether hostility was being directed toward the therapist, whose response was also judged to involve either an approach to the topic or an attempt to avoid dealing with it. The effect of the clinician's approach and avoidance strategies was then related to factors such as supervisors' judgments about the therapists' level of experience, subsequent client behavior, and clients' perceptions of the therapist. This type of response-contingent simplification strategy has been employed by researchers with psychodynamic, humanistic, and behavioral philosophies.

Failures To Isolate Concrete Therapist Traits

Although we have noted therapist characteristics generally thought to be important, the relational nature of psychotherapy has doomed to failure attempts at specifying stable characteristics of the successful therapist, without considering the interactive influences of the client and setting.

Research On "A" And "B" Types. Two large-scale investigative attempts point up the difficulty of isolating specifically curative therapist traits. The first dealt with the isolation of "A" and "B" therapist types by Whitehorn and Betz over more than two decades (Betz, 1967). The observation that certain therapists appeared to be more effective with *schizophrenic patients* was gradually tied to major personality differences as reflected by the Strong Vocational Interest Blank. Successful therapists (A types) were determined to possess genuineness, sensitivity to inner feelings, and expectations for reasonable patient self-determination. According to this view, they also employ an active problem-solving approach in therapy. B-type therapists, who were eventually found to be more effective in resolving *neurotic complaints*, were categorized as more passively permissive, mechanical, and oriented toward symptom reduction.

These findings held great promise since they appeared to permit an optimal matching of therapists and clients. The utility of the typology has been seriously questioned, however. Chartier (1971), in a review of much relevant research on A and B therapist types, reached the following conclusions:

1. Real-life clinical support for the presumed matching was based on a methodologically weak foundation and contaminated by probable socio-economic biases and hospitalization effects.
2. Extensive analogue research using student "therapists" and "artificial" clients represents premature and unwarranted simplification and has yielded inconsistent outcomes.
3. Since the original research, increasingly fewer type-B therapists have been identified, and the widespread use of ataractic drugs exerts an unknown but important impact on success rates.

Chartier characterized the A-B distinction as "elusive" (p. 31) and implied that it could well be illusory.

Research On Accurate Empathy. Attempts by Truax and his associates to measure therapist attributes of genuineness, nonpossessive warmth, and accurate empathy provide an even more graphic illustration of the pitfalls of seeking to isolate therapeutic traits. This line of investigation yielded an immense output suggesting the existence of a causal link between these characteristics and client improvement (Truax and Mitchell, 1971). This conclusion was weakened, however, by the discovery of conceptual confusions and methodological defects in the assessment of accurate empathy (Chinsky and Rappaport, 1970).

Accurate empathy was originally defined as a relational construct involving the therapist's ability to sense and communicate understanding of the client's feelings. In the typical experiment, judges listened to tapes of verbal exchanges between the client and therapist and rated empathy along a nine-point scale. In 1966, Truax published a study demonstrating that raters could reliably code accurate empathy without hearing client responses (1966a).

Chinsky and Rappaport argued that this strategy violated the original meaning of accurate empathy and suggested that raters based their judgments on the vocal characteristics of the therapists. Their conclusion was bolstered by their demonstration that reliability estimates were not based on independent judgments and that reliability dropped dramatically when more than 15 therapists were rated. In a subsequent critique of accurate empathy, Rappaport and Chinsky (1972) noted that emerging research indicated accurate empathy ratings to be reliably related to amount of therapist talking. In addition, while empathy was a good predictor of client ratings of therapist understanding, rater judgments of the presumably independent dimensions of warmth and genuineness were more highly related to clients' perceptions of being understood.

Conclusions About Trait Research. Conclusions drawn about both A and B therapist types and accurate empathy have failed to withstand subsequent empirical scrutiny. While systematic methodological weaknesses aided the demise of both lines of inquiry, failure was ultimately due to the reification of these characteristics into oversimplified trait entities that were presumed to exist apart from the therapeutic relationship. Problems with the trait approach can be more thoroughly appreciated by considering the complexities that underlie the relationship between clinical experience and therapeutic outcome.

Therapist Experience

Therapists commonly acknowledge that they gain competence at the expense of their first clients. On a simplistic level, the acquisition of clinical experience should lead to increased therapeutic competence, if only because postgraduate training proves that these individuals are capable of learning. Literature reviews (e.g., Bergin, 1971) suggest that experienced therapists are generally more successful than beginners.

Relationship Between Experience And Success. The relationship between experience and success is a complex one, however. Experience is not a unitary variable, but, rather, represents a combination of many relational elements. Even though the two concepts are allied, experience does not always insure expert competence. Experience and success are mediated by four interrelated influences that center on (1) therapeutic style, (2) specificity of treatment technique, (3) client expectations, and (4) personal attributes of the therapist.

Variation In Style. A great deal of research stemming from Fiedler's (1950, 1951) initial investigations has indicated that, in comparison to novice clinicians, experienced therapists employ a wider range of therapeutic strategies derived from multiple theoretical inclinations, are more dynamically oriented, less preoccupied with obtaining descriptive information, and place a greater emphasis on historical material. In addition experienced clinicians tend to make more efficient use of therapy contact time, in terms of providing information, exerting control, and subtly directing what occurs during the encounter.

Treatment Specificity. These differences will be less evident when therapy involves more specific change strategies or when they conflict with a therapist's theoretically determined operations. The concrete and standardized specifications of many behavior therapy change procedures, or the Gestalt emphasis on here-and-now experience, for example, tend to mask divergence in therapeutic style.

Client Expectations. Popular stereotypes depicting the therapist as an older person who is always at ease and in control attests to the strength of client expectancies regarding experience. Even relatively unsophisticated consumers of counseling services express very strong preferences for experienced therapists (Tinsley and Harris, 1976). The consequences of violating such expectations are presumably negative, although very little research on this topic currently exists.

Influence Of Personality. Investigation of experience as a determinant of therapeutic success leaves us with a dilemma, particularly when aspects of the therapist's personality are taken into account. *While we know that experience and success are associated, we do not know whether "good" therapists are successful because they are experienced or experienced because they are successful.* Therapeutic failures have been traced to fairly global therapist characteristics. Baekeland and Lundwall (1975) characterize therapists who are likely to drive people out of treatment as being generally aloof, detached, and uninvolved in respect to their clients. Haley (1969a) instructs those who wish to be failures as psychotherapists to practice what he calls the "five B's"—"Be Passive, Be Inactive, Be Reflective, Be Silent, and Beware" (p. 78). This general pattern of passivity and disinterest is in direct contrast to the SAUNA experience provided by therapists who are considered to be generally successful.

The foregoing suggests that experience by itself is neither necessary nor sufficient to insure favorable therapeutic outcome. Clinical experience results from the operation of more specific influences. Novice therapists may offset their lack of experience by approaching their clients with enthusiasm, warmth, genuineness, and concern. These factors help both young therapists and their clients surmount difficulties that arise because of strategic awkwardness.

FINAL WORDS

Our analysis of client characteristics and therapist attributes points up the sterility of the myths about client and therapist uniformity. Psychotherapy is a complex interactive process that occurs between complex human beings. Clients differ from one another along a wide variety of dimensions, just as therapists do. We have made great progress toward uncovering common threads that are associated with success and failure in psychotherapy, but we have much work ahead of us.

One general conclusion that can be drawn from our brief overview is that complicated clinical phenomena deserve more than simplistic analysis and require more than simple answers. If certain types of therapeutic intervention do not appear to be particularly helpful when applied to poor people, older individuals, or any other *class* of client, it is the responsibility of the professional to question this situation and devise strategies which will be of greater benefit. *We cannot afford the convenient luxury of blaming the victims of our therapeutic failures.*

We also cannot afford to lose sight of the interactive nature of the therapeutic process. For many, it would be nice if we could isolate characteristics of the ideal client or attributes of the perfectly effective therapist. Clinical reality, however, is not that simple. The discovery of information that will be ultimately useful in improving therapeutic efficacy will, of necessity, be a long and complicated process.

6
Therapeutic Components II: Setting, Time, and Common Elements

As noted earlier, interactions between the therapist and the client occur in a social context. This is a broad term that encompasses aspects of the physical arrangement of the therapy setting, the time limitations imposed on the therapeutic process, and the elements (or rituals) employed. Throughout history, socially sanctioned healers have possessed an intuitive understanding of the importance of such factors in the healing process. Witch doctors, shamen, soothsayers, physicians, and psychotherapists have deliberately capitalized on these influences in their attempts to cure people who were afflicted by sickness or madness.

For the most part, healing that occurred as a result of a particular therapeutic intervention was explained in terms of whatever theoretical beliefs predominated at a given historical period. The operation of curative influences associated with the social context was masked by prevailing theoretical explanations. If a theory could not provide a satisfying explanation of how change came about, these factors were assumed to have nonspecific effects. That is, although the healers generally appeared to be effective, they could not provide a satisfactory explanation of how they operated.

The effects of social influences are considered to be nonspecific only to the extent that we are unable to adequately describe, predict, and control them. The emergence of more sophisticated techniques of empirical inquiry and novel explanatory frameworks has helped dispel ignorance about these formerly nonspecific influences. In many instances, fairly satisfactory methods of coping with them have been developed. In some cases, we have even begun to systematically exploit them in order to improve our effectiveness as helpers.

In this chapter, we will examine what empirical research has yielded about the operation of the more-or-less nonspecific factors associated with the social context of psychotherapy. Specifically, we will deal with setting and time. Then we will examine some common elements of therapeutic practice. We will focus on therapeutic operations that transcend the techniques employed by therapists with competing theoretical orientations.

CONTRIBUTIONS OF THE SETTING

Early Treatments
Medical historians have conceptualized almost all the treatment procedures employed before the twentieth century as having nonfunctional therapeutic properties in light of present knowledge. Many of these remedies, however, were effective in reducing physical suffering and alleviating emotional distress. Suffering individuals often showed improvement in their afflictions after ingesting "medicines" containing such delicacies as lizard blood, crocodile dung, and frog sperm (Shapiro, 1959). After making religious pilgrimages to places like Lourdes in France (Frank, 1961), others have experienced miraculous recoveries from conditions medical practitioners had diagnosed as hopelessly incurable. On the negative side, observers in many parts of the world have documented that voodoo deaths do indeed occur when people believe that they have been hexed by a more powerful other. Such deaths represent interpersonal influence at long range, often occurring without any face-to-face contact between the antagonists.

Change Attributed To Operations
Whatever changes that occur usually are attributed to the specific operations that were employed. One's sickness was cured because the medicine contained crocodile droppings; someone died because the magic possessed by the enemy was powerful. Failure to change was interpretable in two ways. Either the medicine (or the magic) was not powerful or the person was incapable of profiting from (or able to resist) the intervention. The ancient Greeks used the latter kind of reasoning. Afflicted individuals were brought to a temple where the

priest-healers would implore the gods to remove the ailment. If the conditions did not improve, the sufferers could be accused of being impious and many were put to death. Because the gods were more powerful than mere mortals, their nonintervention was evidence that the victims were at fault.

Although such explanations might appear silly, several similarities to modern therapeutic practices easily can be noted. Therapists attribute improvement in their clients to the specific operations they employ. People improve because they were exposed to a nonpossessive, warm, and accurately empathetic therapist, because they were desensitized, or because they had acquired insight. Failure to improve is explicable in terms of either deficiencies in the therapeutic operation (the therapist did not manifest enough warmth, was not adequately trained in the use of desensitization, or encountered insurmountable unconscious resistance) or deficiencies in the client (who is presumed to possess poor motivation, or the wrong social class, sex, age, racial, or educational qualifications).

Placebo And Expectancy Influences

Defining The Terms And Their History. In conjunction with other conceptual pioneers (e.g., Shapiro, 1959), Jerome Frank (1961) helped dispel existing ignorance about the operation of the interpersonal influence processes mentioned earlier. Frank provided a framework for tying the diverse effects of the healing process to a smaller set of interrelated causes, which he conceptualized in terms of faith and hope. All professional healers, be they witch doctors, psychotherapists, or faith healers, employ complex rituals that contain an aura of mystery. Usually, the rituals include elaborate trappings (e.g., chants, dances, and so on) which add to the mystery. The medicinal ingredients employed often had noticeable effects on the sufferer; they frequently caused bodily discomfort, smelled terrible, and tasted horrid. These rituals have the effect of arousing faith in the ability of the healer and hope that the intervention will be effective.

Although modern psychotherapists do not wear tribal masks or cast spells, strategies that parallel these practices are easy to find. Private therapists work in well-furnished offices and often prominently display diplomas and other credentials of professional competence. These trappings are presumed to strengthen the client's faith in the therapist's ability. Well-appointed surroundings provide a message: the therapist is apparently quite successful. Torrey (1972) categorized the influence of such setting factors as the "edifice complex." The strategic components employed by therapists often have immediately noticeable impact on the client. Systematic muscular relaxation, for example, produces marked physiological changes that include reduction in muscle tension and heart rate. The credibility of the clinician is increased when such changes are predicted in advance and then actually do occur. Accurate predictions of this type provide evidence to the client that the therapist is skilled and competent. The therapist need not even be this active to facilitate positive changes, however. Torrey (1972) suggests that simply providing a descriptive label for the client's difficulty has a therapeutic effect, while Goldstein and Shipman (1961) reported that having clients fill out questionnaires can lead to a reduction in the intensity of the client's presenting problems.

Modern investigators prefer to conceptualize what Frank describes as faith and hope in terms of placebo and expectancy influences. A **placebo** refers to any intervention that is presumed to be without specific activity for the condition being treated (Shapiro, 1971). The term itself has a long and seedy history stemming from its original meaning of an offering to God. It has been used to refer to vespers for the dead, professional mourners who were paid to weep and pray at funerals (many of whom were considered to be parasites), a commonplace medicine, and an inert drug. Shapiro (1971) noted that many physicians react quite defensively when this issue is raised. They suggest that other physicians are guilty of using them three times more often than they admit to using them themselves, and they tend to exclude their specialty area when defining what a placebo is.

Shapiro's definition indicates that a placebo is any *theoretically inert* substance or procedure. Although a placebo often produces specific effects, no theoretical or empirical framework can be employed to satisfactorily explain how it operates. This definition has several important implications with regard to psychotherapy. *First, there exists a constantly shifting boundary between placebo and real therapies.* The presumably active ingredients of some of yesterday's interventions have become today's placebos, while some of today's placebos are emerging as tomorrow's theoretically relevant treatments. *Second, placebos are direct manipulations of the environment which should be distinguished from expectancies.* An **expectancy** is a mediating variable that refers to a belief held by a person that something will happen in a certain way. Expectancies must be inferred from an individual's behavior; they can never be directly manipulated. Placebo manipulations are presumed to affect behavior by changing one's beliefs. Finally, neither term is useful as an explanation of behavior change. It makes no conceptual sense to argue that a person improved because he received a placebo or because the placebo altered his expectancies. When used as explanations, such concepts mask our ignorance of the more proximate causes of change which can be found in contingent arrangements between specific environments, responses, and consequences.

Attempts To Isolate Expectancy And Placebo Effects As Traits. Both placebo and expectancy influences are undoubtedly important in psychotherapy. We have already noted some impressive evidence for this in Chapter 5. Discrepancies between the expectations of therapists and clients were associated with premature termination from psychotherapy in every investigation reviewed by Baekeland and Lundwall (1975). These influences, however, cannot be investigated without taking their response-contingent nature into account. Attempts to isolate expectancy and placebo effects as traits residing inside of people have not proven to be particularly worthwhile. Beyond the very general conclusion that anxiety is a concomitant of placebo effectiveness, those who react positively to placebo manipulations have not been consistently found to be any more suggestible, compliant, dependent, neurotic, or depressed than people who manifest variable or negative reactions (Shapiro, 1971).

Coping Strategies. At the present time, much effort is being directed toward both coping with and exploiting expectancy and placebo influences. The net effect of these attempts has been the discovery and eventual manipulation of the properties of placebos, thus making their formerly nonspecific operation more specific and precise.

As mentioned in Chapter 5, behavior therapists have been by far the heaviest contributors to our knowledge about these influences. Since behavioral clinicians have a primary interest in validating the effectiveness of various therapeutic procedures over and above the contribution made by nonspecific factors, they were forced to devise adequate coping strategies to discount their effects. New and effective therapeutic manipulations have resulted from these coping efforts.

These points can be illustrated by continuing the analysis of research on systematic desensitization which we started in Chapter 4. In general, three types of coping strategies have been employed. In his pioneering investigation, Paul (1966) documented the superiority of desensitization by using the most straightforward approach. He provided a pseudotherapy condition against which to compare changes produced by both insight therapy and desensitization. A second widely used approach has involved desensitizing individuals who are given different kinds of feedback about the effects of treatment. In some cases (e.g., Marcia, Rubin, and Efran, 1969), the participants are provided with false physiological feedback, while, in others (e.g., Leitenberg, Agras, Barlow, and Oliveau, 1969), they are instructed directly about the benefits they can expect. The third strategy has been to present desensitization either as an effective therapeutic procedure or as a method for investigating physiological responsiveness which has little therapeutic relevance (e.g., Rosen, 1974; Tori and Worell, 1973).

In general, each of the strategies has yielded specific, but fairly consistent, conclusions about desensitization, although exceptions can be noted in the literature. Comparison of desensitization against various forms of placebo conditions has usually demonstrated the superiority of this specific technique in alleviating numerous types of evaluative anxiety. The addition of positive instructional sets to the treatment process, however, appears to produce only modest gains in therapeutic effectiveness. Finally, desensitization appears to be more effective when presented as a clinically useful treatment procedure.

Four Components Of Placebo Manipulations. Many of the findings contradictory to these general conclusions are explicable in terms of four components of *placebo manipulations* which influence their effectiveness. These components are (1) credibility of the rationale, (2) context of the therapeutic intervention, (3) extent of the client's anxiety, and (4) complexity of the target behavior.

The first element involves the *credibility of the rationale* presented to participants. Every therapeutic technique is based on a specific theoretical foundation which makes sense to the therapist. Concrete therapeutic operations derive logically from the theory, which also specifies what sorts of changes are expected to occur and how these will come about. One initial task of any therapist is to "sell" the theoretical framework to the client. It is intuitively obvious that certain rationales will make more sense to particular clients than will others. It is also possible, given what we know about placebo influences, that the more believable a client finds the rationale to be, the more effective the therapeutic intervention will be.

In a simple yet brilliantly ingenuous experiment, Borkovec and Nau (1972) began to validate this line of reasoning. They provided college students with the rationales of two "real" therapies (desensitization and implosion) and four placebo treatments, asking them to rate how believable these rationales were. Each subject read two rationales and judged the plausibility of each by answering a series of questions like "How willing would you be to recommend this treatment to a friend?" All possible combinations of the rationales were compared. The participants rated the rationales of the "real" therapies to be the most credible, but they also judged the placebo rationales to be significantly different from one another.

The findings of this study, which were replicated by McGlynn and McDonnell (1974), have some important implications. Borkovec and Nau noted that the placebo used by Paul (1966) was much less credible than the rationale he provided to participants who were desensitized. But, this low-credibility treatment proved to be as effective as insight therapy. A reasonable interpretation of these findings is that some "true" (that is, theoretically based) treatment procedures might not have very plausible rationales. Just because a treatment is derived from a theory does not mean that it will make sense to an individual client. A second consequence of this line of investigation was the discovery that highly plausible placebo treatments are often found to be as effective as desensitization (e.g., Tori and Worell, 1973). Credible placebo manipulations can thus serve as effective interventions in the absence of a theoretical rationale.

A second important component is the *context of the therapeutic intervention*. We have already noted that healing rituals often involve elaborate trappings which are intuitively employed to heighten the sufferer's faith in the treatment process. Contextual features can operate in a wide variety of ways; for example, they can bias the selection of participants for psychotherapy research, particularly the analogue variety, and they can influence the extent to which people being treated show improvement.

The criticism directed against analogue research by Bernstein and

Paul (1971) was based on the contention that few of the participants in these studies were actually phobic. Bernstein (1973) suggested that the assessment of fear of small animals often involves a form of collusion between the subject and the experimenter. Prospective clients are typically screened by having them approach the feared stimulus. Since the subjects have usually indicated that they are fearful before the screening, those who fail the approach test (that is, touch the animal) are likely to lose face. Bernstein provided a graphic illustration of how the context of assessment can influence phobic avoidance behavior.

Women who reported being very afraid of rats were asked to approach and touch a large rodent on two occasions separated by a six-week interval. Assessment for one-half of the sample first occurred in a psychological clinic and was similar to the procedure typically used to screen potential clients for therapy analogue research. The remaining women were first tested in a laboratory setting. These participants were told that telepathic influences on subhuman behavior were being investigated, and they were urged to approach the rat and telepathically direct it to press a bar in its cage. They were allowed to hold the animal if they wished. On the first assessment, 97 percent of the presumably fearful women actually handled the rat in the laboratory setting. In the clinic, only 79 percent of the women touched the rat. Bernstein also found that the degree of self-reported fear was a significant predictor of behavioral manifestations of anxiety and extent of approach. Women who reported being very afraid were observed to be more anxious and stayed farther away from the rat than subjects who had rated their fear as less intense. These consistent relationships, however, were noted *only in the clinical setting.*

McCardel and Murray (1974) provided a striking demonstration of the impact contextual features can have on promoting personality growth. In their study, three differently structured weekend sensitivity-encounter groups were held on a beautiful island off the Florida coast. Participants in these groups completed a series of questionnaires which measured various aspects of personality integration both before and after group sessions. They reported that participants in the group experience manifested significantly more personal growth than was noted in control subjects who remained at home. This finding by itself suggests that encounter groups represent an effective method of fostering beneficial change.

A fourth group was included in this study, however, which per-mitted an entirely different conclusion to be drawn. Members of this group also spent a weekend on the island and were led to believe that they were participating in an encounter group experience. In reality, these people engaged in no group exercises and, instead, spent their time in recreational activities such as dancing and volleyball. McCardel and Murray reported that these individuals also manifested significant personality growth to the extent that they were indistinguishable from those who had participated in the encounter group activities.

A third important element that needs to be considered is the *extent of the client's anxiety*. Practicing therapists generally view a moderate degree of initial client discomfort as an important determi-nant of successful therapy. Clients who are judged to be nonanxious are often undependable and frequently terminate from therapy prema-turely. Overwhelming anxiety, on the other hand, may render the client incapable of engaging in therapeutic discussion, thereby making inter-vention less effective. Reviews of analogue investigations (Bernstein and Paul, 1971; Borkovec, 1973) have suggested that placebo treatments may be less effective with highly fearful individuals, when anxiety is manifested by high autonomic reactivity. Contradictory research find-ings do exist, however.

One source of confusion on this topic resides in how anxiety is measured. Anxiety is a complex phenomenon which may be assessed in many different ways. One useful conceptual framework is to view mani-festations of anxiety as being measurable through three fairly indepen-dent channels. An individual may report feeling anxious in an interview or on a questionnaire, may show noticeable shifts in physiological func-tions, and may be observed to avoid certain situations or to manifest a decline in performance.

Borkovec (1973) has suggested that the extent of conditioned autonomic reactivity is likely to be one critical mediating factor in determining the success of a therapeutic intervention. Placebo manipu-lations seem to produce greater changes in self-reported and observable performance outcome measures. Physiological manifestations of anxiety are less susceptible to nonspecific placebo influences. Results of a comparative investigation of desensitization and study-counseling pro-cedures in alleviating examination anxiety (Allen, 1971) illustrate Borkovec's point. In this study, the effects of four therapeutic interven-

169

tions were assessed by having participants fill out anxiety question-naires just prior to taking examinations before and after treatment. Physiological measures of heart rate and palmar sweating were collected at the same time. Performance changes were measured by analyzing test scores and semester grades.

One of the conditions involved a seemingly credible placebo manipulation in which participants played a variation of the quiz game, "College Bowl." The rationale of this treatment was that exposure to testlike questions in a nonevaluative, gamelike atmosphere would im-prove the participant's ability to focus on the relevant dimensions of test questions in real-life examination situations. Subjects in this condi-tion reported reductions in self-reported anxiety of a magnitude found for participants who were desensitized, who received intensive instruc-tion on improving their study skills, or who received a combination of the latter two interventions. The placebo procedure also produced signi-ficant improvement in college grades, but it did not reduce physio-logically measured anxiety.

The final component that deserves our attention is the *complex-ity of the target behavior*. Psychotherapy is most often aimed at resolv-ing specific difficulties clients encounter. Successfully solving problems requires that therapists attend to both motivational and behavior or skill issues. The prospect of changing, even in adaptive ways, is often frightening to clients. The development of new patterns of action in-volves taking risks and frequently increases the likelihood that others will make new demands on the client. One common element found in all therapeutic systems is providing support to bolster the client's cour-age to risk changing.

Willingness to change is a necessary but not sufficient condition for fostering improvement, however. The client must possess the skills necessary to accomplish meaningful change. A second common helping operation found in all therapeutic systems is the provision of some sort of skill training, although the mechanisms for accomplishing this vary markedly across existing "schools" of psychotherapy. In psycho-analytic and client-centered systems indirect forms of interpersonal feedback are employed, while Gestalt and behavior therapists use more direct training strategies.

Placebo manipulations often provide people with an "excuse" for discarding maladaptive patterns of interaction. That is, they provide a motivational basis for changing. Their effectiveness, however, depends upon two additional factors—the requisite skills already possessed by the client or information contained within the placebo that specifies how such skills can be developed. Both Bernstein (1973) and Borkovec (1976) suggest that placebo manipulations which incorporate simple demands for change are relatively less effective in promoting the acquisition of complex interpersonal skills than they are in reducing fears that are measured in terms of approach. Walking toward a caged snake is a simpler response than emitting behaviors that identify one as an attractive dating partner. It is also considerably less risky since approach tests are conducted in safe laboratory situations. The placebo manipulation employed by Allen (1971) was effective partly because the student participants already had demonstrated that they had enough study-skill abilities to survive their freshman year.

Interaction Of The Four Components. In real-life therapy situations, these four components interact in complex ways. The complexity of the target behavior is mediated by credibility of rationale, contextual features, clients' anxiety level, and channel of assessment employed. Slutsky and Allen (1977) illustrated how these features interact in an investigation of desensitization and placebo effects on public speaking anxiety. In this study, the screening and assessment procedures employed by Paul (1966) were used. After an initial assessment, participants were assigned to receive desensitization, a highly credible placebo, or no treatment. For half of the subjects, treatment was described as therapy and conducted in a clinical setting. Although identical treatment strategies were used with the remaining participants, they were told that the procedures involved a method for experimentally investigating basic fear processes. These subjects, who were treated in a laboratory setting, reported seeing little therapeutic relevance in either the desensitization or the placebo treatments.

Slutsky and Allen reported that desensitization was effective in reducing public speaking anxiety, regardless of the context in which it was administered. Even though laboratory-treated participants believed that the procedure would not have beneficial effects, in actuality, it did. The placebo manipulation, however, proved to be as effective as desensitization, but only in the clinical context. When administered in the laboratory setting, its effects were indistinguishable from those found in the no-treatment conditions. The superiority of desensitization was particularly evident on physiological indices of anxiety, particularly when compared to the laboratory placebo treatment.

Exploitation Of Expectancy And Placebo Influences. Attempts to cope with nonspecific placebo and expectancy influences has led to much knowledge about specific components of placebo manipulations. This knowledge has, in turn, led to the exploitation of placebo effects on two fronts. Some investigators have worked to develop effective treatments from placebo manipulations that were designed to affect client expectancies. Often these strategies are more efficient in terms of therapist involvement than are more traditional procedures. In Allen's (1971) study, test-anxious participants received 10.5 hours of therapeutic intervention. Meichenbaum and Smart (1971) were able to produce substantial improvement in the grades of borderline freshmen through a much less costly expectancy manipulation. In their study, 43 students were divided into three groups, two of which were invited to participate in psychological testing. Members of one group were informed that, on the basis of their test data, they could be considered "late bloomers." Although their academic performance had gotten off to a shaky start, they could expect to show substantial improvement in the near future. The second group was informed that no reliable predictions about their subsequent academic performance could be made.

The "late bloomers" showed greater academic improvement than did either those who were tested and given ambiguous feedback or those who were not tested. In addition, even though no differences in such functional academic behaviors as visiting professors for help or study skills existed between the groups, the "late bloomers" reported believing that their courses were more relevant to their careers and that they found them more interesting.

Other investigators have sought to optimize the matching of clients to therapists by exploiting expectancy and placebo influences. Some form of intuitive matching is carried out at practically all existing treatment facilities. These matches are often not optimal ones, however, because they are heavily influenced by power and status factors within the organization. It is not unusual for the least experienced clinicians to be assigned the most difficult cases.

Optimal matching depends upon identifying *functional* characteristics of both the therapist and client and devising methods to adequately measure them. Goldstein (1975) offered five general elements of a potentially successful therapist-client match:

1. Both participants agree in general about their rights and responsibilities during therapy.
2. Both participants have optimistic expectations about the outcome of therapy.
3. Both participants come from similar socio-economic, racial, and educational backgrounds.
4. Both participants are similar on a variety of personal dimensions, such as flexibility and social awareness.
5. The needs of both participants in terms of exerting power, providing support, and so on are complementary.

Although much has been done to harness emerging knowledge about expectancy and placebo influences to improve the efficacy of therapy, much remains to be accomplished. The relational nature of psychotherapy makes the isolation of functionally relevant characteristics of the therapist and client a difficult process. Systematic inquiry based on simplification strategies does, however, provide a more secure base for enhancing therapeutic effectiveness than has hitherto been possible.

By far the most systematic inquiry into the exploitation of placebo and expectancy factors has been Goldstein's (1971, 1975) research on ways to facilitate mutual interpersonal attraction between the therapist and the client. Goldstein (1975) describes eight strategies for enhancing the therapeutic relationship by fostering mutual liking, respect, and trust between the participants. These elements have the consequences of increasing open and honest communication between therapist and client. The ultimate product of increasing the client's persuasibility is adaptive change.

Borrowing heavily from the work of humanistic (primarily nondirective) clinicians in his focus on the enhancing effects of warmth and empathy, Goldstein has devised specific training packages to teach such skills. In addition, he has been heavily influenced by the social-psychological literature on modeling, imitation, communicator credibility, and expectancy and placebo influences. For example, he describes one simple strategy called *direct structuring*, which is similar to the therapeutic manipulation employed by Meichenbaum and Smart.

Direct structuring simply involves suggesting to a client that she will like the therapist and benefit from therapy. This may be accomplished by simply telling the client that the therapist will be liked, describing some positive characteristics of the clinician, or clarifying what the client might expect to happen during the initial interview. This last strategy is a particularly important one because the therapeutic process is so ambiguous to many people.

LIMITATIONS IMPOSED BY TIME

How Therapeutic Time Is Used

Like all human activities, psychotherapy is bounded by temporal limitations. It is not the passage of time by itself that has relevance for psychotherapy, however. Rather, it is what is done during the time spent in therapy. Our analysis of temporal factors has three aspects. First, we will be concerned with schemes that describe various stages of therapy. Next, our attention will be directed toward how long people stay in therapy. Finally, we will compare the benefits that derive from time-limited versus open-ended interventions.

Psychotherapy obviously has a starting point, middle, and, hopefully, an end. Unfortunately, this scheme tells us nothing about the processes that take place during therapy. The few writers (e.g., Wolberg, 1967) who prefer to categorize the phases of therapy in this way point out that different strategies need to be implemented at each of these stages. Developing an open and trusting relationship requires different types of activity on the part of the clinician than does confrontation or preparing the client for termination.

Identification Of Stages And Processes. The precise nature of the operations involved in bringing about therapeutic change differ depending upon one's theoretical inclinations. Most of the frameworks that describe stages in the therapy process are based on specific and concrete therapeutic operations. For this reason, little correspondence exists between various schemes. White (1956), for example, divides therapy into five stages: (1) establishing a relationship, (2) exploring problems, (3) promoting expression of feelings, (4) facilitating transference, and (5) noting behavior change. White's description of psychotherapy is obviously based on the psychoanalytic model that was dominant at the time he was writing. He clearly indicated that transference is the most crucial aspect of the process; he paid little attention to the social influence mechanisms that bring about behavior change. This was not to White's discredit; at that time, little was known about these processes.

Operating from a much more sophisticated technological base, Brammer (1973) describes eight stages in the therapy process. In this scheme, transference itself is accorded only secondary importance. It is viewed as one possible outgrowth of exploring problems and expressing feelings. Brammer notes that each stage involves specific sets of therapeutic operations, which he describes in detail.

One particularly interesting scheme has been presented by Carkhuff and Berenson (1967), who describe therapy as having two distinctive aspects: (1) downward and inward and (2) upward and outward. The initial phase, involving **downward and inward** strategies, is aimed at developing a good working relationship with the client. The therapist endeavors to build an atmosphere of trust and respect while gathering information related to the client's difficulties. A major concern during this period is providing the client with the support needed to attempt making changes.

The second phase involves the implementation of operations designed to move the client **upward** and **outward**. The goal here is to provide the client with skills that will enable her to function autonomously. The therapist often adopts a more confrontive posture in an attempt to challenge the client to change. An important part of this phase is providing necessary skills to the client. Many of the strategies associated with achieving the goal of autonomy involve active problem solving as a collaborative endeavor between the therapist and client. Several of the major approaches will be examined in Chapter 7.

One especially useful feature of the framework provided by Carkhuff and Berenson (1967) is that it can be used to classify different theoretical approaches to psychotherapy. These writers pointed out that several psychodynamic approaches, particularly psychoanalysis, do not provide the client with coping strategies to move upward and outward. Psychoanalysts, for example, often view treatment as successful when the client nears the end of the downward and inward sequence, that is, achieves insight.

More recent schemes, such as the one presented by Brammer, possess a more technological emphasis than was found in earlier ones. Description of complex processes in very general terms (e.g., establishing a relationship) has been replaced by more precise specification of what the therapist must do to achieve therapeutic goals. This emphasis holds the promise that increasingly more effective methods of training therapists can be continually developed.

Length Of Time In Therapy

Therapeutic intervention is an open-ended affair in that it is impossible to make a general statement about how long an individual will need to remain in treatment. At one extreme, meaningful reduction of distress may occur after a single interview (Goldstein, 1962). At the other, no substantial improvement may be noted after several years of therapy (Grinspoon, Ewalt, and Shader, 1968). Length of therapeutic contact depends upon many of the complex interactional factors we have already described, including characteristics of the client and therapist, the expectations each hold about how long therapy should last, the nature, severity, and duration of the problems clients bring in, and the type of treatment strategies employed.

Investigations Showing Great Variability. Much research has been devoted to this issue, despite the formidable problems that are involved. One clear conclusion that can be drawn from this line of inquiry is that the amount of time people spend in therapy varies to an incredible extent. Contradictions in the literature abound, as indicated in Figure 9. This graph provides information about the mean and median number of visits made by various patient groups. The National Center for Health Statistics (1966) reported that the average number of therapeutic contacts made by close to one million Americans during a one-year period was only 4.7.

Garfield and Kurz (1952) found that 67 percent of the people who entered therapy at a Veterans Administration Clinic terminated before the tenth session, with the median termination occurring between the sixth and seventh session. Garfield (1971), in a comprehensive review, indicated that this figure was an accurate reflection of the attrition rate at facilities around the country. Strupp, Fox, and Lessler (1969) reported that the respondents to their survey of clinic patients had attended an average of 70.4 hours of therapy. This figure is a grossly inflated estimate of attrition for several reasons. Respondents were selected on the basis of having completed at least 25 sessions, and they did not compose a representative sample of the clinic population. An initial survey of private practitioners by Strupp et al. (1969) indicated that their patients averaged 166 sessions over a 28-month period.

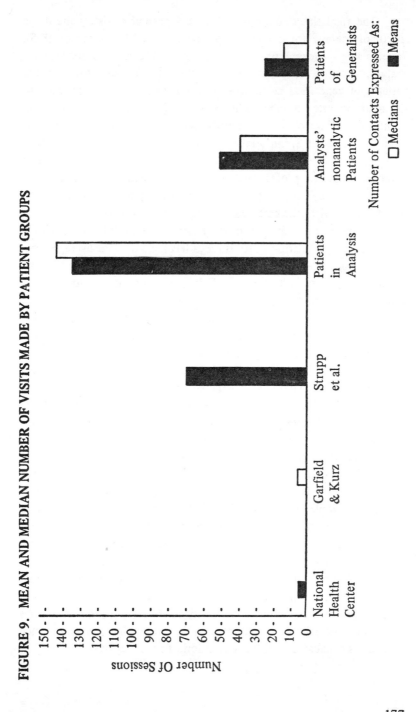

FIGURE 9. MEAN AND MEDIAN NUMBER OF VISITS MADE BY PATIENT GROUPS

177

The final three columns of Figure 9 present statistics about the length of therapy for the patient groups analyzed by Marmor (1975). Patients in psychoanalysis averaged close to 140 visits annually, non-analytic patients of psychoanalysts averaged 51 sessions, and the patients of generalists averaged only 26 sessions. When contrasted to the attrition rates found in clinics, these figures clearly suggest that clients who utilize public and private helping resources live in different worlds. In Chapter 3, important differences in the three patient groups delineated by Marmor were noted. A substantial majority of those in psychoanalysis had professional or high-level managerial positions and earned over $20,000 per year. Those possessing such attributes composed a minority of the caseload of psychiatric generalists.

Figure 9 contains one other relationship of interest. A fairly general finding of attrition rate surveys has been that the average number of sessions attended is higher than the median number. The last two columns demonstrate this point. This occurs because a minority of people remain in therapy for an extended period of time, while a majority terminate after a lesser number of sessions. Interestingly, this general trend is reversed for the patients in psychoanalysis. Figure 10 presents Marmor's data in a way that illustrates the distribution of therapy contacts reported for the three patient groups. As can be seen, a majority of the patients of generalists terminate from therapy before the twentieth session, and a majority of the nonanalytic patients of psychoanalysts terminate before the fiftieth session. In contrast, only 10 percent of those in analysis have terminated by the fiftieth session, while 22 percent are seen at least 200 times during a year.

Relevance Of Termination To Expectancy. These findings have relevance for the issue of premature termination that was discussed in Chapter 5. People appear to have very definite expectations about how long therapy should last. Most people expect therapy to involve brief intervention, and for these individuals, therapy usually does. Both analysts and their patients expect psychoanalysis to take an extensive amount of time, and, again, the actual time investment reflects this belief. In fact, psychoanalysis treatment is the one therapeutic intervention that seems impervious to reality constraints. Termination from therapy can be accurately predicted by knowing when one's insurance coverage is exhausted, with the exception of psychoanalysis.

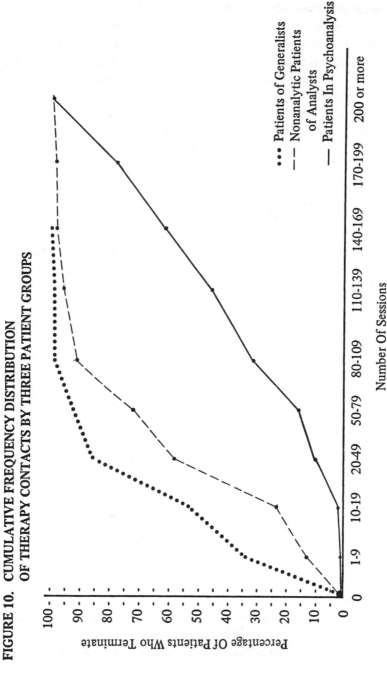

FIGURE 10.   CUMULATIVE FREQUENCY DISTRIBUTION OF THERAPY CONTACTS BY THREE PATIENT GROUPS

Percentage Of Patients Who Terminate

100 -
90 -
80 -
70 -
60 -
50 -
40 -
30 -
20 -
10 -
0

Number Of Sessions

0   1-9   10-19   20-49   50-79   80-109   110-139   140-169   170-199   200 or more

••• Patients of Generalists
– – Nonanalytic Patients of Analysts
—— Patients In Psychoanalysis

Adapted from J. Marmor, *Psychiatrists and their patients*, 1975; with permission from the American Psychiatric Association.

179

Time-Limited Versus Open-Ended Therapy

Movement Toward Short-Term Therapies. Since the time Freud's initial followers began to break away from psychoanalytic orthodoxy, psychotherapists have been concerned with making psychotherapy more efficient as well as more effective. With the possible exception of some classical psychoanalysts, therapists of all theoretical persuasions are embracing short-term therapies as treatments of choice for an increasing number of difficulties. For both logical and practical reasons, there is much to recommend short-term therapy over more open-ended interventions.

Imposing a specific time limit on therapy forces the participants to stay focused on the specific problems the client possesses. The highly structured nature of short-term therapy facilitates collaboration between therapist and client, thus making the latter a more active change agent. Because discrete problems are the focus of intervention, changes can be closely monitored. This enables the therapist to pinpoint ineffective strategies before much time has elapsed and devise potentially more helpful ones.

The practical benefits from the client's point of view are obvious. Structured short-term treatment can result in substantial financial savings. The problem-solving focus can supply the client with relief from stressful debilitations and can provide effective coping strategies for handling problems that arise in the future. About the only criticism of short-term approaches which can be made on theoretical grounds would be to argue that such intervention produces only illusory improvement in one's symptoms. A variant of this argument would be that short-term approaches are unlikely to bring about extensive personality reorganization in people who have been unable to cope with pervasive, long-standing difficulties.

Such theoretical criticisms appear to have little merit. On one hand, they often involve circular reasoning. Long-term difficulties are often defined as those which do not respond to brief intervention, thereby making short-term therapy *by definition* inappropriate for these sorts of problems. On the other hand, we have already noted that most people enter therapy because they cannot adequately cope with the demands imposed by their daily routines. We also have seen that most people expect therapy to last only a short time.

Studies Comparing Short-Term And Long-Term Therapies. The few direct comparisons of brief and longer-term therapies for assorted neurotic outpatients suggest that the former produce at least as much improvement as does open-ended intervention. Shlien, Mosak, and Dreikurs (1962) compared client-centered and Adlerian therapy provided within a limitation of 20 interviews against unlimited interventions that averaged 37 sessions. They found that the briefer therapies produced equivalent improvement to the open-ended ones and obviously produced it more quickly.

Muench (1965) reported that both "short-term" (3 to 7 sessions) and "time-limited" (8 to 19 sessions) therapy were more effective than treatment lasting 20 or more sessions. He also noted that, although improvement was not related to therapist skill or to the extent of clients' pathology, ratings of change by the therapists were discrepant with test data that were used to measure improvement. The results of this study document the contention made earlier about differences between how clients and therapists judge the effective ingredients of therapy. For the clients in Muench's study, more therapy was not better, but his therapists made just the opposite judgment.

Both studies we have mentioned failed to include independent behavioral assessments of client functioning. This has been a very common omission in research comparing various time limits on therapy, with the exception of investigations conducted by behaviorally oriented clinicians. In a review of this topic, however, Luborsky, Singer, and Luborsky (1976) concluded that differences in time limits had no differential effects on outcome. In five of the eight investigations they examined, no differences between brief and open-ended interventions were found; two favored brief therapy; and one favored longer-term treatment. In this latter study (Henry and Shlien, 1958) clients in brief therapy were found to be inferior on a single dimension that was measured by a projective test.

At present, experimental evidence that favors short-term therapy is largely circumstantial. Logically, however, it seems fair to conclude that brief interventions are often the treatment of choice, since they produce benefits that are equivalent to those provided by longer-term intervention. Highly structured, short-term prescriptive interventions definitely are useful with people from the lower socio-economic strata (Goldstein, 1973).

COMMON ELEMENTS IN THE THERAPEUTIC PROCESS

Efforts To Identify Interlocking Theories
And Merging Concepts

Since the pioneering conceptual work of Frank (1961), a great deal of effort has been directed toward specifying basic elements common to all therapeutic approaches. In Chapter 3, we reviewed attempts to accomplish this goal by defining the operations deriving from one therapeutic orientation as being *really* based on operations stemming from other theories. We concluded that arguments, such as "psychotherapy is really behavior therapy," "psychoanalysis is nothing more than operant conditioning," or "systematic desensitization is effective because it activates unconscious merging fantasies," did not add anything to our understanding of basic therapeutic processes. Further, we concluded that attempts to combine competing systems of psychotherapy (e.g., behavioral psychoanalysis) confuse some similarities in concrete technique with essential philosophical differences.

Efforts To Identify Consistencies In Activities

A considerably more profitable approach has involved seeking consistencies in the activities of clinicians which transcend their specific theoretical orientations. Often, common elements are masked by differences in the vocabularies used by therapists with competing theoretical inclinations. Nonetheless, a number of similarities have been discovered by clinicians who operate within an anthropological (Frank, 1961, 1971, 1976; Torrey, 1972) or a linguistic analysis (Bandler and Grinder, 1975; Watzlawick, Beavin, and Jackson, 1967) framework, as well as those who view therapy as a general interpersonal influence process (Marmor, 1976).

Foundations Of Language And Power. Two common foundations underlie all therapeutic encounters. They are language and power. Communication provides the basis for establishing a relationship, providing a treatment rationale, understanding what the client experiences, and assessing change. Psychotherapy without language is impossible to imagine. Skilled therapists have a great deal of respect for the communication process. Communication is rarely simple and straightforward. Words are abstractions from experience; as such, they are often ambiguous. Everyone knows that it is impossible to communicate the full meaning of one's experience to others through words. Language also directs perception and determines human action. What we perceive and how we act are limited by our ability to conceive via language.

Linguistic analysis of psychotherapy (Bandler and Grinder, 1975; Watzlawick et al., 1967) indicates that one common task among all clinicians involves bringing to light hidden meanings in the surface structure of the client's statements. Therapists engage in a very active form of listening. They attend to the *content* of what is being said, and, even more importantly, they analyze the *process* of communication itself. Verbal statements are interpreted within a context of associated cues, including body movements and vocal characteristics. In addition, overall reciprocal patterns of communication are analyzed. A therapist might notice, for example, that statements which imply a client is responsible for making himself miserable are typically followed by an attack on the therapist's competence. The content of the attack can vary widely—the client may declare that the therapist "doesn't understand," may argue that therapy is not helping, or may state that he is incapable of benefitting from therapy. Despite this variability in surface structure or the overt content of what is being said, a common pattern exists in the communication process. Skilled therapists seek to discover these processes and turn them into content. In our example, the clinician might say "Every time I suggest that you are making yourself unhappy, you seem to get angry" and then document this perception with examples. By doing this, the therapist and client can now communicate openly (in terms of content) about an issue that was formerly hidden.

We move to the second common foundation of therapeutic encounters: *power*. Differences in the relative amount of power held by therapists and clients exist in all therapeutic systems. The therapist has access to five sources of power within the therapeutic context (French and Raven, 1959). The social sanctioning of therapists as professional healers and helpers invests them with **legitimate power**. They are granted legal privileges that nonprofessionals do not possess. The specialized knowledge possessed by the professional provides that person with **expert power**. The therapist is usually viewed as being responsible for prescribing the specific operations which presumably would benefit the client.

These socially derived sources of influence give therapists three more personally relevant types of power. The dependency position occupied by clients, together with their desire to obtain help from the therapist, provides the latter with both **reward power** and **coercive power.** Cooperation by the client can be reinforced by the clinician, and noncompliance can be punished in a variety of ways. These two sources of power provide the basis for the operant conditioning that occurs in all forms of psychotherapy, even the most nondirective types (Truax, 1966b). Finally, the therapist frequently comes to serve as a model of adjustment for the client, thus acquiring **referent power.** This source of power provides a foundation for the therapist's ability to use persuasion effectively.

Four Elements In All Psychotherapy. The foundations of language and power support four basic elements found in all forms of psychotherapy (Frank, 1976). Figure 11 shows these four elements and six associated functions they have in the helping process, according to Frank. All socially sanctioned healing involves a **professional relationship,** regardless of whether the healer is a witch doctor, a psychoanalyst, or a behavior therapist. Effective intervention depends upon establishing a relationship that is based on mutual trust and respect.

Intervention is carried out in **impressive settings** which people generally associate with getting effective help. In his discussion of the "edifice complex," Torrey (1972) pointed out that elaborate trappings are an integral part of all professional healing endeavors. The specific type of adornments associated with effective helping must make sense in terms of their cultural context. Treating a phobia by having a witch doctor wear a ceremonial mask and dance around is not likely to provide relief to a fear-crazed resident of New York City, but it is likely to be effective wherever people generally believe the witch doctor has magical powers.

All therapeutic treatment strategies derive part (and in some cases seemingly all) of their effectiveness from the **credibility of their rationale.** The client is provided with an explanatory framework for understanding how the problem developed, and how it can be alleviated. Torrey (1972), in describing this as the "principle of Rumpelstiltskin," suggests that the very act of labelling an individual's dysfunction is therapeutic in itself. The manipulation of the clients' expectancies about future academic performance by Meichenbaum and Smart (1971) illustrates the power that resides in the labelling process.

FIGURE 11. COMMON FOUNDATIONS, ELEMENTS, AND FUNCTIONS FOUND IN ALL PSYCHOTHERAPIES

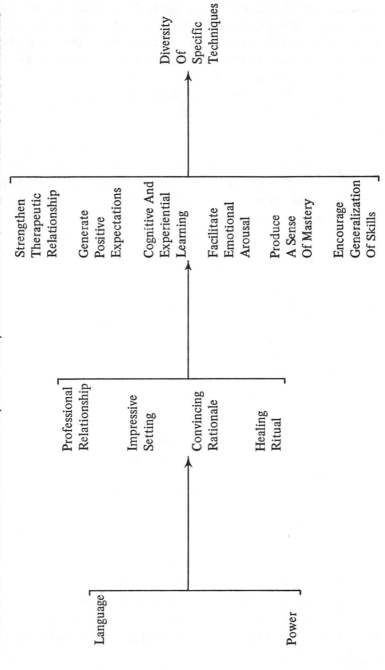

Finally, all therapeutic interventions contain some **healing ritual**. This may consist of chants to various gods, free association, feedback in a group, or systematic desensitization. Like the covering rationale, the ritual must be convincing to the client and must make sense within the cultural context in which it is employed. Our discussion of placebo manipulations illustrates this point.

Six Functions Common To All Psychotherapy. Frank suggests that these four elements combine to produce six therapeutic functions that are common to all systems of therapy (See Figure 11).

1. *They activate therapeutically healing aspects of the relationship.* Being accepted into therapy often reduces an individual's sense of isolation and demoralization. Marmor (1976) suggests that simply being able to talk about one's difficulties in a confidential relationship produces a release of pent up tension.

2. *They generate and maintain positive expectations.* Frank suggests that entry into therapy causes the general affective states of faith and hope to be channeled into more specific expectations. Emotional support provided by the therapist serves to facilitate hope, while the acquisition of new coping skills (or even of insight) helps to strengthen it.

3. *They promote cognitive and experiential learning.* All therapists provide the client with new ways to conceptualize the influences that molded him. Differences between therapeutic systems exist with regard to how directly this information is imparted to the client. In psychoanalysis and in some humanistic therapies, learning is quite indirect; in behavioral interventions, coping strategies are actively taught. Frank points out that, while the learning situation is often structured by the therapist through provision of a rationale, the actual learning process involves activity by the client. Marmor (1976) describes one kind of learning that takes place in therapy as involving *operant conditioning*. This may occur directly or through transmission of more subtle reinforcements and punishments by means of selective attention or interpretations of the client's behavior.

4. *They lead to emotional arousal.* Although behavior therapists generally de-emphasize the role of emotional arousal in therapy, Frank indicates that affective shifts supply the client with motivation to engage in constructive change. One central feature of

demoralization is helplessness. A client who is helped to exchange affects like pathos or anger (both of which contain elements of self-acceptance) for pathological resignation is likely to begin taking courageous risks during therapy.

5. *They foster a sense of mastery and increased self-control.* Working from a foundation of support, therapists of all theoretical inclinations begin to actively challenge the client to change. Torrey's (1972) "principle of Rumpelstiltskin" is based on the premise that being able to name an influence provides a sense of control over it. Once the client begins to attempt changes, success experiences often help establish a benign cycle whereby the client continues to change. Behavior therapists have been particularly active in developing strategies that help insure the success of any attempt at change.

6. *They encourage the generalization of new skills to the larger environment.* As is true with the other five functions, the concrete strategies for implementing this component differ across therapeutic approaches. Within all systems of therapy, however, dialogue between the therapist and client enables the latter to engage in a good deal of reality testing. Clients are encouraged to try out certain ways of acting, "think about" things in new ways, and, in some instances, are asked to carry out homework assignments.

FINAL WORDS

Our analysis of the components that combine to produce a therapeutic encounter points to the sterility of the many uniformity myths that continue to surround psychotherapy. Many of these myths are an offshoot of theoretical pretentiousness. Certain types of therapy are touted as better than other types on a priori theoretical grounds that have no functional utility. Some psychoanalysts (e.g., Tarachow, 1963) would have us believe that psychoanalysis is a superior form of treatment to run-of-the-mill psychotherapy. Some behavior therapists (e.g., Wolpe, 1976a, b) would have us believe that their approach combines all that is good in other forms of psychotherapy with a truly scientific technology that the others do not possess. Others, of various theoretical persuasions, accuse behavior therapists of being cold and manipulative technologists.

Empirical inquiry has yielded much valuable information about the functional relationships that actually exist between clients and therapists within specific settings and definite temporal parameters. In the process of uncovering these relationships, an increasing number of such uniformity myths are being destroyed. The complex interactional nature of these relationships makes it unlikely that one therapeutic system will prove to be superior to others *in general*. Luborsky et al. (1976) reached just this conclusion after comparing (1) client-centered versus other traditional psychotherapies, and (2) behavior therapy versus psychotherapy. In both cases, they reached the verdict that "everybody has won and all must have prizes," (p. 12) after judging pertinent research studies as favoring one or the other approach or as indicating no differences between approaches.

Out of five studies comparing client-centered and other theoretical interventions, four suggested that no differences existed, and one favored a dynamically oriented treatment. Behavior therapy investigations that excluded college student samples fared somewhat better. They proved to produce superior outcomes when compared to other approaches in 6 of 18 investigations, with no differences being noted in the remaining 12 studies. Luborsky et al., however, questioned the methodological adequacy of five of these six studies. The best controlled investigation to date (Sloane et al., 1975) indicated that behavior therapists and more traditionally trained clinicians were equally effective in dealing with an assortment of "neurotic" dysfunctions.

The clients in the Sloane et al. investigation also had some interesting things to say about the unattractive stereotype of the "typical" behavior therapist's personal characteristics. Behavioral clinicians were judged to be as warm and as accepting as the psychodynamic therapists and were rated as showing higher levels of congruence, personal disclosure, and accurate empathy. The only differences between the two clinician groups dealt with the way strategic issues were handled. Behavior therapists spent twice as much time talking during therapy and tended to give more explicit advice and direction than did dynamic therapists.

Given the complexity of the interactions involved in psychotherapy as well as the undeniably strong influence exerted by setting factors, failures to find evidence that supports uniformity beliefs should not be surprising. It would be unfair, however, to argue that psychotherapy is nothing more than the operation of nonspecific curative influences that reside in either the client or the setting. Such influences are nonspecific only to the extent that we remain ignorant of their functional response-contingent properties. Empirical inquiry has enabled us to specify many of these formerly nonspecific influences and harness their effects to improve both the efficiency and the effectiveness of the helping process.

7
Emerging Perspectives

The interpersonal influences that occur during a therapy session are very complex. The clinician must try to understand and direct them to benefit the client. As a therapist gains experience, she typically develops a more sensitive, intuitive "feel" for how these factors affect the course of therapy. These intuitions, in turn, influence the specific activities of the clinician. This aspect of psychotherapy has long been considered artistic.

This chapter will deal with four frameworks involving interpersonal influence in the therapy setting. They are (1) the problem-solving process, (2) attributional analysis, (3) self-evaluative and interpersonal games, and (4) the language of the body. These four frameworks have emerged from artistic clinical intuitions, but they are moving into the realm of scientific endeavor as empirical investigations provide better understanding of them and lead to more skillful use.

PROBLEMS IN APPLYING EMPIRICAL METHODOLOGY
TO THESE FRAMEWORKS

Use Of Terms
Applying empirical methodology to these frameworks has not been a simple task for several reasons. Some of these reasons will be amplified later in the chapter, but we will introduce them here.

First, most of the response-contingent functional relationships between events that occur in therapy are masked by theoretical language. The conceptualizations employed to describe events in therapy (e.g., transference, resistance, accurate empathy) are relational terms. Describing what occurs between the therapist and client as having "broken through a resistance" masks the functional behavioral interactions between the participants. These relationships are masked by describing them with theoretically derived terms, and they are totally obscured when such terms are used as explanations of what has occurred.

Levels Of Interaction

A second problem is that many concrete therapeutic operations are extremely complex, thus making them difficult to define and to reliably measure from an observer's viewpoint. Experienced clinicians frequently analyze their interactions with clients on three levels. On an *overt* level, they respond to the *content* provided by the client. Although overt content is the easiest material to reliably assess, it is often the least important from the viewpoint of the practicing clinician. On a higher level of abstraction, therapists pay attention to the *process* of communication, analyzing this process in terms of recurring interactive patterns. This is considerably more difficult to reliably observe. The most abstract level of analysis involves making sense of *metacommunications*.

Language is a set of symbols for describing experience and a set of rules for combining the symbols. **Meta-language** is the analysis of a linguistic system through use of another symbolic system. **Meta-communication** is taking some of the process inherent in language and turning it into content by discussing it. Since we shall examine meta-communication in detail shortly, for now, we need simply be aware that language can cause many paradoxes in interpersonal relationships. For example, a person who says, "I do not want to be the leader; you be the leader," is giving up the leadership role on an overt level of communication. On a meta-level, however, that individual is actually being the leader because she is directing others.

Paradoxes In Power

In psychotherapy, there are several paradoxes involved in the distribution of power between the therapist and the client. The induction of clients, many of whom have problems relating to dependency, into a dependent relationship which is aimed at fostering independence is perhaps the basic paradox of psychotherapy. This paradox is further complicated by the implicit equation of therapist power and therapist responsibility. Thus, clients often expect to be "treated" (that is, have things done to them by the therapist) while maintaining a passive, uncommitted, or even antagonistic stance toward the therapeutic process. Most therapists, however, readily admit that "treating" someone without that person's active involvement is beyond their ability. When faced with an "uncommitted" client, many therapists will give up by pointing out that there is nothing they can do to make the client change. This strategy is a paradoxical one since it is designed to maneuver the client into accepting responsibility. On a meta-level, the therapist is attempting to gain reward, coercive, and referent power by ostensibly giving these up to the client.

Haley (1963; 1969a, b) has provided insightful analyses of how power paradoxes operate within the major systems of psychotherapy. In psychoanalysis, the client is forced into a "one-down" (or inferior) position compared to the therapist. The client lies on a couch and free associates to a listener who is out of sight and provides little or no feedback. Attempts by the client to go "one up", (e.g., force the therapist to take care of him) on the analyst are met with silence or interpreted as defensive resistances. Power paradoxes in humanistic therapies are even more subtle because the vocabulary of humanistic therapists (e.g., growth, self-actualization, integration, and differentiation) emphasizes self-determination by the client. Yet, even nondirective therapy, according to Haley (1963) is directive on a meta-level because the therapist directs or specifies that it is to be nondirective.

Emergence Of Research Efforts

This discussion of meta-communication and paradoxes in therapy implies that these components would be very difficult to assess in a reliable manner. Nonetheless, they are undoubtedly important ones to consider in our attempt to understand psychotherapy. Of the four frameworks that we will present in this chapter, only the first one, which deals with problem-solving strategies in therapy, does not involve some form of paradoxical communication. It is probably not coincidental that this particular framework has generated more empirical research than have the others. Research on the other three frameworks has begun to emerge in the last decade and is currently having an increasing impact on therapeutic practices. Even the problem-solving framework, however, has its artistic aspects. In fact, the complex interaction between therapeutic art and science can be clearly seen in all four frameworks.

THE PROBLEM-SOLVING PROCESS

Origin And Nature Of The Process

Although behavior therapists have been most vehemently accused of capitalizing on power as a source of influence in psychotherapy, they have been among the most ardent supporters of the problem-solving orientation which seeks to minimize power and status differences between therapist and client. Although the roots of this approach extend to the educational pragmatism of John Dewey, its first systematic clinical application can be traced to Kelly's (1955) conceptualization of psychotherapy as a collaborative undertaking. Kelly believed that people attempt to deal with problems in a manner similar to the empirical methods of hypothesis building and experimentation used by scientists. The goal of therapy was to combine the therapist's general expert knowledge about change mechanisms and processes with the client's expertise about her own life to derive workable intervention strategies. This process demands the active involvement of both participants.

Coping Skills. Even though the importance of problem-solving has been acknowledged in the writings of client-centered and psychodynamic therapists (e.g., Carkhuff and Berenson, 1967; Wolberg, 1967), behavior therapists such as D'Zurilla and Goldfried (1971) can be credited with providing a detailed analysis of the problem-solving sequence applicable in clinical situations. The goal of this orientation is to provide the individual with general coping skills that can be applied to a wide variety of problematic interpersonal situations. The steps or skills are (1) recognizing that a problem exists and believing that it can be effectively dealt with, (2) defining important aspects of the problem, (3) generating various possible alternative solutions, (4) selecting a particular solution after considering the costs and benefits associated with each alternative, (5) actually implementing the solution, and (6) obtaining feedback to verify its effectiveness. The sequence is recycled until the client can use the component skills independently of the therapist (see Figure 12).

FIGURE 12. SOCIAL PROBLEM-SOLVING PROCESSES

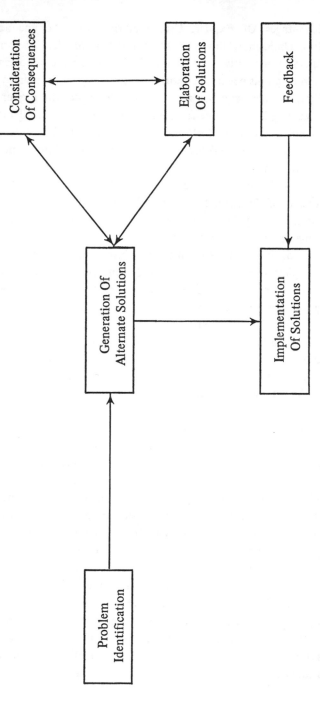

Adapted with permission. G. J. Allen, J. M. Chinsky, S. W. Larcen, J. E. Lochman, and H. V. Selinger. *Community psychology and the schools: A behaviorally oriented multilevel preventive approach.* Hillsdale, New Jersey: LEA Publishers, 1976.

Advantages Of Explicit Use. Traditional psychodynamic and humanistic clinicians claim with some justification that all forms of psychotherapy implicitly use this model. However, some important differences in emphasis occur when this strategy is explicit in therapy.

First, as Allen and his associates (1976) note, the sequence of problem solving is itself value-free, even though the specific dilemmas it may be employed to resolve often have ethical aspects. This characteristic helps both therapist and client clarify their unique philosophical and moral convictions through a more dispassionate examination of how these views influence proposed solutions. This is in contrast to the entanglement of divergent therapist and client values over issues, such as the nature of psychological health, what constitutes a cure, and so on, in some theoretical orientations.

Second, there is a premium on therapist-client collaboration. This feature implies respect for the clients' complaints as conceptualized within their own frameworks. Since two experts are working together to solve problems, mutual respect is fostered and power differences can often be minimized without resorting to interpersonal games. The collaborative nature of therapy helps dispel the magical aspects of diagnosis and treatment. These advantages can be further clarified by examining the use of behavioral diagnosis and therapeutic contracts, both of which are amenable to the problem-solving orientation.

Behavioral Diagnosis

Finding A Thematic Overview. Building diagnostic formulations is a cognitive activity that the clinician begins as soon as therapeutic contact is initiated. He listens to the client's verbal reports of experiences, observing nonverbal mannerisms and nuances of emotional overtones. Clinicians selectively choose particular features and formulate speculative inferences consistent with their theoretical beliefs. To this extent, diagnostic activities of all therapists can be broadly viewed as applied behavior analysis.

Diagnostic formulations provide the therapist with a meta-representation (Bandler and Grinder, 1975) or thematic overview of the client's perceptions of reality. A useful theme weaves events into larger patterns that can be used to successfully predict the client's feelings or actions in other situations. The accuracy of thematic predictions often amazes clients.

Dangers Of A Mystique. Mysteriously accurate predictions occur in all forms of therapy and may increase the client's evaluation of the power, prestige, and ability of the therapist. Two problems are readily apparent when diagnosis is shrouded in mystique. If this sort of clinical wizardry is an art, it can be haphazardly taught at best through a time-consuming apprenticeship. An even larger danger, particularly inherent in some psychodynamic formulations, is that diagnostic artistry may convince the client that the therapist automatically knows what is best. Such a stance is, at best, patronizing, and at worst, fosters passivity in the client. Even though behavioral diagnosis has elements of artistry, it can be more easily taught than psychodynamic therapy.

The Specificity Of Behavioral Diagnosis. The application of behavioral diagnosis enables the therapist and client to stay focused on specific therapeutic goals. Kanfer and Saslow (1965) have outlined seven areas of functioning as appropriate for diagnostic inquiry. They provide a comprehensive and detailed basis for determining the scope and severity of specific problems. The essential element of behavioral diagnosis, namely, clarification of relationships between behaviors and consequences in particular settings, is also an integral component of the problem-solving process.

Advantages Of Behavioral Diagnosis. Behavioral diagnosis has three advantageous features in relation to problem solving. First, the heavy emphasis on discovering sources of strength can provide both rapid relief from distress and a firm foundation upon which to build constructive change. Second, since behavioral diagnosis involves consistent monitoring of progress, it provides a mechanism of isolating the causes of improvement and identifying factors that bring about failure. Third, it breaks problems into manageable components. Many who enter therapy are paralyzed by the perception that their problems are too large to be effectively handled. Feelings of helplessness often result from the client's tendency to lump separate problems together. When this happens, the tangled issues seem to represent an unsolvable mess. Behavioral diagnosis helps dispel this hopelessness by enabling the participants to focus on one concrete issue at a time.

Contractual Negotiations In The Problem-Solving Process
Historically, psychotherapists have operated under a curious double standard with regard to providing services. On one hand, clinicians

clearly acknowledge the importance of defining the responsibilities entailed in entering therapy. It is argued that the very nature of the therapeutic relationship requires that limits and goals be examined. On the other hand, the foundation of psychotherapy as a guildlike, medically allied enterprise has protected therapists from the accountability found in competitive economic markets.

Implicit Contracting. In many ways, all psychotherapy involves some form of implicit contract, whereby the client agrees to pay the therapist for access to his resources. Even a diagnostic statement like, "It seems to me that you will be better able to cope with your difficulties when you learn to be more assertive" can be interpreted as an implicit contract of the form, "You pay me and I will teach you how to better assert yourself. We agree that this would be of benefit to you."

The problem with many such agreements is that their vagueness makes them subject to different interpretations and misunderstandings by the involved parties. In the implicit contract specified above, for example, the participants must decide (1) what is going to be taught, (2) for how long, (3) under what circumstances, and (4) whether they can agree on a means of assessing the effectiveness of training. Since the therapist occupies the position of power in the relationship, many of these decisions are left to her. Thus, although even implicit therapeutic contracts do systematize the interpersonal relationship, many consumer groups are insisting that such invisible agreements often are to the ultimate detriment of the client.

Explicit Contracting. Adams and Orgel (1975) suggest that therapeutic contracts be explicitly drawn up. There is much to recommend this idea. Such a procedure enables both participants to specify concrete therapeutic goals, define their responsibilities to each other, and negotiate the type of evidence that will indicate movement toward the goals. Such negotiations not only take much of the magic out of psychotherapy for the client, but they also release the therapist from the obligation to bring about a magical cure. In addition, contracting is a strategic method of manipulation that a therapist could use to force a client to accept more personal responsibility for changing.

The literature on therapeutic contracting (Homme, Csanyi, Gonzales, and Rechs, 1969; Kanfer, 1975) suggests that certain guidelines should be followed in formulating contracts. Briefly, contracts should have six elements. They should be *fair* in the sense that the effort needed to reach a goal should be balanced by the payoff for having accomplished the task. Second, contracts should be *clear*. Rights and responsibilities should be outlined in detail; it is often a good idea to have both parties summarize their understanding of the final arrangements. Contracts must be *honest* in that the agreement must be mutually binding. Failure by a therapist to live up to the agreed upon specifications can seriously damage credibility and trust. Good contracts seek to build from the client's assets and strengths, hence they are *positive* in nature.

Since a person does not develop severe difficulties overnight, it cannot be assumed that the problems will quickly disappear. A good contract thus must be *systematically implemented* and given time to foster change. Finally, a contract's effects ought to be *assessable* so that both therapist and client can profit from feedback. This last characteristic is what really sets apart implicit and explicit agreements. An explicit contract contains a built-in "fail-safe" mechanism enabling the parties to pinpoint difficulties that emerge during the treatment program and to implement strategies to remedy them.

Some therapists might consider contracting to be dehumanizing, particularly those agreements that contain an aversive consequences clause. It could be argued that many people in therapy are demoralized to begin with, and the last thing they need is additional punishment from the therapist. Such a criticism fails to recognize that contracting is simply an explicit statement of what most therapists believe—*that failure by a client to become actively involved in the change process inevitably has naturally occurring negative consequences.*

When properly used, however, contracting serves to increase the freedom and dignity of the client. The client becomes better able to make a properly informed choice about the services being purchased and is forced to become more active in collaborating on the solution of her difficulties. A final, but infrequently acknowledged advantage of the behavioral contract is that it enables the client to view his problems as more concrete and specific, thus making them easier to approach and to ultimately resolve.

ATTRIBUTIONAL ANALYSIS IN PSYCHOTHERAPY

The Need For Attributional Analysis

A critical part of psychotherapy is examining the client's self-appraisal.

This is assessing how the client *attributes* the cause of events or situations. Discerning the client's attributional view is important not only in deciding how best to help the person but also in predicting how that client will view the outcome of therapy. Conclusions from attribution research point out the necessity of understanding the client's cognitive criteria for success and failure. If this is not done and not taken into account, even a therapeutic intervention that produces spectacular improvement in measurable problem areas might be considered to be of little value by the client.

The problem-solving model of psychotherapy that we have just discussed is based on a rational and pragmatic view of human nature. It assumes a fairly straightforward positive motivation for change on the part of the client. It also assumes that judgments about progress made by both therapist and client will be in general agreement since they are based upon a dispassionate appraisal of the available evidence. Clinical experience teaches us, however, that this is not always the case.

Many people in therapy have curiously lopsided standards for appraising themselves. In many instances, clients will attribute the occurrence of favorable events to luck or other external factors while simultaneously blaming the ills that befall them on personal shortcomings. Other clients will describe situations in which they have behaved very competently but evaluate themselves as having acted inadequately. From the viewpoint of traditional psychiatric diagnosis, these evaluative patterns are often seen as irrational or *neurotic*.

Defining Attribution Theory. Fortunately, the behavioral-analytic features of the problem-solving approach have been extended to the client's cognitive world by borrowing from the work of social psychologists who study how people make interpersonal judgments. A discipline called **attribution theory** has provided systematic examination of the processes by which people appraise their own actions and evaluate the activities of others. Applied attribution research suggests that the tendency for people to evaluate themselves negatively is extremely common.

The Criteria For Making Attributions
The initial basis for making an unfavorable self-appraisal involves being exposed to somewhat unusual experiences that arouse fear, shame, or other sorts of negative affects. When this happens, an individual is faced

with determining whether the unfavorable condition has resulted from external situational influences or is the result of his own personal inadequacy. The choice of one or the other of these possible interpretations depends upon four criteria, which Kelley (1967) labels as *distinctiveness, consistency over time, consistency over place,* and *consensus.* These characteristics interact to lead a person to attribute a particular affective state to either external or internal causes.

A divorced woman, for example, might have doubts about her ability as a sexual partner. Her feelings of inadequacy may stem from the failure of her first marriage but are particularly strong immediately after sexual encounters with her current lover. When she is forced to generate an explanation of these unpleasant feelings, she can choose to attribute them to an inherent personal deficiency (e.g., "I must be a terrible sexual partner"; "I am a lousy lover") or to situational factors external to herself ("Making love at Harold's mother's house really inhibits me"; "No matter how hard I try to get turned on, Harold puts me down").

She is more likely to attribute her feelings to external causes if (1) she experiences them in the presence of a particular person but not in the presence of others (distinctiveness), (2) they consistently occur in the presence of that person, or in a particular situation, and (3) she learns that others feel the same way in the presence of that person or in a certain situation (consensus). Our young woman is more likely to view Harold as the source of her feelings if she finds herself being more uninhibited and involved with other sexual partners, discovers that Harold consistently belittles her, and hears from her friends that Harold's sarcasm makes them uncomfortable. On the other hand, she is likely to conclude that she is an inadequate lover if she feels inhibited with a variety of sexual partners, regardless of how comforting and gentle they are, and her friends tell her that her partners are "good lovers."

The Interplay Of Descriptive And Prescriptive Elements. In this example, a descriptive analysis of events was interpreted to make *prescriptive evaluations.* The woman was using her perceptions to arrive at a judgment about how she *should* be. People frequently do the same thing when making attributions about the actions of other people. In general, one's actions should make sense within the context in which they occur. If they do not, we are likely to evaluate the person who emits the behavior as abnormal. This contextual emphasis adds some prescriptive elements to a system that is initially descriptive.

In 1975, a man made headlines in Connecticut by hijacking a bus and forcing the driver to take him to New York City at gun point. After being apprehended, the man stated that he had been ordered by God to address the United Nations and that his speech was vital in ensuring lasting world peace. The man was immediately committed to a nearby state mental hospital and judged to be insane. This example demonstrates the role of common-sense attributions in determining normality. Stealing a bus was a *distinctive* activity in that most people can specify more effective ways of reaching a destination. However, the theft, while appearing peculiar, was not enough in itself to justify a decision that the man was abnormal. The bizarre nature of the act was highlighted by the failure of those around the man to concur that his intentions were reasonable. If he had explained that stealing the bus was an act of desperation precipitated by having no way to reach a dying relative, he probably would have been placed in jail. While this underlying motive would have led to an illegal act, at least it would have appeared to be reasonable. The man's explanation, however, made what was already a highly distinctive act appear totally bizarre.

Because descriptive and prescriptive elements are tangled when people make attributions, assessment of distinctiveness and consistency does not involve a dispassionate intellectual examination of objective evidence.

Propositions Involving Self-Evaluations. The literature on attribution provides a number of propositions that interlock to suggest that people make evaluations of personal inadequacy in response to unusual or traumatic environmental events. Here are some of those propositions.

1. *Negative attributes have more impact on self-evaluative and interpersonal judgments than positive characteristics.* Unfavorable information about an event is a much more salient and influential determinant of how that event is evaluated than is favorable information (Kanouse and Hanson, 1971). While this tendency may be partially due to the skew of actual life situations toward unfavorable outcomes (e.g., few people win lotteries, but many get sick), it is also reinforced by many negative dispositional terms in our language and is inherent in the bureaucratic functioning of all our major societal institutions. Both behavior therapists and

humanistically inclined family therapists have commented on the wide prevalence of *negative scanning* (i.e., disproportionate attention being directed toward deviant activities) in disturbed family units (Haley, 1963; Stuart, 1968); Ullmann (1967) has noted the damaging effects of similarly skewed reinforcement patterns in producing passivity in both patients and staffs within hospital systems.

2. *Emotional arousal distorts the evaluation of sensory information particularly in ambiguous situations.* Autonomic arousal affects the behavior and attitudes of people to the extent that the physiological changes are explicable in terms of intrinsic or external causes. Research concerning the attribution of affective arousal indicates the desirability of having an individual attribute negative emotional states to extrinsic causes. Failure to do this often eventuates in a vicious spiral whereby worry about the condition causes further emotional arousal and increases subsequent worry and concern (Valins and Nisbett, 1971). For example, severe depressions are often accompanied by specific physiological manifestations such as sleep disturbances. Attributing such complaints to extrinsic environmental factors like unfavorable work-to-reinforcement schedules often helps relieve them. Viewing them as indicants of personal inadequacy, however, often makes them worse.

3. *Actors and observers have divergent perceptions of the causes of behavior.* Jones and Nisbett (1971) note a curious discrepancy between how people view their own activities (from their viewpoint as actors) and the actions of others (as observers). Actors typically acknowledge being more affected by contingent environmental influences, explaining their behavior in terms of purposive values and strategies. Observers, on the other hand, are more likely to explain the behavior of the actor in terms of internal dispositions or traits. At first glance, this proposition appears to contradict the premise that a bias toward attributions of inadequacy exists. This dilemma can be resolved by recognizing that actors also observe and evaluate their own behavior. Typically, evaluation is in the form of self-statements that derive from our trait-dominated linguistic framework. Worry about inadequacy causes people to behave more cautiously in critical

situations. Anxious individuals become critical spectators of their own behaviors, resulting in an inability to function smoothly and freely. The paralysis caused by **spectatoring** is seen as a basic component of all forms of interpersonal dysfunctions including test, speech, and dating anxiety; frigidity; and impotence.

4. *Failure to obtain social consensus increases the subjective importance of unfavorable events.* From early childhood, a person learns to interpret the meaning of experience by obtaining the opinions of others. It is obviously easier to conclude that a frightening or unusual occurrence is a normal experience if a person learns that others have found themselves in similar situations. Failure to seek consensual validity for subjective experiences is the most important determinant of emotional disorders from an attributional perspective (Valins and Nisbett, 1971). Unfortunately, several of the previously mentioned factors often combine to inhibit a person from obtaining and profiting from consensual feedback. Even when an individual overcomes these impediments, emotional arousal can cause the person to selectively distort attributions provided by others. This distortive tendency can be facilitated by the observer's use of trait characterizations which may carry implicit accusations. Consider, for example, the supposedly helpful response, "Sure, I was impotent myself once or twice, but I know I am a strong person so I didn't worry about it." The afflicted individual may interpret this to mean, "It wasn't a problem to him *because* he is a strong person. But I am a weak person so I cannot overcome this terrible problem." The attributional framework has relevance for understanding both the diagnostic activities of physicians and psychotherapists and the remedial strategies clinicians employ with clients.

Other Schemes For Understanding Attribution. Self-attributions of inadequacy and abnormality are invariably discernible from a client's behavior during initial therapeutic contacts. Expression of these sentiments are typically categorized by therapists as faulty or irrational thinking, but they make perfectly logical sense within the client's conceptual framework. Clinicians are less concerned with whether these attributions accurately reflect objective reality than they are about their debilitating and paralyzing effects. Several other specific schemes have been developed which enable the clinician to understand detrimental attributions in more detail. The linguistic analysis approach of Bandler and Grinder (1975), Ellis' (1962) system of irrational ideas, and Beck's (1970) categorization of maladaptive thinking patterns are among the more influential schemes.

Beck suggests that maladaptive behavior arises as a result of faulty attributions of inadequacy that, in turn, are manifestations of four interrelated thought distortions. **Dichotomous reasoning** describes an individual's tendency to interpret events as extremes. Something is either wonderful or it is awful; there is no middle ground. **Magnification** refers to the tendency to blow things out of proportion. Usually, the events that are magnified are negative ones. **Minimization** occurs when a person constantly belittles her strengths and successes. One important feature of minimization is that the causes of a success are externalized to factors that are independent of the individual's behavior. **Overgeneralization** involves making a categorical judgment about a diverse class of people or events after having sampled only a few. If the woman in our example had concluded that she was sexually inadequate solely on the basis of interacting with one lover, she would have been guilty of overgeneralizing. These four tendencies often combine to cause an individual to make **arbitrary inferences** about the causes of an unpleasant affective state. Like Ellis (1962), Beck maintains that these evaluative distortions cause and sustain difficulties in living.

One particular value in this type of attributional approach is that it can be applied to the self-appraisals made by therapists as well as to those of clients. A supervisory session the author once held with a beginning psychotherapist illustrates this point well. After three intake interviews, none of the clients returned for a subsequent session. Even though nothing was observed that indicated the novice therapist was driving her clients away, she interpreted these events to mean that she was an incompetent failure. One portion of our discussion suggested quite clearly that the therapist had fallen into the cognitive traps described by Beck:

Therapist: "It's the most important thing in the world for me to be a really competent therapist," (*magnification*) "but (sigh) I guess I should stick to research." (*dichotomous reasoning*)

Supervisor: "What makes you feel that way?"

Therapist: "Well, since none of my initial contacts returned, I must have done something to make them not want to come

205

back." (*arbitrary inference*)

Supervisor: "Specifically, what did you do to drive them away?"

Therapist: "I'm not sure; maybe I should have been warmer or more directive or something. I suppose you are going to tell me that I didn't make any major mistakes, but that can't be right. No one else had this happen." (*arbitrary inference*) "I guess I'll never be a decent therapist." (*overgeneralization*)

Like the problem-solving approach, the attributional framework has a nonprescriptive emphasis. Moralistic judgments of behavior in terms of "right-wrong" or "good-bad" are thought to paralyze people, keeping them from acting freely and spontaneously. Detailed study of attributions invariably reveals that even the most seemingly bizarre or unreasonable actions make logical sense from the client's point of view. The attributional framework allows the therapist to dispense with traditional diagnostic labelling practices, and it provides a solid basis for implementing and assessing therapeutic interventions.

Medical And Psychiatric Diagnoses

In the foregoing discussion of attribution we have been concerned with various schemes for understanding attribution. The application of these schemes has mainly focused on behavioral therapy in this discussion. Now we will examine how medical and psychiatric diagnoses relate to these schemes.

Diagnosis involves observation and inference, and, because both descriptive and prescriptive elements are inherent in drawing inferences, diagnosis tends to be biased toward discovering the unusual, bizarre, or pathological. Three factors foster this bias among professionals, as can be clearly seen in the activities of physicians.

Nature Of The Disease Process. The first centers on the nature of the disease process. Physicians view *health* as having meaning only in relation to the absence of demonstrable pathology. People are healthy if they are not diseased. Since no one can observe a disease process directly, identification of sickness represents an attributional process. Disease is caused by some foreign agent which upsets internal bodily functioning. The agent may be identified by various surface manifestations or symptoms that are assessable by diagnostic devices. These symptoms will normally cluster into identifiable patterns which are distinct from the clusters caused by other disease organisms. Noting the distinctive nature of the symptoms is the first step in diagnosis. A tentative diagnosis receives further justification to the extent that the symptoms consistently interrelate to form syndromes and follow a particular pattern over time. Knowledge of these consistencies allows medical specialists to reach consensus about the prognosis of the disease and a course of treatment.

Clearly identifiable disease processes thus manifest high degrees of distinctiveness, consistency, and consensus—the three characteristics which lead to an external attribution; in this case, a foreign pathological entity is considered to be responsible for the manifestation of an illness. If the process does not possess these characteristics, a more tentative diagnostic formulation may implicate the person as "malingering" or as being "hypochondriacal."

Concept Of Health And Sickness. The second factor involves the contrast between health as a unitary state and the many forms of sickness which have been identified. The term *health* actually describes many possible conditions without making clear situational specifications. Our language, however, contains innumerable terms to describe the thousands of diseases afflicting people. As medical science advances, more pathological conditions are continually being discovered. Since diagnosing health depends upon excluding all forms of pathology, this judgment becomes progressively less likely as the number of disease entities multiplies.

Training Of Physicians. The third source of bias toward the pathological derives from the training of physicians as well as the conditions under which they practice medicine. The standard medical procedure of intervening to change ongoing disease processes tends to foster a conservative stance toward diagnosis, which is begun during the training of physicians (Scheff, 1966).

Medical specialists infer the existence of a disease from various diagnostic signs. Based upon the presence or absence of observable manifestations, the physician will decide whether an individual actually has a particular ailment. Two types of errors may occur as a result of this inferential process. The first type results if the person is actually sick, and the physician fails to diagnose pathology; the second type occurs when the physician mistakenly concludes that a disease exists when in fact it does not. Scheff points out that the consequences of making the first type of error are much more serious for the physician:

A physician who dismisses a patient who subsequently dies of a disease that should have been detected is not only subject to legal action for negligence and possible loss of license for incompetence, but also to moral condemnation from his colleagues and from his own conscience for delinquency [Reprinted by permission. T. J. Scheff. *Being mentally ill: A sociological theory.* Aldine, 1966, p. 111].

The second type of error is generally perceived as involving a nuisance to the patient and might even be applauded as healthily conservative.

These three sources of influence also dispose mental health professionals to diagnose pathology when in doubt. Making conservative decisions is also sound diagnostic practice for psychiatrists and psychologists. It is stressed in their training. Many once specialized psychiatric terms (e.g., neurotic, schizophrenic, phobia, anxiety) have become part of our common vocabulary.

Client's Desire For Magical Interventions. When discussing the medical model in Chapter 2, we suggested that its general acceptance was partly a consequence of the political power wielded by institutional psychiatry. Viewing life difficulties as stemming from disease processes gives psychiatric practice the aura of scientific respectability. In addition, it often provides an explanation that meets the emotional needs of those who have the problems.

Many clients in therapy seek immediate resolution of their difficulties through the "magical" intervention of the therapist. Berne (1966) characterizes this orientation as the client's quest for the "magic orb," which is hidden in the therapist's desk. The magic orb insures a problem-free existence to the person who possesses it, but it does not require any active involvement on the part of the client. Conceptualizing life difficulties as analogous to disease processes often implies that they can be resolved through physical treatments (e.g., drugs, megavitamins) administered by the therapist to an individual who simpiy remains passive. As already indicated, disease explanations often provide comfort to the client, even though many therapists view them as illusory pseudo-explanations.

SELF-EVALUATIVE AND INTERPERSONAL "GAMES" IN PSYCHOTHERAPY

Whatever its underlying theoretical rationale, psychotherapy is human communication. This intuitively simple realization has led to a concerted focus on the role communication patterns play in maintaining and alleviating human distress. Pioneers in exploring the relationship between "psychopathology" and communicational dysfunctions include Bateson, Haley, Jackson, and Ruesch. Their work in the 1950's has provided an important conceptual framework for understanding the course of therapy. Paralleling the serious study of these issues has been a dramatic upsurge of popular interest in the interpersonal "games" played by therapists and clients as well as the cognitive "games" people play with themselves.

Assumptions About Human Communication

Although many definitions of "games" can be found, they all suggest that behavior is cycled through interpersonal feedback loops in rule-governed and repetitive patterns. A foundation for understanding game-playing can be derived by examining five assumptions about human communication provided by Watzlawick, Beavin, and Jackson (1967):

1. *It is impossible not to communicate.* All human behavior provides information to an observer, in the form of verbal content, style of delivery, emotional nuances, gestures, distance, or facial and postural cues. Even attempts not to communicate result in the delivery of messages to others. In many cases, discrepancies occur between these sources of information.

2. *Every communication conveys information about both the content of a message and the relationship between participants.* A message not only provides information but also implicitly commands a response from those who receive it. Mode of delivery is viewed as a **meta-communication,** that is, a communication which qualifies or disqualifies the content meaning of the message. For example, the words "Stop it!" may mean exactly that if delivered in an angry tone of voice, but they may be interpreted as "Keep it up" if sandwiched between giggles. In the first instance, nonverbal aspects of communication qualify the statement; in the second, nonverbal cues disqualify the content meaning. Similarly, the statement "Shut the door" can be accompanied by context cues that help identify the relationship among the communicants as parent-child, employer-employee, friend-to-friend, lover-to-

lover, and many others. Thus, the nature of any interpersonal relationship is determined by both the content and contextual command aspects of a communication.

3. *The adequacy of ongoing relationships is determined by how the participants punctuate the communication process.* Human communication is a continual interpersonal influence process. As children, we learn to follow certain grammatical rules that enable us to segment this ongoing flow into discrete units. This is obvious when we write in "sentences" that we organize into "paragraphs," "sections," and "chapters." We segment the flow of written words into somewhat arbitrary units, each of which has a beginning and an end. We do this by using various forms of punctuation.

It is less obvious that we do the same thing when we communicate verbally. If you listen to speech, you will discover that people lower their voices at the end of sentences. In terms of meta-communication, this tendency provides a message to the listener that says in effect, "It is now your turn to talk." Violation of this rule causes the listener to become annoyed, because she "cannot get a word in."

We also use contextual command characteristics (e.g., nonverbal cues) to punctuate longer communication sequences, but we often encounter problems when these characteristics are disqualified by the content of language. For example, we can characterize a person as being "submissive," and imply that this is a trait that the individual possesses. Linguistic analysts, however, argue that it is impossible to be submissive except in contrast to being "dominant." Both terms refer to descriptions of an interaction between people rather than to traits that the participants possess. They argue also that all of our linguistic distinctions, such as "leader-follower," "stimulus-response," or "cause-effect," are relational constructs that we find convenient in helping to punctuate the ongoing communication process.

Watzlawick et al. (1967) suggest that disharmony in interpersonal relationships often occurs when the participants punctuate the same ongoing communication sequence at different points. They illustrate this contention by describing how a wife and husband might punctuate a sequence of nagging and withdrawal. The wife may view her nagging as a response to withdrawal, while the husband may believe his withdrawal is caused by his wife's nagging. Both spouses generate conflicting views of what causes the annoying response of the partner by arbitrarily punctuating the ongoing communication process at different points.

4. *The meaning of a communication is determined by both verbal and nonverbal messages.* Verbal communication is possible because people who speak a particular language agree to follow specific grammatical conventions. Failure to follow the rules of proper syntax produces verbal behavior that may be labelled "crazy talk." Assigning meaning to a particular statement, however, also involves attending to nonverbal messages. It is possible to say "I love you, too" in a way that conveys the message, "I hate you." Unfortunately, no general grammatical rules for determining the meaning of nonverbal cues exist.

Communication difficulties arise when the verbal component of the message is disqualified by its nonverbal aspects, or *vice versa*. Watzlawick et al. point out that translating verbal messages into nonverbal ones produces a loss of relevant information, but attempts to express messages that are being received nonverbally do not readily fit into conventions of grammar and syntax. Thus, it becomes very difficult to talk about the relationship being defined between speaker and listener.

5. *All communication sequences are based on defining the relationship as symmetrical or complementary.* A **symmetric** relationship assumes that the participants have equal power and status and seeks to minimize differences between them. A **complementary** relationship maximizes differences between participants. Attempts to control a relationship often involve two additional relational patterns. In the first type, called a **meta-complementary** encounter, one person assumes control by letting or forcing the other person to take command. Haley (1963), for example, notes that while the statement, "Tell me what to do," implies being in an inferior position, it is really an implicit command showing that the speaker possesses the actual power.

The second type, called **pseudo-symmetric**, involves the person in the superior position letting or forcing the other to be an equal. This relationship may be found in sensitivity-training groups in which employers demand that their employees treat them "just like I am one of you." The paradoxical nature of this relationship does little to encourage open and honest feedback.

Interpersonal interactions are characterized by continual maneuvers designed to redefine the nature of the relationship. *These five assumptions can be used to help identify symptoms as interpersonal influence strategies and to appreciate the paradoxes involved in psychotherapy.*

Symptoms As A Method Of Interpersonal Control

Freud conceptualized symptoms as having both intrapsychic and interpersonal components, which were categorized as primary and secondary gain, respectively. Game analysts (Berne, 1966; Haley, 1963) give almost total emphasis to the interpersonal aspects of "symptoms." They believe symptoms are derived from paradoxical conflicts in communication. The author once worked with a 40-year-old man who lived with his parents and was unable to hold a job, even though he had a master's degree in a specialized field. Our encounters suggested that he was the recipient of many paradoxical messages from his parents. On one hand, they urged, and even continually nagged him to "Get a job so that you can move away from home." He also constantly heard, "Daddy and Mommy are getting too old to take care of you." These messages however, were disqualified by the way the client's parents treated him. At one point, he obtained work in another city. Both his parents helped him select an apartment, and his mother would drive about 80 miles three times a week to literally "tuck my little darling into bed." They also encouraged him to come home whenever "anybody at work is mean to you."

This client was in a *double-bind* situation in which his parents' demands that he be independent were disqualified by their treating him as though he were a helpless child. Their tendency to infantilize him is reflected also in the choice of words they used to communicate with him. Parents rarely refer to themselves as "Daddy and Mommy" when talking to their middle-aged children, nor do most parents typically tuck their 40-year-old darlings into bed. Even the word "mean" has a hidden connotation, implying an adult-to-child relationship. Adults can be "mean" to children; with other adults they are usually described as thoughtless, insensitive, or nasty.

The client responded to being in this sort of meta-complementary relationship by acting as though he were totally incompetent. This strategy was frustrating for everyone involved, leading the parents to complain that their son was "lazy" and causing the client to greatly resent his parents. The client responded to the paradoxical message of "obey us and be competent, but act as we treat you—incompetently" by developing "symptoms" whenever confronted with a stressful situation. He would dutifully obtain job interviews, but he would impress the interviewer with his incompetence, so he would rarely be offered a job. Whenever his parents pressed him too hard, he would begin to talk "crazy." This would frighten them and they would leave him alone for awhile. This cycle would eventually repeat itself, however.

His development of "symptoms" was a particularly effective strategy because, from a traditional psychiatric view, symptoms are considered to be involuntary. The client "could not help" acting crazy, and thus was relieved of responsibility for these outbursts. From the viewpoint of linguistic analysis, the development of symptoms simultaneously fills the contradictory demands to act competently and to act helplessly. This viewpoint is very similar to Perls' (1973) contention that sickness is an interpersonal tactic which people can use to control others around them.

The Paradox Of Power In Psychotherapy

From the perspective of game analysts, the therapeutic encounter involves a complementary relationship that resembles other complementary relationships in the client's life. Because of this similarity, clients will often resort to many of the games that they use to control others. For example, clients may demand the therapist to resolve difficulties without actively cooperating themselves. Despite the power position occupied by therapists, they do not have the ability to produce magical changes sought by clients. If the therapist tacitly accepts the responsibility demanded by the client, a meta-complementary relationship is being established. The client occupies the superior position by insisting the therapist take command in dealing with the client's presenting problems. In this meta-complementary relationship the client is in the superior position while appearing to be in the one-down position.

Skilled therapists are very sensitive to this sort of ploy and use numerous counterstrategies to avoid being placed in this position. Therapy itself is viewed as a series of games designed to (1) neutralize the self-defeating nature of symptomatic maneuvers and (2) allow clients to examine the rules of the games they play to (3) develop more effective interpersonal maneuvers. The therapist's first strategy is to place the client in a meta-complementary relationship whereby the client is directed to behave spontaneously. This is itself paradoxical. By requiring spontaneous behavior on the part of the client, the therapist occupies the position of power by turning it over to the client. Haley (1969b) illustrates the difference between complementary and meta-complementary power by contrasting how two hypothetical therapists dealt with a client's attempt to get "one up":

> If a patient insists that he is God, the Bull will insist that *he* is God and force the patient to his knees, thus getting one-up in a rather straightforward way. To handle a similar claim by a patient, The Lady of the Lodge will smile and say, "All right, if you wish to be God, I'll let you." The patient is gently put one-down as he realizes that no one but God can *let* anyone else be God [Reprinted by permission. J. Haley. The art of psychoanalysis. In J. Haley (Ed.), *The power tactics of Jesus Christ and other essays.* Grossman Publishers, 1969, p. 22-23].

The statement by the client in this example has many possible meanings regarding the relationship with the therapist. It could represent an attempt to avoid the topic under discussion or to force the therapist to acknowledge that the client is not responsible for his behavior. On the level of meta-language it represents an attempt to wrest control from the therapist, and both clinicians viewed it as such. The Bull's response was to deal with the client's claim by saying in effect, "I am in charge here," which illustrates a straightforward complementary power play. The Lovely Lady, on the other hand, established a meta-complementary relationship. She demonstrated her control over the client be essentially giving him permission to act as he did, forcing the client to take responsibility for his control strategy. A logical follow-up to the Lovely Lady's strategy would be to ask the client, "Now that you are God, what do you want to do about your problem?"

Specific Game Sequences During Psychotherapy

Game analysts acknowledge the contradiction in conceptualizing psychotherapy as a series of games designed to neutralize the destructive games that the client plays elsewhere. Their position, however, is based on the assumption that the therapist is a more skilled strategist than the client and can create therapeutic double binds which foster improvement. The goals of the therapist within this framework are (1) to neutralize the effectiveness of the maladaptive games being played in therapy and (2) to help the client realize how pervasive and consistent similar modes of interaction are in other life areas. Once this is accomplished, the client is taught more adaptive game strategies (Berne, 1966).

Straightforward attributional analysis can be translated into game terminology. It is easy to translate, for example, Beck's (1970) scheme of thought distortions into cognitive games. Two of the most frequently encountered games can be labelled inappropriate comparisons and success equals failure. In the **inappropriate comparisons game**, a client compares his attributes against those possessed by significant others in an arbitrary manner. The others selected for comparison typically are the best at a particular skill; different people are chosen for each attribute. Thus, clients conclude that they are inadequate because they cannot do X as well as person A, and they cannot do Y as well as person B, and so on.

The **success equals failure game** is a variant of inappropriate comparisons, in which clients compare any progress they have made against their own ultimate goals, rather than against the perceived strengths of other people. Since improvement does not mean that the client has actually achieved the desired goal, it is perceived as a failure rather than as a success. For example, a man who is uncomfortable talking to women may be encouraged by his therapist to initiate a conversation. Rather than view this exercise as a success, the client may rob himself of the victory by qualifying the situation to minimize its importance. A statement such as, "Well, I talked with her . . ." may be qualified by the responses listed in Table 4.

People who habitually employ these one-sided standards of comparison place themselves in the position of eternal losers. Feelings of hopelessness and behavioral paralysis are inevitable consequences of these games, since people are unlikely to take the risks necessary for improvement if they think their efforts are doomed before they attempt them. Therapists employ various forms of linguistic analysis (Bandler and Grinder, 1975; Ellis, 1962; Meichenbaum, 1974) to break these self-defeating patterns.

TABLE 4. EXAMPLES OF VERBAL QUALIFIERS THAT
A MALE CLIENT COULD USE TO MINIMIZE
HIS SUCCESS IN SPEAKING TO A WOMAN

Qualifier	Subjective Meaning
but she was easy to talk to	it was the woman's positive or negative qualities that enabled me to be successful
but she wasn't that attractive	
because it was part of my homework in therapy	the special and unique nature of the situation determined my success
but that was in class; on a date, I wouldn't know what to say	
however, after five minutes, I couldn't think of anything else to say	my performance was not a success because I did not achieve my more ultimate goals
except that when I thought about asking her for a date, I froze	

Game theorists emphasize that these cognitive games have interpersonal consequences relating to control in psychotherapy. Berne (1966) notes that a client may attempt to execute a therapist's suggested intervention in a way that will sabotage its effects. This strategy allows the client to turn the "success equals failure" game into either the "look what you made me do" or "schlemiel" game (Berne, 1966). The **look what you made me do game** involves blaming the therapist (or more indirectly therapy) for making the client worse. The **schlemiel game** is designed to enable the client to apologize and seek the therapist's forgiveness. The unwary therapist who becomes defensive in response to the first ploy or provides forgiveness as a consequence of the second is tacitly assuming unwarranted responsibility for solving the client's problems (which only the client can solve) and thus is forfeiting the most therapeutically helpful position of empathetic distance. By accepting a client's apology for messing up an intervention, without pointing out how the client is hurting himself, the therapist may be condoning such sabotage.

The client's verbalizations contain many hidden messages that structure the meaning of the therapeutic relationship, as illustrated in Table 5. The use of "why" questions can pose a subtle interpersonal dilemma. Regardless of their therapeutic orientation, clinicians learn that "why" questions are typically less functional in gathering information than "who, what, how, when," and "where" questions. "Why" questions are not only difficult to answer, but they also often convey a motivational accusation (e.g., "Why did you do that" equals "What a stupid thing to do"). This situation also exists when a client asks a question like "Why am I like this?" The question may reflect a legitimate request for information or a self-critical motivational indictment which really means "I should not think, feel, or behave as I do right now." In either case, the expertise of the therapist is being tested. As was pointed out in Chapter 4, what serves as an adequate explanation for some people will be completely inadequate for others. Skillful therapists will probe the client to determine what sort of response will provide an explanation that is satisfying before answering a "why" question. They will also attempt to help the client translate such inquiries into more helpful "what," "who," "when," "where," and "how" questions.

One element that runs through all games is an attempt by the client to force the therapist to assume responsibility for the client's improvement. *In all therapeutic systems, including behavior therapy, the therapist seeks to employ communication paradoxes in order to free clients from the debilitating effects of the games they play and to develop more constructive modes of relating to others. This goal can be accomplished only if the therapist can discriminate between maneuvers that represent honest attempts to cope with difficult life situations and those that are designed to evade responsibility for meeting the challenges of life.* If a client's maneuvers reflect the latter situation, the task-oriented aspects of social problem-solving that occur in therapy

TABLE 5. EXAMPLES OF HIDDEN MESSAGES TO THE
THERAPIST CONTAINED IN CLIENT STATEMENTS

Statements	Implicit Messages
These homework assignments never seem to work out.	You are pushing me too hard.
	Despite what you say, I really am incompetent.
Well, Doctor, what should I do?	Give me some advice; let's explore alternatives.
	It's your responsibility to fix me; solve my problems for me.
I did what you suggested, but now I feel worse.	I'm sorry I am such an incompetent bungler, please forgive me (and accept me as I am).
	You are responsible for messing me up.
Why am I like this?	(This is a legitimate but misconstrued attempt to obtain information.)
	Nobody has problems like I do.
	Let's see how well you really understand (or like) me.

can be impeded. Before effective collaboration between the participants in therapy can take place, the clinician must deal with these issues. Although impediments related to the client's willingness to change have been conceptualized quite differently by psychodynamic (i.e., as resistance) and behavioral (i.e., as relationship enhancement) therapists, a thorough understanding of the hidden dimensions of communication is employed by clinicians of all theoretical persuasions in an attempt to overcome such difficulties.

THE "LANGUAGE OF THE BODY" IN PSYCHOTHERAPY

Early Efforts To Understand Nonverbal Cues

Psychoanalysts were the first to assign special importance to nonverbal cues in psychotherapy. The psychoanalytic assumption that specific gestures and postures were closely linked to particular affective states led to attempts by some therapists to change feelings by directly manipulating the body. Wilhelm Reich, for example, sought to free his patients from their "body armor" through massage and relaxation exercises. This emphasis also can be found in the "games" Gestalt therapists use to help people overcome their inability to give and to receive physical affection.

Some of the parallels psychoanalysts draw between affect and behavior (e.g., "upright" posture suggests "uptight" attitudes; Mahl, 1968) were based on commonly held intuitive similarities, while others (leftward motion on projective drawing tests indicates a pathological flight from one's own environment) were derived from more specialized conventions.

Conceptual Difficulties
In Studying Body Language

No System Of Assigning Meaning. Understanding how nonverbal cues affect the communication process has been a difficult conceptual endeavor for several reasons. First, no widely held conventions about the grammar or syntax of nonverbal language exist. Viewing nonverbal messages as a language necessitates that specific behaviors can be formed into recognizable patterns which have generally agreed upon meanings. Although we can agree that placing a noun before a verb forms a sentence, we have difficulty formulating rules for how the meaning of nonverbal sequences are to be defined. Several systems to achieve this aim have been devised, but they are quite esoteric and their ultimate utility remains speculative.

Contradictions And Combinations. Second, body messages that are emitted from different localities may convey contradictory meanings or combine in numerous ways to provide distinctly different meanings than they do when transmitted singly. The very complexity of these interactions poses a third problem, namely, the meaning of nonverbal cues is situationally specified.

Research on body language has been conducted in five major areas: (1) bodily posture and gesture (called *kinesics*), (2) vocal characteristics and qualities (*paralanguage*), (3) personal boundaries and space (*proxemics*), (4) clothes and cosmetics (*body artifacts*), and (5) modalities involving touch and smell. The discovery of basic relationships in each area depends upon holding constant many of the variables which may potentially interact with the focus of the investigation. Thus, the conclusion that people who like each other will maintain more eye contact than people who dislike one another is mediated by influences such as the sex of the participants, their perceived status, topic of conversation, distance between them, and many other factors. At present, we have no general theoretical models comprehensive enough to describe consistent patterns among these many sources of influence.

Despite these difficulties, emerging knowledge about body language enables the therapist to more effectively accomplish two important tasks: interpreting nonverbal cues from clients to better understand their subjective states and using nonverbal cues to convey warmth and respect to the clients.

Bodily Communication Of Emotions And Intentions

Skilled therapists recognize that the body messages of any particular individual are bound to be highly unique. Such messages will, however, form constantly recurring patterns in response to specific environmental changes. As the therapeutic relationship develops, the association between these patterns and verbal statements provides interpretative meaning about what the client is experiencing, provided the therapist knows what to look for. Expert clinicians typically have a variety of analytic perspectives to use sequentially or in combination for improving their understanding of the client's feelings and intentions.

Facial Expressions And Body Movements. Working within a psychodynamic framework, Mahl (1968) has indicated that the gestures and postural positions emitted by people in psychotherapy are suggestive of specific attitudinal orientations. Folding one's arms tightly or clutching one's body is indicative of attempts to provide self-protection or is an expression of fear or withdrawal; playing with one's rings suggests frustrations about marriage or home conflict. The way individuals cross their legs also has significance, according to Mahl. High tight crossing suggests sexually related inhibitions, but loose, exhibitionistic crossing may represent flirtation.

It has generally been concluded more general body movements occur during discussions of highly charged emotional material. Often these movements serve several functions. They may be indicative of the client's attempt to censor what is about to be said, or they may punctuate a meta-message, such as the client's ambivalence or confusion over certain issues.

The face is an especially fruitful source of information about one's emotional state, but it also is an interpretative nightmare for two reasons. Facial expressions change dramatically in as rapidly as one-fifth of a second (Haggard and Isaacs, 1966), and these expressions of emotional states are dependent upon many possible configurations of the forehead and eyebrows; the eyes, lids, and bridge of the nose; and lower nose, mouth and jaw. Ekman, Friesen, and Ellsworth (1971) have developed a coding system that provides associations between configurations among these three facial areas and subjective affect. They found fear to be primarily reflected by the eyes, while disgust was most easily interpretable from mouth positions. More complex emotions involve combinations of these areas, with anger being deducible from cues on the mouth, jaws, eyebrows, and forehead; and sadness being inferable from numerous configurations of the eyebrows, eyes, and mouth.

It is difficult to tell whether one is being deceived by facial messages, however. The face is obviously better equipped to support deceptive maneuvers than any other part of the body, since people have generally developed control over the impressions their facial cues provide. Ekman and Friesen (1969) suggest that the best clues to deception often are found in leg tensions and repetitive foot movements. They also report that the hands tend to indicate lies of omission. The pleasant meaning of smiling in a nervous person, for example, may be contradicted by hand tremors, picking of fingernails, and other manifestations of tension.

Distance Between Communicators. Distance between communicators also provides important interpretative cues. Hall (1966), in his pioneering work on proxemics, has identified four zones of personal space. While people in our society appear to be most comfortable interacting at a distance of 4 to 6 feet, Hall has noted that more intense personal encounters (involving hostility and intimacy) usually occur at closer distances. Intimate contact occurs at less than 18 inches, while therapy sessions typically are conducted in what Hall calls the personal (1.5 to 4 feet) or social distance (4 to 12 feet) zones. This spacing optimizes visual feedback and verbal communication. Clients may attempt to erect "barriers" at various times between themselves and their therapist. Clouds of cigarette smoke, for example, may invariably thicken whenever certain topics are discussed. Fisher (in press) reports that men typically position themselves across from liked others, while women place themselves adjacent to those they prefer. While the choice of seating arrangements in therapy often is not possible, shifts in the positioning of chairs often have interpretative meaning. Thus, movement toward less face-to-face body orientation may represent a withdrawal from intimacy by a client.

Paralinguistic Cues

Therapists have also extensively studied paralinguistic cues to help them understand the client's experience. Speech blockage and disturbances have been frequently noted to occur when clients discussed distressing topics. This has led psychoanalysts to believe such manifestations indicate conflict over the emergence of repressed material. The emphasis given to certain words within a spoken sentence supplies potentially different meanings about the statement. "I *think* therapy is helping me" might well suggest doubt and confusion by a client, while the statement, "I think therapy is *helping* me," may indicate surprised delight.

Oswald (1963) identified four patterns of voice inflection to be characteristic of particular classes of mental disorders. "Neurotics" were found to have the "sharp" vocal characteristics often noted in querulous whining and complaining. Dependent and depressed individuals typically had a "flat," sickly vocal style, while brain-damaged patients had lifeless, "hollow" voices. Oswald noted that psychotherapy produced more resonant, confident, and "robust" vocal characteristics in those receiving treatment.

The ability to accurately identify emotional undertones from paralinguistic cues varies greatly across people. Davitz (1964) identifies sensitive listeners as having (1) knowledge about the vocal characteristics of emotional expressions, (2) well-developed abstractive abilities, (3) exposure to a wide range of vocal expressions, and (4) ability to accurately portray their own emotions through vocal and facial cues. These characteristics parallel client descriptions of what constitutes sensitivity in a therapist.

Experience gives clinicians opportunities to enhance their ability to interpret emotional meaning from subtle vocal characteristics. Beginning therapists usually can accurately identify straightforward emotional states such as anger, but they typically need supervised experience to intuit more complex affective meanings (e.g., shame). How a clinician chooses to interpret the many messages of the body is largely a matter of theoretical preference, but the fact remains that failure to utilize them is likely to retard therapeutic progress.

The Communication Of Therapist Attitudes

Therapeutic encounters are mutual influence processes. Therapists not only receive subtle nonverbal messages from their clients, but they also emit meaningful cues. In discussing the communication of affect, Mehrabian (1971) has concluded that facial expressions have almost eight times as much impact as verbal statements, and vocal characteristics are roughly five times more influential. Thus, it is very important for therapists to insure that the kinds of body messages they transmit do not contradict statements designed to facilitate client liking and self-respect. Research by Mehrabian and others clearly indicates that warmth is communicated by a forward lean, smiling, direct eye gaze and relaxation in the limbs. Mehrabian (1971) designates such actions as immediacy cues, and he notes that these messages increase liking between people. He also notes that the persuasibility of a communicator is enhanced when a verbal message is delivered with more volume, greater intonation, and a faster rate and when it is accompanied by forceful (but not extravagant) gestures.

Although close physical proximity facilitates intimacy and interpersonal attraction, violation of personal space arouses unpleasant emotions in both the violator and violated (Fisher, in press). Inappropriate intrusion into the client's zone of comfort will typically lead to compensatory strategies (e.g., aversion of the eyes, less direct body orientation) to reduce intimacy.

One caution must be kept in mind when deciding to employ nonverbal behaviors to facilitate therapeutic progress. No optimal strategy exists apart from the requirements of the specific situation. Empirical research tells us that too little eye contact retards intimacy and liking, but too much (i.e., staring) is likely to have the same unfavorable effects. What may be perceived as a violation of personal space when talking about an irrelevant issue may not be an intrusion at another time.

FINAL WORDS

The four frameworks we have reviewed are in reality terribly complex. In theory, each can be applied by the therapist to effectively resolve difficulties clients bring into therapy. In addition, each provides a number of derivative strategies that can facilitate the development of an effective working relationship. Simply occupying the role of therapist, however, provides no guarantee that an individual can use these strategies in an adept manner. The ability to use them in an optimal way depends upon several factors.

First, the therapist must possess an understanding of their theoretical and empirical underpinnings. Because each framework is systematic, each provides a method of organizing observations in a coherent manner. Familiarity with the frameworks enables the clinician to direct her perception to important aspects of the therapeutic encounter that would otherwise remain hidden.

Having general knowledge about the frameworks is not enough in itself, however. The therapist must be able to translate this global understanding into more specific forms that pertain to what actually occurs in the therapy session. Like scientists, clinicians operate in both the context of discovery and the context of justification. Vague hunches and insights that are based on the clinician's perceptions need to be formulated into hypotheses and tested. Although clinical hypothesis testing is not as methodologically rigorous as the validation strategies employed by researchers, both types require some systematic alteration in the therapist's behavior and careful assessment of changes in the client.

A beginning therapist may have the vague feeling of being outmaneuvered by a client. By becoming familiar with the literature on interpersonal games, the therapist can develop a clearer understanding of what is occurring. The clinician can then use this information to develop hypotheses of the form, "If I act in this way, the client will engage in that maneuver." The next step involves attempting to validate the hypotheses by systematically altering specific therapeutic maneuvers and noting what the client does. If a hypothesis proves correct, the therapist will be able to predict the client's behavior before carrying out a particular strategy. After the therapist has enough evidence to document that a certain pattern of interaction consistently takes place, she can discuss this interpersonal influence pattern with the client.

The therapist must expect to make mistakes when beginning to experiment with a new conceptual framework. Mistakes may consist of either continuing to hold a particular perspective on some process issue in the face of overwhelming contradictory evidence, or they may involve abandoning an interpretation without having obtained sufficient contradictory evidence. Both types of errors are less likely to occur, however, if the therapist is willing to seek feedback from the clients and openly discuss the reasons that they hold a particular viewpoint. Therapy involves communication, and it is only through communication that therapists learn to exploit the hidden dimensions of these frameworks.

8
Moral and Ethical Issues

Professional healers have always been among the elite of any society. Their functions are socially sanctioned in ways that provide them with great power. In exercising this power, however, the professional often becomes obligated to help maintain the *status quo* and cannot deviate too radically from the generally held expectations about his functions. Those whose activities depart from these expectations are castigated as charlatans or quacks and are ostracized by their colleagues.

From this perspective, it clearly follows that psychotherapeutic practices not only reflect the predominate values in a given society, but they also can be employed to subtly indoctrinate members of that culture into accepting the legitimacy of those beliefs. Radical feminists, for example, have accused the male-dominated mental health establishment of directing psychotherapy toward helping women accept the basic inequities of marriage, rather than toward enabling women to improve the circumstances of their lives.

This situation is not a static one, however. In our society, values change rapidly, vary from place to place, and often conflict with one another, particularly those held by competing social groups. This state of affairs has led to confusion among the participants in psychotherapy about the role moral and ethical issues ought to, and actually do, play in the helping process.

This chapter opens by examining the issue of exploitative practices in psychotherapy. Following the major theme of the book, exploitation is examined as a relational term whose meaning changes over time and across situations. The controversial nature of exploitation is next highlighted by an examination of sexism and racism in psychotherapy. The chapter ends by summing up the many facets of psychotherapy that have been examined and emphasizes the importance of viewing the process from a relativistic standpoint. The major theme of this chapter, however, is the necessity of having both therapist and client accept personal responsibility in combatting exploitative practices in the therapeutic process.

THE NATURE AND BASIS OF EXPLOITATION
IN PSYCHOTHERAPY

By now, it should be obvious that a psychotherapist is not simply a "mechanic of the mind." The belief that a therapist can adjust maladaptive patterns of thought and action in a detached, aloof manner is a myth. Psychotherapy is an active, persuasive process during which individuals share their resources to solve problems and to promote growth toward full human potential. Even though humanistic therapists have been most insistent in contending that effective therapy is based upon mutual respect and involvement, genuine caring, and empathic concern; these features are an integral part of successful psychodynamic and behavioral interventions. Despite attempts by classical analysts to act as nondistorting blank screens or contentions by some behavior therapists that they simply remove maladaptive responses, all forms of psychotherapy are interpersonal influence processes. From this perspective, it is impossible to conduct therapy in a value-free vacuum that exists apart from real-world constraints on the therapist and client.

Amorality And Self-Sustaining Therapist Beliefs

Range Of Stances For The Therapist. There has been considerable controversy about the interplay between the values held by the therapist and client in psychotherapy. At first, debate centered on whether therapy was a value-free enterprise. It is now very apparent that avoiding the intrusion of values into the therapeutic process is impossible. Therapists frequently serve as models of adjustment for their clients; their legitimate and expert power heighten their influence as change agents.

The current debate has shifted to how the therapist can most responsibly use this persuasive power. This is a complex issue. The range of possible coping strategies stretches from pretending that psychotherapy is value-free to explicitly indoctrinating the client with a particular set of values. Both extremes hamper the quality of the therapeutic services being rendered. On one hand, therapists who refuse to provide information or take stands on particular issues for fear of imposing their own moral judgments are not providing the kind of help many clients seek. In addition, they are likely to be perceived as unhelpful, disinterested, and incompetent. On the other hand, therapists who attempt to coerce their clients into accepting their moral beliefs are guilty of abusing their power and frequently are viewed as manipulative and overbearing.

The concept of amorality occupies a middle position along this dimension. It implies that the therapist can neither ignore the issue of values by refusing to take explicit positions toward the real-life dilemmas faced by the client nor seek to impose a specific moral philosophy on the client. **Amorality** presupposes that the therapist serves as a model of adjustment for the client and that the therapist accepts the position of power this implies. Amorality also is based on the assumption that no person's moral philosophy is adequate for any other person. One's moral philosophy is a combination of many specific prescriptive beliefs about how the world is and ought to be. Since its development is a gradual process that encompasses both intellectual and emotional aspects, many beliefs will logically conflict with one another, and all will be bounded by situational determinants. A belief in the ultimate importance of life, for example, may be mediated by valuing euthanasia as an option for those suffering from terminal illness, or it may conflict with another belief concerning the right of women to undergo abortions.

An amoral stance also implies that the therapist and client have responsibilities toward each other, although the greater power and status of clinicians impose larger burdens upon them. Therapists need to be aware of their own basic values and how these influence their therapeutic activities. They must also be able to articulate their moral philosophies to the client, but, at the same time, clearly indicate that their views represent personal beliefs rather than universal moral imperatives.

By being straightforward in describing the ethical beliefs that influence how strategic decisions are arrived at, the therapist provides a concrete framework to which the client can react. Portions of the perspective will make sense to the client who might then incorporate these elements into the decision making process, while other aspects may well be rejected. Even if the therapist is in conflict about an issue, elaborating the sources of conflict can enable the client to make a more informed choice and can facilitate active collaboration between the participants in therapy. Explicit discussion of conflicting beliefs and outcomes has the additional benefit of demonstrating to clients that many options may be open to them and that no single option is morally compelling in and of itself. Growing concern with the therapist's "hidden agenda" among even the most nondirective humanistic clinicians suggests that they are recognizing their responsibility to explicitly structure the directive features inherent in all forms of psychotherapy.

The Need To Examine Beliefs. These responsibilities require therapists to constantly examine the self-protective beliefs that develop as a result of clinical experience. Such beliefs provide a source of stability for therapists by providing frameworks for analyzing their successes and failures. Any theoretical orientation contains many such beliefs, but the value judgments of any particular clinician extend beyond theoretical boundaries to encompass the therapist's moral view of the world. Some of the more important self-protective beliefs clinicians hold may be presented as dimensions that center on:

1. How tough or fragile are clients in their ability to cope with discomfort and manage their own affairs?
2. How much (if any) of a financial burden should therapy impose to instill the client with motivation to improve?
3. Who is ultimately responsible for bringing about constructive change in the client?
4. What events during psychotherapy actually represent a real crisis?
5. Does psychological disturbance result from internal dynamic forces, faulty belief systems, or behavioral inadequacies?
6. Must the client experience pain as an integral part of the process of personal growth?
7. Do clients benefit from hearing therapists discuss the formative experiences that helped mold them?
8. Are women basically stronger or weaker than men?
9. Can the poor or old people profit from psychotherapeutic services?
10. Is continual education and formal training necessary for providing effective psychotherapy?

These issues are not simple ones to resolve, as can be illustrated by examining any one of them. Consider the diversity of beliefs about the relationship between a financial burden and motivation to improve. Little empirical research on this important topic has been conducted. Despite this vacuum in our knowledge, some therapists adamantly maintain that people should "pay until it hurts." Others contend with equal vehemence that, if change is dependent upon the decision to pay, then the therapeutic procedures themselves must be inconsequential. Still others would argue about the relationship between "motivation to improve" and actual behavior change. Other therapists would be likely to substitute the notion of imposing some form of existential burden (e.g., the belief that meaningful change cannot come about without experiencing pain) for the notion of a financial burden. The issue becomes even more complicated when we consider that ability to pay is often correlated with other characteristics of the client (e.g., socio-economic status, education) that affect therapeutic outcome.

The Effects Of The Therapist's Beliefs. Individual therapists undoubtedly take very different positions on these and other hidden belief issues, and their responses could not be accurately predicted solely on the basis of the theoretical views they possess. *The importance of understanding self-protective beliefs lies in the fact that they have very real consequences for how therapy is conducted.* Unfortunately, coming to grips with this interplay is difficult for two reasons.

First, the manifestations of a self-sustaining belief may have unintentional negative consequences. Therapists who act on the assumption that clients are basically delicate and fragile are likely to be nurturant and supportive rather than critically analytical. This style may, however, subtly communicate the therapist's magnified fears that the client is too weak to be appropriately challenged. This position is patronizing because it is based on the therapist's assuming that the client is an inadequate individual. If this belief becomes a tacit underpinning of treatment, both therapist and client can become locked into defensive positions of mutual paralysis (Gauron and Rawlings, 1973). The therapist is reluctant to challenge the client to change because the latter might fall apart, and the client is fearful of change for the same reason. A self-fulfilling prophetic myth is thus established, whereby the client's *perceived* weakness prevents him from meeting the challenges necessary to grow, thereby proving that the client is inadequate. The only "evidence" for inadequacy, however, comes from the client's reaction to being treated as a fragile creature by the clinician.

A second source of difficulty in tracking the effects of self-sustaining beliefs is that numerous values are intertwined so that they either reinforce or disqualify one another. For example, two therapists might hold similar beliefs about women being somehow weaker than men. One therapist might attribute this situation to inherent biological or psychic inferiorities, while the other might believe that the weakness is due to a woman's acceptance of societal myths that devalue women. The views of the first therapist could result in a contemptuous, patronizing stance toward female clients. The conceptual framework of the second clinician, however, could be reflected in an appropriate balance between supporting women as oppressed and challenging a female client to change her self-defeating perceptions.

The reason these beliefs are called *self-sustaining* and *self-protective* is that they provide the therapist with a sense of stability and continuity in dealing with complex interpersonal dilemmas. Obviously, the therapist must possess firm convictions about human nature, the goals of therapy, and what influences cause change to come about. Without the sense of direction provided by such beliefs, a clinician would be reduced to nothing more than a human alchemist—trying "a little of this and a little of that" (White, 1956) and hoping that change will somehow miraculously occur.

The danger of any self-sustaining belief is that it will become an overly protective one for the therapist. Often, therapists use beliefs to insulate themselves from the painful process of critically examining their clinical encounters, particularly unsuccessful ones. In all too many instances, if a client does not improve, it is that person, rather than therapeutic strategies, who is blamed. Often, this is accomplished in an indirect manner that implicates some personal characteristic that the client is presumably unable to control. A therapist who cites "unconscious resistance" as the cause of a therapeutic failure is *implicitly* blaming the client, since it is the client who possesses this attribute. But, since the resistance is unconscious, the client is presumably not aware of it, and therefore, not *really* responsible.

Testing Of Beliefs By Peer Review. This is exactly the same sort of slanted perception that exists among scientists who declare that those who hold different views are inadequately trained, misguided, or do not know what they are talking about. Researchers, however, are at least able to subject controversial issues to empirical analysis, although this strategy does not always produce unequivocal answers. An increasing number of clinical practitioners are adopting similar methods of seeking consensual validation from their colleagues by means of clinical case conferences and peer review.

Peer review panels at many clinics and hospitals consist of clinicians who are elected by their colleagues. All clinicians on the staff are expected to present cases before the panel, which makes suggestions about how the quality of intervention might be improved. Ideally, presentations are to involve situations in which therapy is stalled or which confuse or frustrate the therapist. Peer review provides a useful feedback mechanism that can enhance professional competence. Unfortunately, it is not conducted on a widespread scale at this time. Many private practitioners are unable (and sometimes unwilling) to take advantage of peer review.

Elements Of Exploitation

Freedom Of Therapists. One implication of our attempt to define a professional in Chapter 1 is that most professionals deal with complex human problems which often involve conflict between people. The professional possesses expert knowledge in a specialized area as well as a great deal of autonomy and freedom. As professionals, psychotherapists are expected to act in the ultimate best interests of the client, but within this broad constraint, they are free to employ a wide variety of strategies. This flexibility, in combination with the power possessed by the therapist, raises the possibility that exploitation can occur during psychotherapy. *The essence of an exploitative relationship is an abuse of the power possessed by the therapist whereby the client is used to gratify some needs of the clinician.* Clear prohibitions against taking advantage of clients to satisfy the therapist's financial, sexual, or psychic needs can be found within all therapeutic systems as well as in professional ethical codes that transcend the "schools" of therapy.

Factors In Exploitation. The nature of exploitation is more involved than it first appears for a number of reasons.

1. *Exploitation is a relativistic concept.* No clear standards exist for judging whether exploitation has occurred. No single therapeutic activity is exploitative in and of itself. Psychotherapy is a reflection of generally accepted social mores, which vary across time

and place and are in rapid flux. In addition, what one therapist views as being ethically justifiable on theoretical or empirical grounds may be considered as inappropriate by others who hold competing beliefs. Long-term psychoanalytic treatment may be considered as a form of financial exploitation by clinicians who interpret research on psychoanalysis to indicate that this treatment is generally ineffective. Analysts, however, could just as easily suggest that brief behavioral interventions are a financial rip-off because they produce only symptomatic improvement. Differences in theoretical orientation often underlie the conflicting contentions that antagonists raise in front of ethical boards of inquiry established by various professional groups.

2. *Exploitation and its documentation are two different things.* When dealing with a professional, clients are expected to discard the common rule of the market place, "let the buyer beware," and accept the belief, "let the buyer trust" (Lynn, 1965). Trust implies uncertainty. The therapist cannot guarantee that intervention will be successful but is pledged to provide her best efforts to facilitate positive changes. For this reason, therapy that is ineffective cannot automatically be categorized as exploitative.

Attempting to prove that exploitation has occurred is essentially an adversary process that involves litigation between people. One individual believes that he has been wronged by another and attempts to document this by gathering whatever evidence is available. The validity of the evidence is usually the basic criterion for rendering a verdict. In malpractice lawsuits, two types of evidence are typically offered.

The first type of evidence involves attempting to prove that the professional has acted in a manner inconsistent with commonly accepted practices. The nature of what is considered a commonly accepted practice, however, is difficult to define, particularly in the realm of psychotherapy where so many diverse practices coexist.

The second type of evidence involves attempting to prove that the therapist has acted deceitfully. Since deceit involves a discrepancy between a professional's actions and his intentions, its existence is almost impossible to prove. Our analysis of psychotherapy as a series of interpersonal games suggests that therapists will often say one thing and intend exactly the opposite. The use of various paradoxical therapeutic double-bind techniques is not considered to be deceitful, if the therapist deems that they are in the best interests of the client (Watzlawick et al., 1967). In addition, certain therapeutic interventions may not appear to be in the client's best short-term interests, but they are considered to be beneficial in terms of longer-range outcomes.

The difficulty of assessing the existence of deceit can be seen also by considering the therapist who deliberately withholds a potentially painful or damaging interpretation because she believes the client is unprepared to handle it. The therapist is caught in a bind between full and painful honesty, which might damage progress, and a lie of omission that might be in the best interests of both participants. Again, this strategy is not typically judged to be deceitful, if justified as being in the client's best interest and if the therapist does not appear to materially profit from the client's loss.

3. *Exploitation may stem from and/or satisfy hidden psychic needs in the therapist.* Psychoanalysts were the first to recognize that exploitation might result from inappropriate attempts by the therapist to satisfy personal needs (such as psychic voyeurism or unconscious sadism), which do not readily appear to provide gratification to an outside observer. Within this theoretical perspective, determining whether the therapist's comments are interpretations or indicative of countertransference is based on judging the appropriateness of the statements relative to the need systems of both the analyst and patient. Interpretation is considered to involve feeding back the analyst's impressions in an undistorted manner, while countertransference is indicated by confusion between the referential perspectives of the analyst and patient. This judgment is often made by a more experienced analyst or left to the analyst involved in the encounter. Proving the existence of countertransference is particularly difficult if the analyst chooses to verbally deny its existence, since its documentation then must rest on subtle nuances. Although an exploitative practice need not be conceptualized as countertransference, the same inferential problems are found in all theoretical systems.

4. *Exploitation may result from unintentional technical or personal*

inadequacies. Some change strategies that others may regard as exploitative could have been attempted with the most sincere intentions of good will toward the client. The therapist, however, may simply lack the technical skills or general competence necessary to effectively employ particular strategies. Again, whether this is exploitative is a controversial question. There is little disagreement that therapists who represent themselves as something they are not (e.g., unlicensed or uncertified individuals describing themselves as psychiatrists or psychologists) are acting irresponsibly and, in many states, illegally. The same is true of professionals who employ procedures that are reserved for members of other professions, such as psychologists who prescribe medication.

Although it is agreed that such activities are clearly unethical, different ethical dilemmas arise when therapists operate beyond their range of personal competence while remaining within the legal or conventional boundaries of their professional practice. For example, any person who is licensed as a physician is legally entitled to practice any branch of medicine, including psychiatry, without any additional training. Adams and Orgel (1975) suggest that consumers seek psychiatrists who have been certified by the American Board of Psychiatry and Neurology, but they note that only 33 percent of the practicing psychiatrists in this country have earned this credential. On one hand, professional growth can be accomplished only by challenging and extending one's frontiers of technical skill. On the other hand, therapists may be inadvertently stomping on the psyches of their clients while obtaining new skills. This dilemma is further complicated by the development of novel psychotherapeutic frameworks and strategies which necessitate that the therapist continually learn new skills.

Ethical Dilemmas—A Case History. A very courageous presentation by Kovacs (1974), in which he describes a painful therapeutic failure, illustrates some subtleties in the points just mentioned. Kovacs treated Gwen, a "deadly cute" 19-year-old woman in response to her presenting complaint of anxiety attacks in one of her college courses. Her immediate problem involved believing that one of her instructors was subtly trying to embarrass and seduce her. The deeper roots of her difficulty appeared to stem from a brutalized childhood that included being raped by her own father. These experiences left her incredibly conflicted about her own sexuality. Projecting her conflicts led her to oscillate from being seductive and sexually provocative to being frightened and enraged that men would dare respond to her seductiveness.

Therapy for Gwen was based on two basic beliefs held by Kovacs; namely, that people should attend to and actualize the secret longings of their hearts and that interpersonal difficulties could be resolved by full and authentic confrontation. Kovacs himself drew strength from these beliefs to deal with the shame and paralysis associated with terminating his disintegrating marriage. He consequently got Gwen to confront her instructor about the issues that troubled her. She received paradoxical messages from her teacher; his cold and defensive denials conflicted with the warm hug he gave her at the end of the confrontation. At her next therapy session, Gwen furiously accused Kovacs of having taken sadistic pleasure from humiliating her. She then started to persecute Kovacs with obscene early morning phone calls.

At this point, Kovacs' narrative suggests that he and Gwen found themselves in a state of interpersonal confluence. She dropped in and out of group and individual therapy, frequently engaged Kovacs in screaming battles, attacked him physically, and wrecked his office on several occasions. Gwen's violence and hatred were not directed solely at Kovacs. She physically assaulted eight other therapists during a single month and managed to get herself thrown out of therapy with several other clinicians. Her fights with Kovacs contained clearly mixed sexual overtones, as if she were attempting to fight off his influence while "asking him" to have sexual relations with her.

In analyzing this case, it is not our purpose to pass judgment on Kovacs. Most therapists keep the pain of their failures private. The author views his decision to publicize this failure as a sign of intellectual courage and integrity and as an example others will hopefully follow.

The case does highlight some of the complexities related to ethical issues, so it is valuable for this purpose. It should also be mentioned that the following analysis does not do full justice to the intricacies of the involvement between Kovacs and Gwen.

As a starting point, it is suggested that both the therapist and client were engaged in an endless and unintentional game of mutual exploitation. Kovacs clearly did not deceitfully or detachedly manipulate Gwen to gain his own ends. Rather, the exploitation involved subtly maneuvering one another around the psychic themes of shame, guilt, and anxiety. Kovacs apparently found it impossible to maintain enough emotional distance from Gwen to prevent her "craziness" from wreaking havoc with his personal life. They continually inflicted painful experiences on one another without any apparent attempt to integrate these into a framework of greater awareness. Thus, neither could use these experiences to grow personally or to help the other better cope with life difficulties. Gwen appeared to have a remarkable ability to assault Kovacs' greatest vulnerabilities and thus paralyze him. Indeed, this seemed to be her major problem in dealing with everyone.

A second issue involved Kovacs' ambivalence about *consistently* employing a coherent model of human functioning in treating Gwen. His stable beliefs suggest a humanistic orientation. Lacking appropriate personal distance, however, caused him to get entangled in her projections. During a group session, for example, she accused him of sitting with his legs apart to compel her to stare at his crotch. He admitted that he had probably approached her in an inadvertently provocative manner, mentioning that he had fantasized about her as a sexual partner. His account of this description suggests that he had implicitly bought into the psychoanalytic position that "the thought is the deed." His admission led her to later accuse him of humiliating her in front of the group. By letting his own needs become enmeshed with hers, Kovacs appeared unable to provide the detached position which is indispensable for enabling a client to sort out the fantasy and reality components of his projections. His description of his own feelings toward her as "fearful," "furious," and even "murderous" attests to his inability to maintain a detached position of empathy.

A final issue centers on the complex interrelationship between technical competence and exploitation. By any standard, Gwen was an incredibly difficult client. Her problems fed into her therapist's greatest weaknesses at this particular point in his life. Given this potentially damaging situation, seeking consultation from one's colleagues or referring Gwen to another therapist would have been advisable. The major point to be emphasized from this perspective is that even the most technically skilled therapist may not be personally suited for effectively providing psychological services to particular clients at certain times.

Freely Giving And Taking In Psychotherapy

The Nature Of Interaction. Clinical training usually imprints a strong awareness of and aversion to exploitation in psychotherapists. Yet, we have just seen that this issue is a very complex one in reality. Some beginning therapists interpret what they learn about exploitation to mean that psychotherapy requires constant, altruistic giving and the avoidance of all forms of taking. This position clearly is contrary to what actually goes on during psychotherapy. The very nature of therapy as an interpersonal encounter necessitates that the participants continually give to and take from each other. One aspect of the exploitation issue involves what is given and received and for what reasons.

Psychotherapy has many of the elements of friendship, but it is, in some ways, more than friendship and in other ways, less. Friendships are based on mutual support within symmetric interpersonal relationships where friends coact as equals. Psychotherapy is founded on support, but it also involves using this foundation as a basis for challenging the client to change within a professional, complementary relationship.

Perls' (1973) distinction between sympathy, empathy, and apathy is relevant for understanding the relationship between giving, taking, and exploitation in psychotherapy. **Sympathy** represents a state of confluence whereby the need systems of two people become meshed. When one friend expresses sympathy for another, that person becomes entangled in the latter's experiential frame of reference. Sympathy is a means of providing support, but because the two friends are so close, the sympathizer does not have the emotional distance to challenge the other to cope with the difficulty that provoked sympathy. **Empathy**, on the other hand, conveys support to another by acknowledging that the problem is understood while providing enough distance to permit the person to challenge the other and thereby facilitate growth. Apathy, as a cold, detached state of retroflection, is a form of exploitation and has no place in either friendship or psychotherapy.

Analysis of giving and taking emphasizes that therapists have legitimate needs that are met by the practice of psychotherapy, and often these needs mesh compatibly with those of the client. Perhaps one of the biggest hidden psychic needs of the therapist is to be needed. Being able to provide what the client desperately needs promotes feelings of competence and self-esteem in therapists. There is a subtle trap inherent in the need to be needed, however, in that it may make the therapist reluctant to take what the client freely wishes to give (Dolliver and Woodward, 1974).

Clinicians who fail to realize that taking from their clients simultaneously provides a form of giving may be inadvertently robbing their clients of a chance to enhance their self-esteem. Failure to graciously accept what the client wishes to offer may subtly communicate that the client is not worth taking from. The client then might interpret this message as an indication that he is indeed worthless.

Contributions Of The Client. Clients can give to the therapist in many ways. One of the most common expressions of giving involves expressing gratitude to the therapist. Often, the client will imply that the therapist is responsible for having produced beneficial changes. Many therapists do not view this as an accurate reflection of their role as facilitators of change. Nonetheless, they will accept such compliments graciously and simultaneously point out the part played by the client in fostering improvement. Such a strategy represents an appropriate form of therapist taking. It acknowledges the clinician's realistic contribution and reinforces the active involvement of the client.

Dealing With Exploitation In Psychotherapy

Efforts By The Profession And Government. On a broad social level, flagrant exploitation by even a few individuals reflects badly upon the psychotherapy helping professions as a whole. The intricacies of psychotherapeutic intervention combine with the potential to create serious damage to dictate that helping services be provided by competent and responsible individuals. This issue has both social and personal aspects.

The seriousness of the responsibility borne by the therapist is reflected in the development of state laws regulating who may practice psychotherapy. Every state currently evaluates the credentials of physicians before allowing them to practice medicine; clinical psychologists are similarly screened prior to licensing or certification as help providers. Regulatory statutes restrict the terms *physician, clinical-counseling,* or *consulting psychologist* so that only those who are licensed or certified may apply the descriptions to themselves.

While these safeguards are undoubtedly important, they suffer from a number of serious deficiencies. First, being licensed or certified guarantees only that an individual has satisfied minimal training requirements, and standards vary from state to state. Second, once granted, renewal of the certificate is generally automatic. Thus, there is no assurance that individuals who were licensed or certified years ago have actually retained or refined their technical competence. Finally, most states do not restrict people from labelling themselves in other ways which suggest their fitness as service providers. In most states, people may legally call themselves "marriage," "family," or "personal counselors," without having to demonstrate even minimal competence in their purported areas of expertise.

Professional organizations have attempted to deal with these deficiencies in a variety of ways. Ethical review boards have been established to hear complaints of malpractice and exploitation. These groups are also beginning to formulate regulations that require their members to seek continual education in their specialty areas. In addition, many practitioner agencies are beginning to adopt various forms of peer review, as we have mentioned earlier. In some agencies, peer panels are empowered to require the therapist to seek therapy or to obtain further training; they may withhold the assignment of new cases until these demands have been fulfilled. While these strategies represent realistic attempts by responsible mental health professionals to police themselves, they have no impact on therapists who are not part of the regulating society, and their adequacy remains to be determined.

Efforts By Individual Therapists And Clients. In the final analysis, combatting exploitation requires that both therapist and client assume personal responsibility for what occurs between them. The superior position of power and status that therapists occupy places greater demands on them. The clinician can help combat exploitation by working toward his own professional and technical growth. These two areas—professional and technical growth—are thoroughly intertwined and can be realized only by accepting the challenges presented on two levels that follow.

Clinicians must continually examine their self-sustaining beliefs, particularly in terms of the consequences they entail for the individuals they treat in psychotherapy. Facing up to therapeutic inadequacies is often a very painful experience. Personal growth, however, can occur only if therapists are courageous enough to explore these issues, seek guidance from others, and modify their beliefs after open-minded appraisal of viewpoints.

Even the most personally nurturant and committed therapists can augment their effectiveness by acquiring greater technical competence.

The incredible complexity of psychotherapy and the rapidity with which new perspectives emerge obligate therapists to continually sharpen their expertise and acquire new technical skills. Strategic growth can be obtained by reading, attending training seminars, and participating in experiential growth opportunities.

Although they have considerably less power, clients also have some specific responsibilities. Feelings of being exploited need to be discussed openly and honestly with the therapist. Failure to do this is likely to perpetuate the uncomfortable situation and also may provide a meta-communication that the therapist is too weak, fragile, or insulated to profit from honest feedback. If such attempts at open discussion meet with excessive resistance from the therapist, the client can always terminate the relationship and seek another therapist. Finally, flagrant ethical or moral violations can be brought to the attention of professional societies or redressed in courts of law. Concrete action by both therapist and client is the only way to reduce the hazards caused by exploitation.

Recognizing The "Isms"

Some forms of exploitation have become institutionalized as "isms" in psychotherapy. An ism is based on the acceptance of widespread societal stereotypes that devalue certain people because they belong to particular groups or possess specific characteristics. The general societal devaluation is often justified by the generation of "scientific" evidence that is interpreted to support the stereotype. The "facts" are interpreted in such a way that they help maintain devaluation while simultaneously justifying discriminatory practices by individuals. We thus have a closed loop in which stereotypes bring about devaluation and provide the assumptions for empirical inquiry to produce the evidence which supports discriminatory practices that reinforce stereotyping. While the operation of discriminatory practices can affect many groups who seek psychotherapy (e.g., old people), most attention has been directed toward examining sexism and racism in the helping process.

SEXISM IN PSYCHOTHERAPY

Male Dominance Of The Field

Although sexual exploitation during psychotherapy is invariably a controversial issue from an applied point of view, the impact of the radical feminist movement has generated additional polemical tension. The practice of psychotherapy has always been a male-dominated enterprise. It is estimated that men comprise about 90 percent of the membership of the American Psychiatric Association, and 85 percent of currently practicing clinical psychologists (Barrett, Berg, Eaton, and Pomeroy, 1974). Although women outnumber men in the field of psychiatric social work, more men appear to be entering this profession and seem to achieve supervisory positions more rapidly than women. Men also dominate the professional training programs that mold the therapeutic practices of both male and female clinicians in all three professions.

Female Majority Of Clientele

Most psychotherapeutic services, however, are provided to women, who have been found to manifest higher rates of "neurotic" maladjustment. For example, women are twice as likely to be afflicted by severe depression (Beck and Greenberg, 1974), four times more likely to suffer phobic complaints (Marks, 1969), and comprise about two-thirds of the case loads carried by private therapists (Barrett et al., 1974). These statistics have been interpreted in a variety of ways that range from implying inherent psychic deficiencies in women to suggesting that women are victimized by the sex-role conflicts imposed by a male-oriented society. Understanding sexism requires that the phenomenon be examined from three interrelated perspectives—general social values, theoretical and scientific stances, and the attitudes and behaviors of individual psychotherapists.

Societal Attitudes About Women

The Hidden Assumptions. The role of the woman in our society is obviously conflict-ridden. In practically every culture, men have had much greater access to all forms of military, political, and economic power and thus were able to embed institutions which served their purposes deep within the fabric of society (Chesler, 1972). The "traditional" roles for women have centered on child-care and domestic responsibilities as institutionalized in courtship, marriage, and family-centered rituals.

The consciousness-raising efforts of creative feminism have largely been directed toward exploring the hidden assumptions upon which many existing social institutions operate. Such analyses start with the premise that the imbalance of power between men and women has led to numerous paradoxical double-bind situations that ultimately deny women freedom and thwart their growth.

Such a paradoxical situation can be clearly seen in the hidden relational assumption that binds married women to child-care responsibilities. This "womanly" role is set up as being of crucial importance in maintaining the well-being and stability of society. It is further assumed that properly fulfilling this vital role necessitates a great deal of effort and self-sacrifice (which may be read as "loss of freedom"). On another level, however, the child-care role is devalued, because it is seen as economically unproductive. The women in this situation thus become the recipients of a paradoxical message from men which states, "Your role is of fundamental importance to our ultimate well-being, but my career is really more important than what you do."

Historically, marriage has been synonymous with dependency, helplessness, timidity, security, and home-orientation for women. Fodor (1974) has suggested that a woman can deal with the frustrations found in marriage through adopting one of three basic options. She may give in and become obedient, sacrificing her needs to martyr herself for other family members. She may leave the relationship, but this often is a painful and shameful experience, which leaves her financially insecure. The third option is to "get sick." Haley (1963) provides a graphic example of this strategy in describing how a woman's hand-washing compulsion freed her from the petty tyranny exercised by her husband. Because her symptoms were "involuntary," she was not held responsible for her failure to keep a spotlessly clean house. In addition, her symptoms forced her husband to pay attention to her by engaging in such activities as rationing out soap and following her around to insure that she would not begin her compulsive washing. The fact that most women in therapy are educated, middle-class housewives and mothers (Fabrikant, 1974) suggests that many opt for this third alternative.

The development of alternative career choices for women has increased the frustration potential of this double-bind situation in two ways. Extensive questionnaire surveys about women's roles (Steinmann, 1974) suggest that a growing awareness of liberation philosophy among both men and women has occurred over the past 20 years. Some contradictions in Steinmann's results, however, suggest that the same basic paradox now operates in more subtle ways. She noted, for example, that both men and women endorse the belief that women have the right to seek rewarding career opportunities but seem to have a tacit understanding that such independence is permissible only if the *wife's* family responsibilities are discharged beforehand. Given this hidden agreement, her finding that women appeared not to believe the liberal comments made by men is not surprising.

A second source of current frustration is that the values underlying alternative career choices often conflict with the more traditional values of the "wife-mother" role. The subtle nature of the new, more liberal double-bind situation tends to accentuate feelings of self preciation among women. Kronsky (1971) notes that women in therapy frequently blame themselves for being angry at the limitations of their roles, feel guilty about being assertive, and label themselves as unfeminine or as castrating females.

Reflection Of Society's Values In Psychotherapy. Since psychotherapy is a social enterprise that reflects the values of a particular society, domination of the mental health helping professions by men is simply an extension of male power in other social areas. Feminists have critically attacked the psychotherapy establishment for failing to comprehend the unique difficulties faced by women. Chesler (1971) noted some striking similarities between the institutions of marriage and psychotherapy. Both are complementary relationships, in which men exercise most of the power and influence, thus tending to maintain women's dependence upon them. She argued further that psychotherapists seek to change women to better fit into their situations rather than supplying them with the support, knowledge, and courage to change their environments. From this perspective, psychotherapists are seen as supporting the hidden inequities in marriage.

Theoretical Stances And Feminine Values

Psychoanalytic Theory. Men not only dominate the practice of psychotherapy, but they also have developed most of the theories of personality that underlie the many "schools" of therapy. In recent years, the consequences of these theories for women have begun to be carefully explored. Again, analysis has been in terms of examining the

245

hidden assumption that most theories present a largely masculine view of human nature. Psychoanalytic theory has been declared to be one of the primary culprits in this regard. Some feminists have asserted that Freud's notion of penis-envy, for example, implies that women are second class creatures, and use of this concept places women in the double bind of equating assertive career activities with neurosis. Other feminist writers (e.g., Mitchell, 1974), however, contend that the basic fault with the psychoanalytic position lies less in Freud's writing than in the assumption of certain stereotypes about women that arise from a superficial analysis or a reification of Freud's position. In other words, his theorizing became an ideology which generated widely accepted self-fulfilling myths about the "inherent" distinctions between men and women.

One myth that continues to persist is the belief that a vaginal orgasm is better than a clitoral orgasm. This distinction derived from the psychoanalytic view that a clitoris was an inferior penis and that the woman can be fulfilled only through incorporating a man's penis or symbolically, by becoming pregnant. Thus clitoral orgasms came to represent an ineffective method of coping with penis envy, while vaginal orgasms signalled the woman's readiness to adopt a more "mature" (which many feminists equate with "passive") stance toward receiving and child bearing. Although the double-bind implications of this position are obvious, its self-fulfilling consequences are less clear. Many women who suffer from sexual dysfunctions have been found to be anxious about their ability to achieve vaginal orgasms. If the anxiety is severe, it may inhibit any type of orgasm from occurring. The source of anxiety stems from the woman's acceptance of this myth and the paralysis caused by believing that she is incapable of doing something she *should* be able to do.

This example also points out one characteristic of psychoanalytic theory that is not possessed by any other theoretical system. Psychodynamic terms and concepts pervade our everyday vocabulary and have much greater impact on our thinking than humanistic or behavioral viewpoints. The pervasive influence of this perspective has the unfortunate consequence of providing people with many detrimental labels that may be applied to their thoughts and actions. Even though some of these terms make little theoretical sense (e.g., fathers were viewed as the castrating agents in psychoanalytic theory, not "castrating women"), they may cause a woman to become enmeshed in a debilitating self-fulfilling prophecy.

Other Orientations. Rice and Rice (1973) have castigated not only psychoanalytic conceptions but also client-centered theories for reinforcing patterns of passivity and dependence in women. Behavior therapy formulations, with their emphasis on problem solving and direct action, have generally escaped these sorts of criticisms. In line with this action orientation has been a growth of techniques to expand the behavioral repertoires of both men and women (e.g., assertive training). Combining behavioral treatment strategies with cognitive restructuring and attributional approaches contains the added benefit of enabling women clients to actively explore the realities of their sex-role conflicts without the patronizing imposition of a framework that dictates the way things should be.

Attitudes And Behaviors Of Psychotherapists

Role Of The Individual Clinician. In the final analysis, the tenets of any theory must be applied to treating individuals. The possibility of sexist treatment is thus less of a theoretical issue than a practical, experiential one that results from how therapy is conducted. Therapists do not patronize or discriminate because they hold particular theoretical views but, rather, do so because of the kind of people they are. The most insidious aspect of sexist treatment is that a therapist's contempt for women usually is not recognized by female clients because it is congruent with the clients' negative self-appraisal.

Subtle Devaluation. A survey requesting information about sexist practices in psychotherapy by a Task Force on Sex Bias established by the American Psychological Association (1975) provided five broad themes relating to this issue. We have already noted two of these; namely, the sexist use of psychoanalytic concepts and the use of therapy to maintain traditional sex roles. A third area of concern was the extent to which therapists may subtly devalue women. In a pioneering investigation of this issue, Broverman, Broverman, Clarkson, Rosenkrantz, and Vogel (1970) had 46 male and 33 female therapists rate the characteristics of a healthy man, a healthy woman, and a healthy adult. They reported that a close parallel existed between judgments of a healthy male and a healthy adult, both being rated as independent, ambitious, assertive, objective, unemotional, and so on. The healthy woman, on the other hand, was viewed as having different and less desirable traits than the healthy adult, being perceived as less aggressive or adventurous, more dependent, emotional, excitable, and conceited. Even more surprising was the discovery that women therapists shared this negative stereotype of ideal feminine functioning. The double bind inherent in this situation is obvious. Therapy for women may not be directed toward enabling them to function as healthy adults.

The devaluation of women also appears to extend to female therapists in a variety of ways. Often, female therapists are perceived as intruders into a male-dominated profession rather than as colleagues. Women clients seem to prefer male therapists, often perceiving being assigned to a female therapist as indicative of receiving second-class treatment. Fabrikant (1974) noted that female clinicians themselves share this view. In his survey, 82 percent of a sample of women therapists who were themselves in therapy sought treatment from a man and remained in therapy almost twice as long (3.5 years) as men therapists (1.8 years) who underwent psychotherapy. Fabrikant's replication of the Broverman et al. (1970) study, however, does indicate that this situation may be improving. Responses to his adjective rating questionnaire suggest that more favorable and liberal attitudes toward women are being reported by both male and female therapists.

Exploitation As Sex Objects. The final two themes of the task force report centered on the interlocking problems of sexually exploiting female clients and treating them as sex objects. The task force noted that, although these problems were less common than attempts to foster stereotyped sex roles in therapy, they represented more emotionally charged and controversial issues. Most respondents branded the practice of having sexual relationships with clients as clearly exploitative and as detrimental to therapeutic progress. One female member of the task force, however, argued that the majority position was patronizing to women by its implication that they were incapable of making responsible sexual choices.

An overwhelming majority of the evidence, however, supports the majority contention that sexual relations between client and therapist are countertherapeutic. Chesler (1972) described 11 women who had sexual relations with their therapists as intellectually insecure, sexually fearful and compulsive, and as having difficulty in expressing their anger. The presence of these characteristics suggests that such women would have difficulty in making a free and informed choice about this matter. In addition, responding to subtle coercion by the therapist leaves the female client in a particularly vulnerable position. Attempts to prove that sexual relations with the therapist actually had occurred could be met with the charge that the woman was "fantasizing," "projecting," "distorting reality," or just plain "crazy."

More subtle exploitation of women clients as sex objects is a much harder issue to come to grips with. Chesler (1971) suggests that the male therapist receives a substantial psychological service from female clients because their interactions allow him to exercise his control and allow him to feel superior to the women he treats. Chesler (1972) provides a striking documentation of this position by contrasting the therapeutic histories of 54 women who were designated as (1) having had sex with their therapists, (2) being lesbians, (3) feminists, (4) third-world minority group members, and (5) having been hospitalized in a mental asylum. Altogether, these women had seen a total of 136 therapists divided about equally between male and female clinicians.

Lesbians were committed at the youngest average age and remained institutionalized over three times as long as women who had sex with their therapists. Chesler interprets this finding to indicate that lesbianism is perceived as an extreme rejection of the woman's feminine role and hence is severely punished. Women in the mental asylum group were older than members of the other groups when first hospitalized. Since most of these women had obtained private psychotherapy before being committed, it is possible that they were perceived as increasingly worthless and therefore expendable as they grew older.

Of major interest was the finding that, with the exception of third-world women who may have been viewed as less desirable candidates for psychotherapy, females remained in treatment almost twice to three times as long with male therapists than with female clinicians. The women in Fabrikant's (1974) sample also stayed in therapy more than twice as long (5.7 versus 2.3 years) than male clients. While it is possible that the women in both these studies were more severely handicapped, it is equally plausible to speculate that their continuation in therapy met some hidden needs of the male therapists.

Combatting Sexism In Therapy
The widespread and serious nature of this problem requires that it be

addressed on many levels. The suggestions for dealing with perceived exploitation are relevant to this issue. In addition, the task force has recommended that therapists be exposed to various consciousness-raising activities to become more fully aware of possible sexist practices in diagnosis and treatment. Employing male and female clinicians as cotherapists in problem-solving group therapies has also been suggested (Rice and Rice, 1973).

In addition to promoting changes within the mental health establishment, many less formal strategies are arising around the country. Numerous women's organizations are systematically soliciting comments from those who have sought mental or physical health care and providing this information to prospective clients. Although these innovations are important first steps in overcoming sexism, the ultimate responsibility for laying this problem to rest belongs to the people actually involved in therapy.

RACISM IN PSYCHOTHERAPY
A full understanding of racism in psychotherapy also rests upon analyzing it on the levels of societal devaluation, "scientific" support for existing stereotypes, and the activities of individual therapists.

The Effects Of Stereotyping
We have all grown up with strong stereotypes about *black* and *white* and encounter these in our daily lives. *White* is associated with heaven, angels, purity, and clean laundry, while *black* connotes dirt, filth, and other undesirable impurities.

These general stereotypes can be found in much of the "scientific" literature on racial differences. In a widely quoted study, Kardiner and Ovesey (1951) noted that the psychodynamic investigation of black clients revealed their personality structures to contain many unappealingly negative traits, including apathy, resignation, desire to be white, identification with feces, promiscuity, disorderliness, inclinations to gamble, drink, and live for the moment, as well as unconscious resentment and hostility. Gardner (1971) has characterized much of the psychodynamic literature on the black personality as "patronizing and paternalistic" (p. 79). He also notes a fascinating shift in this literature over the past decade.

It was initially argued that these strong negative characteristics were inherent in the black personality structure as a result of genetic and constitutional deficiencies. The more current variation of this theme states that these attributes result from oppression and discrimination black people experience. Thus, the basically negative view of the black personality structure has not radically changed, only the reasons for its existence. The stereotype itself, however, actually represents yet another uniformity myth.

Racial Influences In The Therapeutic Encounter

Unconscious Prejudice. Many writers (e.g., Gardner, 1971; Riess, 1971) suggest that most instances of discrimination in therapy are not motivated by maliciousness, but, rather, are the result of unconscious prejudice. Riess provides an interesting example of this. Upon hearing a speaker characterize placing hands on the heads of black children as a discriminatory activity, he realized he typically did this while visiting a day-care center. He also recalled learning as a child that rubbing a black child's head brought good luck. This realization was shocking to him and probably resulted in a drastic change in his behavior.

Cross-Racial Therapy. The salience of race often causes a confluent situation in cross-racial therapy situations. Confluence arises because the impact of racial differences often represents a hidden agenda for both the therapist and the client. One primary task of the therapist is to help clients distinguish between what they do and what they are. An individual may get into trouble because she is hostile and suspicious. That person's race may be one formative influence in the development of these characteristics. The task of sorting out these contributing factors becomes more difficult in therapy that involves a black therapist and a white client, or *vice versa*. Gardner (1971) indicates that black therapists may have particular anxieties about maintaining a white clientele and therefore act in an ingratiating manner which inhibits their ability to challenge the client. He also notes that some black therapists may act out their anger and frustration as a form of reverse racism. White clients often seek black therapists because they are too ashamed to deal with certain issues with a white therapist. The hidden message in this situation is that clients have such low self-esteem that they don't deserve first-class therapy. The implications of this position are obviously patronizing to the therapist. Finally, Gardner points out that many white clients are preoccupied that their black therapist will detect latent racism in them. Oversensitivity to this concern by the client can lead to a patronizing oversolicitousness that hampers free and honest communication.

The same confluent situation can exist when a white therapist works with black clients. Wilson and Calhoun (1974) describe three common strategic errors that can result from this form of confluence. The therapist may accept the *illusion of color blindness* whereby any reference to racial differences is avoided. These authors point out that this strategy represents:

> a capitulation to racism in that viewing a black client as "just another client" is equivalent to viewing him as a white client, hence automatically labelling deviations from the white middle-class standard as evidence of behavioral pathology [Reprinted by permission. W. Wilson and J. F. Calhoun. Behavior therapy and the minority client. *Psychotherapy: Theory, Research and Practice*, 1974, *11*, 319].

A second error is *being blinded by color*. Here, the therapist assumes that all of a client's problems result from being oppressed because of racial discrimination. This strategy ignores the fact that people differ because they have unique experiences. It is also patronizing to black clients because it assumes that "they" are not like other people.

The final error has been labelled by Wilson and Calhoun as *the great white father syndrome*. It involves an overconcern on the part of therapists that they will be perceived as bigots. They therefore bend over backward to present themselves as benevolent providers who can "fix" the client. This strategy also is patronizing and prevents the therapist from effectively challenging the client to change and grow.

All the experts on this issue agree on the necessity of having therapists critically examine their beliefs and attitudes about race. In addition, therapists must be courageous enough to risk appearing to be racist at times to challenge the client by saying the difficult things that often need to be said. Ultimately, the success of cross-racial therapy depends upon establishing a warm, honest, and trusting relationship between the people involved in the therapeutic encounter. These goals can be facilitated by seeking experience with clients of different ethnic backgrounds, but in the final analysis, involves dealing with people as people rather than as whites, blacks, Hispanics, oldsters, and so on.

FINAL FINAL WORDS

We have examined the process of psychotherapy from many different perspectives, encountering numerous contradictions and paradoxes in our attempt to make sense out of the helping endeavors. The consequences resulting from this confusion have been to generate frustration and controversy on one hand and to foster an atmosphere of electric excitement and humility, on the other.

The uniform nature of psychotherapy is for many a myth caused by our language which designates the process as an entity. Yet, others have argued that "it" does contain elements that transcend theoretical, political, and social boundaries. Whether one chooses to accept this latter position, it is clear that the practice of psychotherapy has been torn by numerous controversial schisms. Many of these, such as wrangling over how psychotherapy ought to be defined and who is qualified to conduct "it," came about as a result of the specialization of helping functions throughout history and have been aggravated by the political maneuvering of different professional organizations. These controversies are multifaceted because they combine historical, political, and economic elements that receive partial justification from existing psychological theories and scientific investigations.

We also have seen, however, that a complex interplay exists between politics, theory, and science. Both theory and science themselves represent arbitrary simplifications of clinical reality that are affected by more general social values. This situation led to another series of controversies, such as deciding whether psychotherapy was effective and whether "it" is an artistic or a scientific enterprise. These schisms fostered the development of numerous, more novel ways to conceptualize psychotherapy in terms of power, problem solving, interpersonal games, and attributional analysis, to mention just a few.

Despite the many conflicts and controversies that currently surround our attempts to understand psychotherapy, we know much more about this complex phenomenon than we did 30, or even 20, years ago. Our knowledge has been extended because we have challenged some basic assumptions about the nature of that knowledge itself. Scientific investigators have begun to question the belief that they can discover immutable truths about psychotherapy. We realize that any framework of understanding, whether it be historical, political, theoretical, or empirical, represents an arbitrary simplification of the larger reality. With this realization, we have come to understand that while any framework might ultimately provide a clearer view of some aspects of psychotherapy, its use will blind us to other aspects.

This understanding is perhaps the one basic truth we possess about psychotherapy. If we accept a belief in the relativistic nature of psychotherapy, we are left with two starting points for increasing our understanding.

First is the necessity of taking personal responsibility for the many decisions that arise in the clinical process or in investigation of it. Various forms of orthodoxy often provide useful frameworks for understanding what goes on, but it must always be remembered that any orthodox ideology is incomplete. The ultimate decision of any of the numerous choice points resides with the individuals involved.

The second starting point rests upon tolerance. It is clear that our knowledge about psychotherapy remains incomplete to the extent that we arbitrarily rule out certain frameworks without considering what they have to offer. Many uniformity myths surrounding psychotherapy still exist; these relate to theoretical perspectives as well as to the characteristics of the people involved. Discarding alternative frameworks because of tradition, early professional training, or on the basis of authority limits one's ability to grow as a therapist or as a researcher.

Although we have learned a great deal about psychotherapy, we have much more to understand. Our ability to provide more effective helping services in the future must begin with tolerance for all varieties of existing knowledge, the humility to accept that knowledge as fragmentary and incomplete, and the willingness to make systematic inquiries into therapeutic processes and practices until our curiosity is satisfied.

References

Adams, S. and Orgel, M. *Through the mental health maze.* Washington, D.C.: Public Citizen's Health Research Group, 1975.

Albee, G. The uncertain future of clinical psychology. *American Psychologist,* 1970, *25,* 1071-1080.

Albee, G. To thine own self be true: Comments on "Insurance reimbursement." *American Psychologist,* 1975, *30,* 1156-1160.

Alexander, F. G., and Selesnick, S. T. *The history of psychiatry.* New York: Harper and Row, 1966.

Allen, G. J. Effectiveness of study counseling and desensitization in alleviating test anxiety in college students. *Journal of Abnormal Psychology,* 1971, *77,* 282-289.

Allen, G. J.; Chinsky, J. M.; Larcen, S. W.; Lochman, J. E.; and Selinger, H. V. *Community psychology and the schools: A behaviorally oriented multilevel preventive approach.* Hillsdale, New Jersey: LEA Publishers, 1976.

American Board of Psychiatry and Neurology. Annual report-1974. *American Journal of Psychiatry,* 1975, *132,* 1121-1123.

American Psychiatric Association. *Diagnostic and statistical manual of mental disorders, 2nd Ed. (DSM-II).* Washington, D.C.: American Psychiatric Association, 1968.

American Psychological Association Task Force on Sex Bias. Report of the task force on sex bias and sex-role stereotyping in psychotherapeutic practice. *American Psychologist,* 1975, *30,* 1169-1175.

Andrews, L. M., and Karlins, M. *Requiem for democracy?* New York: Holt, Rinehart, and Winston, 1971.

Apfelbaum, D. *Dimensions of transference in psychotherapy.* Berkeley: University of California Press, 1958.

Asher, J. Psychiatrists oppose key bill. *APA Monitor*, 1974, *5*, No. 7, 1.

Astin, A. W. The functional autonomy of psychotherapy. *American Psychologist*, 1961, *16*, 75-78.

Ayllon, T. Intensive treatment of psychotic behavior by stimulus satiation and food reinforcement. *Behaviour Research and Therapy*, 1963, *1*, 53-61.

Baekeland, F., and Lundwall, L. Dropping out of treatment: A critical review. *Psychological Bulletin*, 1975, *82*, 738-783.

Bandler, R., and Grinder, J. *The structure of magic*. Palo Alto, California: Science and Behavior Books, 1975.

Bandura, A.; Lipsher, D. H.; and Miller, P. E. Psychotherapists' approach-avoidance reactions to patients' expressions of hostility. *Journal of Consulting Psychology*, 1960, *24*, 1-8.

Barrett, C. J.; Berg, P. L.; Eaton, E. M.; and Pomeroy, E. Implications of women's liberation and the future of psychotherapy. *Psychotherapy: Theory, Research and Practice*, 1974, *11*, 11-15.

Barron, F., and Leary, T. F. Changes in psychoneurotic patients with and without psychotherapy. *Journal of Consulting Psychology*, 1955, *19*, 239-245.

Beck, A. Cognitive therapy: Nature and relation to behavior therapy. *Behavior Therapy*, 1970, *1*, 184-200.

Beck, A., and Greenberg, R. L. Cognitive therapy with depressed women. In V. Franks and V. Burtle (Eds.), *Women in therapy: New psychotherapies for a changing society*. New York: Brunner/Mazel, 1974.

Bergin, A. E. The effects of psychotherapy: Negative results revisited. *Journal of Counseling Psychology*, 1963, *10*, 244-250.

Bergin, A. E. The evaluation of therapeutic outcomes. In A. E. Bergin and S. L. Garfield (Eds.), *Handbook of psychotherapy and behavior change*. New York: Wiley, 1971.

Bergin, A. E., and Strupp, H. H. *Changing frontiers in the science of psychotherapy*. Chicago: Aldine-Atherton, 1972.

Berne, E. *Principles of group treatment*. New York: Oxford University Press, 1966.

Bernstein, D. A. Behavioral fear assessment: Anxiety or artifact? In H. Adams and P. Unikel (Eds.), *Issues and trends in behavior therapy*. Springfield, Illinois: Charles Thomas, 1973.

Bernstein, D. A., and Paul, G. L. Some comments on therapy analogue research with small animal "phobias." *Journal of Behavior Therapy and Experimental Psychiatry*, 1971, *2*, 225-238.

Berscheid, E., and Walster, E. Physical attractiveness. In L. Berkowitz (Ed.), *Advances in experimental social psychology, Vol. 7.* New York: Academic Press, 1974.

Betz, B. J. Studies of the therapist's role in the treatment of the schizophrenic patient. *American Journal of Psychiatry*, 1967, *123*, 963-971.

Birk, L. Intensive group therapy: An effective behavioral-psychoanalytic method. *American Journal of Psychiatry*, 1974, *131*, 11-16.

Blanck, G. Psychoanalytic technique. In B. B. Wolman (Ed.), *The therapist's handbook: Treatment methods of mental disorders.* New York: Van Nostrand Reinhold, 1976.

Bockoven, J. S. *Moral treatment in American psychiatry.* New York: Springer, 1963.

Bordin, E. S. Simplification as a strategy for research in psychotherapy. *Journal of Consulting Psychology*, 1965, *29*, 493-503.

Bordin, E. S. Free association: An experimental analogue of the psychoanalytic situation. In L. A. Gottschalk and A. H. Auerbach (Eds.), *Methods of research in psychotherapy.* New York: Appleton-Century-Crofts, 1966.

Borkovec, T. D. The role of expectancy and physiological feedback in fear research: A review with special reference to subject characteristics. *Behavior Therapy*, 1973, *4*, 491-505.

Borkovec, T. D. Investigations of fear and sleep disturbance: Methodological, measurement, and theoretical issues in therapy outcome research. In G. E. Schwartz and D. Shapiro (Eds.), *Consciousness and self-regulation: Advances in research.* New York: Plenum, 1976.

Borkovec, T. D., and Nau, S. D. Credibility of analogue therapy rationales. *Journal of Behavior Therapy and Experimental Psychiatry*, 1972, *3*, 257-260.

Brammer, L. M. *The helping relationship.* Englewood Cliffs, New Jersey: Prentice-Hall, 1973.

Broverman, K.; Broverman, D.; Clarkson, F.; Rosenkrantz, P.; and Vogel, S. Sex role stereotypes and clinical judgments of mental health. *Journal of Consulting and Clinical Psychology*, 1970, *34*, 1-7.

Butler, J. M., and Haigh, G. V. Changes in the relation between self-concepts and ideal concepts consequent upon client-centered counseling. In C. R. Rogers and R. F. Dymond (Eds.), *Psychotherapy and personality change.* Chicago: University of Chicago Press, 1954.

Carkhuff, R. R., and Berenson, B. G. *Beyond counseling and psychotherapy.* New York: Holt, Rinehart, and Winston, 1967.

Cartwright, D. S. Note on "changes in psychoneurotic patients with and without psychotherapy." *Journal of Consulting Psychology,* 1956, *20,* 403-404.

Chartier, G. M. A-B therapist variable: Real or imagined? *Psychological Bulletin,* 1971, *75,* 22-33.

Chesler, P. Patient and patriarch. In V. Gornick and B. K. Morgan (Eds.), *Women in a sexist society.* New York: Basic Books, 1971.

Chesler, P. *Women and madness.* Garden City, New York: Doubleday, 1972.

Chinsky, J. M., and Rappaport, J. Brief critique of the meaning and reliability of "accurate empathy" ratings. *Psychological Bulletin,* 1970, *73,* 379-382.

Colby, K. M. Experiment on the effects of an observer's presence on the imago system during psychoanalytic free association. *Behavioral Science,* 1960, *5,* 197-210.

Colby, K. M. Psychotherapeutic processes. *Annual Review of Psychology,* 1964, *15,* 347-370.

Condon, T. J. *Systematic desensitization: An evaluation of a psychoanalytic model of its effectiveness.* Storrs, Connecticut: Unpublished Doctoral Dissertation, University of Connecticut, 1976.

Cooper, A.; Furst, J. B.; and Bridger, W. A brief commentary on the usefulness of studying fears of snakes. *Journal of Abnormal Psychology,* 1969, *74,* 413-414.

Cross, H. J. The outcome of psychotherapy: A selected analysis of research findings. *Journal of Consulting Psychology,* 1964, *28,* 413-417.

Dailey, W. F.; Dailey, R.; Allen, G. J.; Chinsky, J. M.; and Veit, S. W. Patterns of volunteer visits to institutionalized retarded children. Storrs, Connecticut: University of Connecticut, Unpublished Manuscript, 1975.

Davitz, J. R. *The communication of emotional meaning.* New York: McGraw-Hill, 1964.

Dolliver, R. H., and Woodward, B. T. Giving and taking in psychotherapy. *Psychotherapy: Theory, Research and Practice,* 1974, *11,* 66-70.

D'Zurilla, T. J., and Goldfried, M. R. Problem solving and behavior modification. *Journal of Abnormal Psychology,* 1971, *78,* 107-126.

Ekman, P., and Friesen, W. V. Nonverbal leakage and clues to deception. *Psychiatry*, 1969, *32*, 88-106.

Ekman, P.; Friesen, W. V.; and Ellsworth, P. *The face and emotion: Guidelines for research and an integration of findings.* New York: Pergamon, 1971.

Ellenberger, H. F. *The discovery of the unconscious.* New York: Basic Books, 1970.

Ellenberger, H. F. Psychiatry from ancient to modern times. In S. Arieti (Ed.), *American handbook of psychiatry, 2nd Ed.,* Vol. 1. New York: Basic Books, 1974.

Elliott, P. *The sociology of the professions.* New York: Herder and Herder, 1972.

Ellis, A. *Reason and emotion in psychotherapy.* New York: Lyle Stuart, 1962.

Ellis, A. Should some people be labelled mentally ill? *Journal of Consulting Psychology*, 1967, *31*, 435-446.

Ellis, A. *Humanistic psychotherapy.* New York: McGraw-Hill, 1973.

Eysenck, H. J. The effects of psychotherapy: An evaluation. *Journal of Consulting Psychology*, 1952, *16*, 319-324.

Eysenck, H. J. Learning theory and behavior therapy. *Journal of Mental Sciences*, 1959, *105*, 61-75.

Eysenck, H. J. The effects of psychotherapy. In H. J. Eysenck (Ed.), *Handbook of abnormal psychology.* New York: Basic Books, 1961.

Eysenck, H. J. The outcome problem in psychotherapy: A reply. *Psychotherapy: Theory, Research and Practice*, 1964, *1*, 97-100.

Eysenck, H. J. The contributions of clinical psychology to psychiatry. In J. G. Howells (Ed.), *Modern perspectives in world psychiatry, Vol. 2.* New York: Brunner/Mazel, 1971.

Fabrikant, B. The psychotherapist and the female patient: Perceptions, misperceptions, and change. In V. Franks and V. Burtle (Eds.), *Women in therapy: New psychotherapies for a changing society.* New York: Brunner/Mazel, 1974.

Feather, B. W., and Rhoads, J. M. Psychodynamic behavior therapy: I. Theory and rationale. *Archives of General Psychiatry*, 1972, *26*, 496-502 (a).

Feather, B. W., and Rhoads, J. M. Psychodynamic behavior therapy: II. Clinical aspects. *Archives of General Psychiatry*, 1972, *26*, 503-511 (b).

Fenichel, O. *The psychoanalytic theory of neurosis.* New York: Norton, 1945.

Ferster, C. B., and Meyer, M. K. A method for the experimental analysis of the behavior of autistic children. *American Journal of Orthopsychiatry*, 1962, *32*, 89-98.

Fiedler, F. A comparison of therapeutic relationships in psychoanalytic, nondirective and Adlerian therapy. *Journal of Consulting Psychology*, 1950, *14*, 436-445.

Fiedler, F. Factor analyses of psychoanalytic, nondirective and Adlerian therapeutic relationships. *Journal of Consulting Psychology*, 1951, *15*, 32-38.

Fish, J. M. *Placebo therapy.* San Francisco: Jossey-Bass, 1973.

Fisher, J. D. Environmental and social behavior. In R. Baron and D. Byrne (Eds.), *Social psychology: Understanding human interaction, 2nd Ed.* Boston: Allyn and Bacon, In Press.

Fodor, I. G. The phobic syndrome in women. In V. Franks and V. Burtle (Eds.), *Women in therapy: New psychotherapies for a changing society.* New York: Brunner/Mazel, 1974.

Frank, J. D. *Persuasion and healing.* Baltimore: Johns Hopkins Press, 1961.

Frank, J. D. Therapeutic factors in psychotherapy. *American Journal of Psychotherapy*, 1971, *25*, 350-361.

Frank, J. D. Restoration of morale and behavior change. In A. Burton (Ed.), *What makes behavior change possible?* New York: Brunner/Mazel, 1976.

Franks, C. M., and Wilson, G. T. The nature of behavior therapy: Recurring problems and issues-commentary. In C. M. Franks and G. T. Wilson (Eds.), *Annual review of behavior therapy, Vol. 2.* New York: Brunner/Mazel, 1974.

French, J. R. P., and Raven, B. The bases of social power. In D. Cartwright (Ed.), *Studies in social power.* Ann Arbor, Michigan: University of Michigan Press, 1959.

Freud, S. On psychotherapy (1905). *The standard edition of the complete works of Sigmund Freud, Vol. VII.* London: The Hogarth Press, 1959.

Freud, S. The question of lay analysis (1926). *The standard edition of the complete works of Sigmund Freud, Vol. XX.* London: The Hogarth Press, 1959.

Gardner, L. H. The therapeutic relationship under varying conditions of race. *Psychotherapy: Theory, Research and Practice*, 1971, *8*, 78-87.

Garfield, S. L. Research on client variables in psychotherapy. In A. E. Bergin and S. L. Garfield (Eds.), *Handbook of psychotherapy and behavior change.* New York: Wiley, 1971.

Garfield, S. L., and Kurtz, R. Clinical psychologists in the 1970's. *American Psychologist,* 1976, *31,* 1-9.

Garfield, S. L., and Kurz, M. Evaluation of treatment and related procedures in 1216 cases referred to a mental hygiene clinic. *Psychiatric Quarterly,* 1952, *26,* 414-424.

Gauron, E. F., and Rawlings, E. L. The myth of the fragile patient. *Psychotherapy: Theory, Research and Practice,* 1973, *10,* 352-353.

Goldfried, M. R., and Kent, R. N. Traditional versus behavioral personality assessment: A comparison of methodological and theoretical assumptions. *Psychological Bulletin,* 1972, *77,* 409-420.

Goldstein, A. P. *Therapist-patient expectancies in psychotherapy.* New York: Pergamon Press, 1962.

Goldstein, A. P. *Psychotherapeutic attraction.* New York: Pergamon Press, 1971.

Goldstein, A. P. *Structured learning therapy: Toward a psychotherapy for the poor.* New York: Academic Press, 1973.

Goldstein, A. P. Relationship-enhancement methods. In F. H. Kanfer and A. P. Goldstein (Eds.), *Helping people change.* New York: Pergamon Press, 1975.

Goldstein, A. P., and Shipman, W. G. Patients' expectancies, symptom reduction and aspects of the initial psychotherapeutic interview. *Journal of Clinical Psychology,* 1961, *17,* 129-133.

Grinspoon, L.; Ewalt, J. R.; and Shader, R. Psychotherapy and pharmacotherapy in chronic schizophrenia. *American Journal of Psychiatry,* 1968, *124,* 1645-1652.

Gurin, G.; Veroff, J; and Feld, S. *Americans view their mental health.* New York: Basic Books, 1960.

Haggard, E. A., and Isaacs, K. S. Micromomentary facial expressions as indicators of ego mechanisms in psychotherapy. In L. A. Gottschalk and A. H. Auerbach (Eds.), *Methods of research in psychotherapy.* New York: Appleton-Century-Crofts, 1966.

Haley, J. *Strategies of psychotherapy.* New York: Grune and Stratton, 1963.

Haley, J. The art of being a failure as a therapist. In J. Haley (Ed.), *The power tactics of Jesus Christ and other essays.* New York: Grossman Publishers, 1969 (a).

Haley, J. The art of psychoanalysis. In J. Haley (Ed.), *The power tactics of Jesus Christ and other essays.* New York: Grossman Publishers, 1969 (b).

Hall, E. T. *The hidden dimension.* Garden City, New York: Doubleday, 1966.

Hamilton, S. W. The history of the American mental hospitals. In J. K. Hall (Ed.), *One hundred years of American psychiatry.* New York: Columbia University Press, 1944.

Hancher, M. The science of interpretation and the art of interpretation. *Modern Language Notes,* 1970, *85,* 791-802.

Haughton, E., and Ayllon, T. Production and elimination of symptomatic behavior. In L. P. Ullmann and L. Krasner (Eds.), *Case studies in behavior modification.* New York: Holt, Rinehart, and Winston, 1965.

Heller, K. Laboratory interview research as an analogue to treatment. In A. E. Bergin and S. L. Garfield (Eds.), *Handbook of psychotherapy and behavior change.* New York: Wiley, 1971.

Hempel, C. G. *Aspects of scientific explanation.* New York: Free Press, 1965.

Henry, W. E., and Shlien, J. M. Affective complexity and psychotherapy: Some comparisons of time-limited and unlimited treatment. *Journal of Projective Techniques,* 1958, *22,* 153-162.

Holmes, D. S. Dimensions of projection. *Psychological Bulletin,* 1968, *69,* 248-268.

Holmes, D. S. Investigations of repression: Differential recall of material experimentally or naturally associated with ego threat. *Psychological Bulletin,* 1974, *81,* 632-653.

Homme, L.; Csanyi, A. P.; Gonzales, M. A.; and Rechs, J. R. *How to use contingency contracting in the classroom.* Champaign, Illinois: Research Press, 1969.

Jones, E. E., and Nisbett, R. E. *The actor and the observer: Divergent perceptions of the causes of behavior.* Morristown, New Jersey: General Learning Press, 1971.

Jones, M. C. A laboratory study of fear: The case of Peter. *Pediatrics Seminar,* 1924, *31,* 308-315.

Kadushin, C. *Why people go to psychiatrists.* New York: Atherton, 1969.

Kanfer, F. H. Self-management methods. In F. H. Kanfer and A. P. Goldstein (Eds.), *Helping people change.* New York: Pergamon Press, 1975.

Kanfer, F. H., and Saslow, G. Behavioral diagnosis: An alternative to diagnostic classification. *Archives of General Psychiatry*, 1965, *12*, 529-538.

Kanouse, D. E., and Hanson, L. R., Jr. *Negativity in evaluation*. Morristown, New Jersey: General Learning Press, 1971.

Kaplan, A. *The conduct of inquiry: Methodology for behavioral science*. San Francisco: Chandler, 1964.

Kardiner, A., and Ovesey, L. *The mark of oppression*. New York: Norton, 1951.

Kelley, H. H. Attribution theory in social psychology. In D. Levine (Ed.), *Nebraska Symposium on Motivation, 1967*. Lincoln, Nebraska: University of Nebraska Press, 1967.

Kelly, E. L. Clinical psychology-1960. Report of survey findings. *Newsletter of the Division of Clinical Psychology*, 1961, *14*, 1-11.

Kelly, G. A. *The psychology of personal constructs*. New York: Norton, 1955.

Kiesler, C. A. Editorial: The training of psychiatrists and psychologists. *American Psychologist*, 1977, *32*, 107-108.

Kiesler, D. J. Some myths of psychotherapy and the search for a paradigm. *Psychological Bulletin*, 1966, *65*, 110-136.

Kirsch, I. The definition of artificial constructs: A "malcontent" replies. *Journal of Behavior Therapy and Experimental Psychiatry*, In Press.

Kline, P. *Fact and fantasy in Freudian theory*. London: Methuen and Company, 1972.

Knight, R. P. Evaluation of the results of psychotherapy. *American Journal of Psychiatry*, 1941, *98*, 434-466.

Kovacs, A. L. Through the valley of the shadow . . . *Psychotherapy: Theory, Research and Practice*, 1974, *11*, 376-382.

Krasner, L. The therapist as a social reinforcement machine. In H. H. Strupp and L. Luborsky (Eds.), *Research in psychotherapy, Vol. 2*. Washington, D.C.: American Psychological Association, 1962.

Krasner, L. On the death of behavior modification: Some comments from a mourner. *American Psychologist*, 1976, *31*, 387-388.

Krasner, L., and Ullmann, L. P. *Behavior influence and personality*. New York: Holt, Rinehart, and Winston, 1973.

Kronsky, B. J. Feminism and psychotherapy. *Journal of Contemporary Psychotherapy*, 1971, *3*, 89-98.

Kuhn, T. S. *The structure of scientific revolutions*. Chicago: University of Chicago Press, 1962.

Lambert, M. J. Spontaneous remission in adult neurotic disorders: A revision and summary. *Psychological Bulletin*, 1976, *83*. 107-119.

Landy, E. E. Sex differences in some aspects of smoking behaviour. *Psychological Reports*, 1967, Vol. 20, 578-580.

Lang, P. J., and Lavovik, A. D. Experimental desensitization of a phobia. *Journal of Abnormal and Social Psychology*, 1963, *66*, 519-525.

Lazarus, A. A. The results of behaviour therapy in 126 cases of severe neurosis. *Behaviour Research and Therapy*, 1963, *1*, 69-79.

Lazarus, A. A. Multimodal behavior therapy: Treating the "basic id." *Journal of Nervous and Mental Disease*, 1973, *156*, 404-411.

Lehner, G. F. Defining psychotherapy. *American Psychologist*, 1952, 7, 547.

Leitenberg, H.; Agras, W. S.; Barlow, D. H.; and Oliveau, D. C. Contribution of selective positive reinforcement and therapeutic instructions to systematic desensitization therapy. *Journal of Abnormal Psychology*, 1969, *74*, 113-118.

Levine, D. S., and Willner, S. G. The cost of mental illness-1974. *National Institute of Mental Health Statistical Note No. 125.* Washington, D.C.: Government Printing Office, 1976.

Levitsky, A., and Perls, F. S. The rules and games of Gestalt therapy. In I. Shepherd and J. Fagen (Eds.), *Gestalt therapy now.* Palo Alto, California: Science and Behavior Books, 1970.

Lindner, R. The girl who couldn't stop eating. In H. Greenwald (Ed.), *Great cases in psychoanalysis.* New York: Jason Aranson, 1973.

Lorion, R. P. Socioeconomic status and traditional treatment approaches reconsidered. *Psychological Bulletin*, 1973, *79*, 263-270.

Lorion, R. P. Patient and therapist variables in the treatment of low income patients. *Psychological Bulletin*, 1974, *81*, 344-354.

Luborsky, L.; Singer, B.; and Luborsky, L. Comparative studies of psychotherapies: Is it true that "everybody has won and all must have prizes?" In R. L. Spitzer, and D. F. Klein (Eds.), *Evaluation of psychological therapies.* Baltimore: Johns Hopkins Press, 1976.

Luborsky, L., and Spence, D. P. Quantitative research on psychoanalytic therapy. In A. E. Bergin and S. L. Garfield (Eds.), *Handbook of psychotherapy and behavior change.* New York: Wiley, 1971.

Lynn, K. S. *The professions in America.* Boston: Houghton-Mifflin, 1965.

Mahl, G. F. Gestures and body movements in interviews. *Research in Psychotherapy*, 1968, *3*, 295-346.

Mahoney, M. *Cognition and behavior modification*. Cambridge, Massachusetts: Ballinger, 1974.

Mahoney, M. *Scientist as subject: The psychological imperative*. Cambridge, Massachusetts: Ballinger, 1976.

Mahoney, M.; Kazdin, A. E.; and Lesswing, N. J. Behavior modification: Delusion or deliverance? In C. M. Franks and G. T. Wilson (Eds.), *Annual review of behavior therapy, Vol. 2*. New York: Brunner/Mazel, 1974.

Mahrer, A. R. The goals and families of psychotherapy: Summary. In A. R. Mahrer (Ed.), *The goals of psychotherapy*. New York: Appleton-Century-Crofts, 1967.

Marcia, J. E.; Rubin, B. M.; and Efran, J. S. Systematic desensitization: Expectancy change or counterconditioning? *Journal of Abnormal Psychology*, 1969, *74*, 382-387.

Marks, I. *Fears and phobias*. New York: Academic Press, 1969.

Marmor, J. *Psychiatrists and their patients*. Washington, D.C.: American Psychiatric Association, 1975.

Marmor, J. Common operational factors in diverse approaches to behavior change. In A. Burton (Ed.), *What makes behavior change possible?* New York: Brunner/Mazel, 1976.

Martin, R. *Legal challenges to behavior modification*. Champaign, Illinois: Research Press, 1976.

McCardel, J., and Murray, E. J. Nonspecific factors in weekend encounter groups. *Journal of Consulting and Clinical Psychology*, 1974, *42*, 337-345.

McGlynn, F. D., and McDonnell, R. M. Subjective ratings of credibility following brief exposure to desensitization and pseudotherapy. *Behaviour Research and Therapy*, 1974, *12*, 141-146.

McGuire, W. J. Suspiciousness of experimenter's intent. In R. Rosenthal and R. L. Rosnow (Eds.), *Artifact in behavioral research*. New York: Academic Press, 1969.

Meehl, P. Discussion of H. J. Eysenck. The effect of psychotherapy. *International Journal of Psychiatry*, 1965, *1*, 156-157.

Mehrabian, A. *Silent messages*. Belmont, California: Wadsworth, 1971.

Meichenbaum, D. *Cognitive behavior modification*. Morristown, New Jersey: General Learning Press, 1974.

Meichenbaum, D., and Smart, I. Use of direct expectancy to modify academic performance and attitudes of college students. *Journal of Counseling Psychology*, 1971, *18*, 531-535.

Meltzer, M. L. Insurance reimbursement: A mixed blessing. *American Psychologist*, 1975, *30*, 1150-1155.

Meltzoff, J., and Kornreich, M. *Research in psychotherapy*. New York: Atherton, 1970.

Mitchell, J. *Psychoanalysis and feminism*. New York: Random House, 1974.

Moore, W. E. *The professions: Roles and rules*. New York: Russell Sage, 1970.

Muench, G. A. An investigation of the efficacy of time-limited psychotherapy. *Journal of Consulting Psychology*, 1965, *12*, 294-298.

National Center for Health Statistics. *Characteristics of patients of selected types of medical specialists and practitioners: United States July 1963 - June 1964*. Washington, D.C.: Government Printing Office, Publication No. 1000, Series 10, No. 28, 1966.

Oswald, P. F. *Soundmaking*. Springfield, Illinois: Charles Thomas, 1963.

Paul, G. L. *Insight versus desensitization in psychotherapy*. Stanford, California: Stanford University Press, 1966.

Paul, G. L. Strategy of outcome research in psychotherapy. *Journal of Consulting Psychology*, 1967, *31*, 109-118.

Paul, G. L. Behavior modification research: Design and tactics. In C. M. Franks (Ed.), *Behavior therapy: Appraisal and status*. New York: McGraw-Hill, 1969 (a).

Paul, G. L. Outcome of systematic desensitization. II: Controlled investigations of individual treatment, technique variations, and current status. In C. M. Franks (Ed.), *Behavior therapy: Appraisal and status*. New York: McGraw-Hill, 1969 (b).

Perls, F. *The Gestalt approach and eyewitness to therapy*. Palo Alto, California: Science and Behavior Books, 1973.

Perls, F.; Hefferline, R. F.; and Goodman, P. *Gestalt therapy: Excitement and growth in the human personality*. New York: Julian Press, 1951.

Quay, H. The effect of verbal reinforcement on early childhood memories. *Journal of Abnormal and Social Psychology*, 1959, *59*, 254-257.

Rachman, S. The treatment of anxiety and phobic reactions by systematic desensitization psychotherapy. *Journal of Abnormal and Social Psychology*, 1959, *58*, 259-263.

Rachman, S. Spontaneous remission and latent learning. *Behaviour Research and Therapy*, 1963, *1*, 133-137.

Rachman, S. The effects of psychological treatment. In H. J. Eysenck (Ed.), *Handbook of abnormal psychology*. New York: Basic Books, 1973.

Rapaport, D. A historical survey of psychoanalytic ego psychology. (Introduction to E. H. Eriksen, *Identity and the life cycle, Vol. I*, pp. 5-17). *Psychological Issues,* 1959, *1*, (Monograph No. 1). New York: International Universities Press, 1959.

Rappaport, J., and Chinsky, J. M. Accurate empathy: Confusion of a construct. *Psychological Bulletin*, 1972, *77*, 400-404.

Raths, L. E.; Harmin, M.; and Simon, S. B. *Values and teaching: Working with values in the classroom.* Columbus, Ohio: C. E. Merrill Books, 1966.

Reichenbach, H. *Experience and prediction.* Chicago: University of Chicago Press, 1938.

Reinehr, R. C. *The machine that oils itself.* Chicago: Nelson-Hall, 1975.

Rice, J. K., and Rice, D. G. Implications of the women's liberation movement for psychotherapy. *American Journal of Psychiatry*, 1973, *130*, 191-196.

Riess, B. F. Observations of the therapist factor in interethnic psychotherapy. *Psychotherapy: Theory, Research and Practice*, 1971, *8*, 71-72.

Rogers, C. R. *Counseling and psychotherapy.* Boston: Houghton-Mifflin, 1942.

Rogers, C. R. *Client-centered therapy.* Boston: Houghton-Mifflin, 1951.

Rogers, C. R. The case of Mrs. Oak: A research analysis. In C. R. Rogers and R. F. Dymond (Eds.), *Psychotherapy and personality change.* Chicago: University of Chicago Press, 1954.

Rogers, C. R. The necessary and sufficient conditions of therapeutic personality change. *Journal of Consulting Psychology*, 1957, *21*, 95-103.

Rogers, C. R. A theory of therapy, personality and interpersonal relationships as developed in the client-centered framework. In S. Koch (Ed.), *Psychology: A study of a science, Vol. 3.* New York: McGraw-Hill, 1959.

Roos, P. Human rights and behavior modification. *Mental Retardation*, 1974, *12*, 3-6.

Rosen, G. M. Therapy set: Its effects on subjects' involvement in systematic desensitization and treatment outcome. *Journal of Abnormal Psychology*, 1974, *83*, 291-300.

Ryan, W. *Blaming the victim.* New York: Vintage Books, 1971.

Santostefano, S., and Kahn, M. Clinical psychology in the United States. In J. R. Braun (Ed.), *Clinical psychology in transition.* Cleveland: World Publishing Company, 1966.

Sarason, I. G., and Ganzer, V. J. Concerning the medical model. *American Psychologist*, 1968, *23*, 507-510.

Sarbin, T. R. On the futility of the proposition that some people be labeled "mentally ill." *Journal of Consulting Psychology*, 1967, *31*, 447-453.

Sargent, H. D. Intrapsychic change: Methodological problems in psychotherapy research. *Psychiatry*, 1961, *24*, 93-108.

Scheff, T. J. *Being mentally ill: A sociological theory*. Chicago: Aldine, 1966.

Schofield, W. *Psychotherapy: The purchase of friendship*. Englewood Cliffs, New Jersey: Prentice-Hall, 1964.

Shapiro, A. K. The placebo effect in the history of medical treatment—implications for psychiatry. *American Journal of Psychiatry*, 1959, *116*, 298-304.

Shapiro, A. K. Placebo effects in medicine, psychotherapy, and psychoanalysis. In A. E. Bergin and S. L. Garfield (Eds.), *Handbook of psychotherapy and behavior change*. New York: Wiley, 1971.

Shlien, J. M.; Mosak, H. H.; and Dreikurs, R. Effect of time limits: A comparison of two psychotherapies. *Journal of Counseling Psychology*, 1962, *9*, 31-34.

Silverman, L. H. Psychoanalytic theory: The reports of my death are greatly exaggerated. *American Psychologist*, 1976, *31*, 621-637.

Silverman, L. H.; Frank, S. G.; and Dachinger, P. A psychoanalytic reinterpretation of the effectiveness of systematic desensitization: Experimental data bearing on the role of merging fantasies. *Journal of Abnormal Psychology*, 1974, *83*, 313-318.

Sjoberg, G. Politics, ethics, and evaluation research. In M. Guttentag and E. L. Struening (Eds.), *Handbook of evaluation research, Vol. 2*. Beverly Hills, California: Sage Publications, 1975.

Skinner, B. F. *Beyond freedom and dignity*. New York: Alfred Knopf, 1971.

Skinner, B. F. *About behaviorism*. New York: Alfred Knopf, 1974.

Skinner, B. F.; Solomon, H. C.; Lindsley, O. R.; and Richards, M. E. *Studies in behavior: Status Report I*. Waltham, Massachusetts: Metropolitan State Hospital, 1953.

Sloane, R. B.; Staples, R. F.; Cristol, A. H.; Yorkson, N. J.; and Whipple, K. *Psychotherapy versus behavior therapy*. Cambridge, Massachusetts: Harvard University Press, 1975.

Slutsky, J. M., and Allen, G. J. The influence of contextual cues on the efficacy of desensitization and a credible placebo in alleviating public speaking anxiety. Storrs, Connecticut: Unpublished manuscript. University of Connecticut, 1977.

Steinmann, A. Cultural values, female role expectancies and therapeutic goals. In V. Franks and V. Burtle (Eds.), *Women in therapy: New psychotherapies for a changing society*. New York: Brunner/ Mazel, 1974.

Stevenson, I. Processes of "spontaneous" recovery from the psychoneuroses. *American Journal of Psychiatry*, 1961, *117*, 1057-1064.

Strean, H. S. *The social worker as psychotherapist*. Metuchen, New Jersey: The Scarecrow Press, 1974.

Strupp, H. H. A multidimensional comparison of therapist activity in analytic and client-centered therapy. *Journal of Consulting Psychology*, 1957, *21*, 301-308.

Strupp, H. H. *Psychotherapists in action*. New York: Grune and Stratton, 1960.

Strupp, H. H. The outcome problem in psychotherapy revisited. *Psychotherapy: Theory, Research and Practice*, 1963, *1*, 1-13.

Strupp, H. H. What is psychotherapy? *Contemporary Psychology*, 1967, *12*, 41-42.

Strupp, H. H. The erosion of excellence. *The Clinical Psychologist*, 1975, *28*, No. 2.

Strupp, H. H.; Fox, R. E.; and Lessler, K. *Patients view their psychotherapy*. Baltimore: Johns Hopkins Press, 1969.

Stuart, R. B. Token reinforcement in marital treatment. In R. D. Rubin and C. M. Franks (Eds.), *Advances in behavior therapy, 1968*. New York: Academic Press, 1968.

Stuart, R. B. *Trick or treatment*. Champaign, Illinois: Research Press, 1970.

Szasz, T. S. *The myth of mental illness*. New York: Harper and Row, 1961.

Tarachow, S. *An introduction to psychotherapy*. New York: International Universities Press, 1963.

Thomas, C. L. (Ed.), *Taber's cyclopedic medical dictionary, 12th Ed.* Philadelphia: F. A. Davis, 1973.

Tinsley, H. E. A., and Harris, D. J. Client expectations for counseling. *Journal of Counseling Psychology*, 1976, *23*, 173-177.

Tori, C., and Worell, L. Reduction of human avoidant behavior: A comparison of counterconditioning, expectancy and cognitive information approaches. *Journal of Consulting and Clinical Psychology*, 1973, *40*, 69-77.

Torrey, E. F. *The mind game: Witchdoctors and psychiatrists*. New

York: Emerson Hall Publishers, 1972.

Trotter, S. Psychology pushes for recognition by JCAH. *APA Monitor*, 1976, *7*, No. 9-10.

Truax, C. B. Influence of patient statements on judgments of therapist statements during psychotherapy. *Journal of Clinical Psychology*, 1966, *22*, 335-337 (a).

Truax, C. B. Reinforcement and non-reinforcement in Rogerian psychotherapy. *Journal of Abnormal Psychology*, 1966, *71*, 1-9 (b).

Truax, C. B., and Carkhuff, R. R. *Toward effective counseling and psychotherapy: Training and practice.* Chicago: Aldine, 1967.

Truax, C. B., and Mitchell, K. M. Research on certain therapist interpersonal skills in relation to process and outcome. In A. E. Bergin and S. L. Garfield (Eds.), *Handbook of psychotherapy and behavior change.* New York: Wiley, 1971.

Ullmann, L. P. *Institution and outcome.* New York: Pergamon Press, 1967.

Ullmann, L. P. Behavior therapy as social movement. In C. M. Franks (Ed.), *Behavior therapy: Appraisal and status.* New York: McGraw-Hill, 1969.

Ullmann, L. P., and Krasner, L. Introduction: What is behavior modification? In L. P. Ullmann and L. Krasner (Eds.), *Case studies in behavior modification.* New York: Holt, Rinehart and Winston, 1965.

Valins, S., and Nisbett, R. E. *Attribution processes in the development and treatment of emotional disorder.* Morristown, New Jersey: General Learning Press, 1971.

Watson, J. B. The place of the conditioned reflex in psychology. *Psychological Review*, 1916, *23*, 89-116.

Watson, J. B. *Behaviorism.* Chicago: University of Chicago Press, 1924.

Watson, J. B., and Rayner, R. Conditioned emotional reactions. *Journal of Experimental Psychology*, 1920, *3*, 1-14.

Watzlawick, P.; Beavin, J. H.; and Jackson, D. D. *Pragmatics of human communication.* New York: Norton, 1967.

Wexler, D. B. Token and taboo: Behavior modification, token economies, and the law. *California Law Review*, 1973, *61*, 81-109.

White, R. B. Psychoanalysis: An evaluation. In J. G. Howells (Ed.), *Modern perspectives in world psychiatry, Vol. 2.* New York: Brunner/Mazel, 1971.

White, R. W. *The abnormal personality, 2nd Ed.* New York: The Ronald Press, 1956.

Wilkins, W. Expectancy for therapeutic gain: An empirical and conceptual critique. *Journal of Consulting and Clinical Psychology*, 1973, *40*, 69-77.

Wilson, W., and Calhoun, J. F. Behavior therapy and the minority client. *Psychotherapy: Theory, Research and Practice*, 1974, *11*, 317-325.

Winder, C. L. Psychotherapy. *Annual Review of Psychology*, 1957, *8*, 309-330.

Wolberg, L. R. *The technique of psychotherapy, Vol. 1, 2nd Ed.* New York: Grune and Stratton, 1967.

Wolpe, J. *Psychotherapy by reciprocal inhibition.* Stanford, California: Stanford University Press, 1958.

Wolpe, J. Behavior therapy and its malcontents-I. Denial of its bases and psychodynamic fusionism. *Journal of Behavior Therapy and Experimental Psychiatry*, 1976, *7*, 1-6 (a).

Wolpe, J. Behavior therapy and its malcontents-II. Multimodal eclecticism, cognitive exclusivism and "exposure" empiricism. *Journal of Behavior Therapy and Experimental Psychiatry*, 1976, *7*, 109-116 (b).

Zubin, J. Technical issues: Discussion. In P. H. Hoch and J. Zubin (Eds.), *The evaluation of psychiatric treatment.* New York: Grune and Stratton, 1964.

Index

uses of, 43, 45, 145
problems with, 45-47
Medicine, 17-18
diagnostic processes in, 206-208
Mental illness, 45-47, 79-80, 148. *See also* Medical model
Merging fantasies, 66-67, 92, 118, 182
Meta-complementary relationship, 211, 213-214. *See also* Interpersonal games
Meta-language, 192, 209-212, 213-214, 242. *See also* Language; Linguistic analysis
Moral treatment, 12

National Center for Health Statistics, 176
Negative scanning, 203
Neurosis, 59-60, 79-80, 101, 200
Nonpossessive warmth, 77, 108, 135, 136, 153, 156, 163, 173, 223, 252. *See also* Accurate empathy

Paradigms, 6-8, 38-39
prescriptive nature of, 38-39
Paralanguage, 8, 220, 222-223. *See also* Kinesics; Proxemics
Peer review, 232-233, 241
Placebo, 115, 134, 136, 142, 163-174
components of, 166-172
definition of, 163-165
exploitation of, 172-174
Power, 182, 183-184, 227-229, 233, 242, 243
paradoxes of, 192-193
sources of, 183-184
Premature termination, 138, 141-142, 169, 178
Principle of Rumpelstiltskin, 184, 187
Professionals, 15-18, 47-48, 153-154, 183, 227, 233-236
characteristics of, 15-17
Projection, 65, 80, 134, 238
Proxemics, 8, 220, 221-222. *See also* Kinesics; Paralanguage
Psychiatric social work, 25-27, 151-152
Psychiatrists, 47, 50, 70, 149-150, 208
Psychiatry, 4-5, 14, 18-21, 41, 208
Psychoanalysis, 13, 21, 23-24, 33, 57-73, 101-102, 105, 120-121, 123-124, 145, 147, 151, 170, 174-175, 178, 182, 186, 187, 193, 219, 222, 228, 234, 235, 245-247
assumptions of, 60-61, 127
effectiveness of, 101-102, 105
limitations of, 71-73
role of therapist in, 134, 193
Psychodynamic psychotherapy, 55-73, 158, 197, 219, 220-221, 238
Psychodynamic therapists, 9-10, 70, 74, 93-94, 96-98, 111, 119-121, 134-135, 153, 192-193
Psychologists, 24-25, 47, 50, 70, 96-98, 150-151
Psychotherapy, 2, 9, 29-33, 48-52, 101-111, 121-124, 133, 192-194, 213-214, 238-240
and friendship, 239
common elements in, 182-187
cost of, 50-52
definitions of, 29-33
paradoxes in, 192-193, 213-214
time limits on, 141-142, 161, 174-181
ultimate and mediate goals of, 121-124
Public Citizen's Health Research Group, 49-50

ABOUT THE AUTHOR

Dr. Allen has been teaching at the University of Connecticut since 1970, after completing his doctoral study at the University of Illinois. He is currently an associate professor in the clinical psychology training program and a licensed clinical psychologist. His research interests center upon assessment of psychotherapeutic processes and outcomes, as well as behavioral interventions in naturalistic settings. In addition to having published widely in a variety of professional journals, he has been the recipient of two awards for distinguished research contributions—from the American Personnel and Guidance Association in 1972, and the Division of Consulting Psychology of the American Psychological Association in 1974. Dr. Allen is a member of the Association for the Advancement of Behavior Therapy and also serves on the editorial board of the journal *Behavior Therapy*. He recently co-authored the book *Community Psychology and the Schools*, which describes the interface between applied behavioral and community mental health approaches.